'Reade him, therefore; and againe, and againe: And if then you do not like him, surely you are in some danger, not to understand him...

John Hemming
Henry Condell

Preface to the 1623 Folio Edition

Shakespeare Made Easy

Contents

Introduction

Shakespeare Made Easy is intended for readers approaching the plays for the first time, who find the language of Elizabethan poetic drama an initial obstacle to understanding and enjoyment. In the past, the only answer to the problem has been to grapple with the difficulties with the aid of explanatory footnotes (often missing when they are most needed) and a stern teacher. Generations of students have complained that 'Shakespeare was ruined for me at school'.

Usually a fuller appreciation of Shakespeare's plays comes in later life, when the mind has matured and language skills are more developed. Often the desire to read Shakespeare for pleasure and enrichment follows from a visit to the theatre, where excellence of acting and production can bring to life qualities which sometimes lie dormant on the printed page.

Shakespeare Made Easy can never be a substitute for the original plays. It cannot possibly convey the full meaning of Shakespeare's poetic expression, which is untranslatable. *Shakespeare Made Easy* concentrates on the dramatic aspect, enabling the novice to become familiar with the plot and characters, and to experience one facet of Shakespeare's genius. To know and understand the central issues of each play is a sound starting point for further exploration and development.

Discretion can be used in choosing the best method to employ. One way is to read the original Shakespeare first, ignoring the modern translation or using it only when interest or understanding flags. Another way is to read the translation first, to establish confidence and familiarity with plots and characters.

Either way, cross-reference can be illuminating. The modern text can explain 'what is being said' if Shakespeare's language is particularly complex or his expression antiquated. The Shakespeare text will show the reader of the modern paraphrase how much more can be expressed in poetry than in prose.

The use of *Shakespeare Made Easy* means that the newcomer need never be overcome by textual difficulties. From first to last, a measure of understanding is at hand – the key is provided for what has been a locked door to many students in the past. And as understanding grows, so an awareness develops of the potential of language as a vehicle for philosophic and moral expression, beauty, and the abidingly memorable.

Even professional Shakespearian scholars can never hope to arrive at a complete understanding of the plays. Each critic, researcher, actor or producer merely adds a little to the work that has already been done, or makes fresh interpretations of the texts for new generations. For everyone, Shakespearian appreciation is a journey. *Shakespeare Made Easy* is intended to help with the first steps.

William Shakespeare

His life

William Shakespeare was born in Stratford-on-Avon, Warwick-shire, on 23 April 1564, the son of a prosperous wool and leather merchant. Very little is known of his early life. From parish records we know that he married Ann Hathaway in 1582, when he was eighteen, and she was twenty-six. They had three children, the eldest of whom died in childhood.

Between his marriage and the next thing we know about him, there is a gap of ten years. Probably he became a member of a travelling company of actors. By 1592 he had settled in London, and had earned a reputation as an actor and playwright.

Theatres were then in their infancy. The first (called *The Theatre*) was built by the actor James Burbage in 1576, in Shoreditch, then a suburb of London. Two more followed as the taste for theatre grew: *The Curtain* in 1577 and *The Rose* in 1587. The demand for new plays naturally increased. Shakespeare prob-ably earned a living adapting old plays and working in collaboration with others on new ones. Today we would call him a 'freelance', since he was not permanently attached to one theatre.

In 1594, a new company of actors, The Lord Chamberlain's Men was formed, and Shakespeare was one of the shareholders. He remained a member throughout his working life. The Com-pany was regrouped in 1603, and re-named The King's Men, with James I as their patron.

Shakespeare and his fellow-actors prospered. In 1598 they built their own theatre, *The Globe*, which broke away from the tradi-tional rectangular shape of the inn and its yard (the early home of travelling bands of actors). Shakespeare described it in *Henry V* as 'this wooden O', because it was circular.

Many other theatres were built by investors eager to profit from the new enthusiasm for drama. *The Hope, The Fortune, The Red Bull*, and *The Swan* were all open-air 'public' theatres. There were also many 'private' (or indoor) theatres, one of which (*The Blackfriars*) was purchased by Shakespeare and his friends because the child actors who performed there were dangerous competitors. (Shakespeare denounces them in *Hamlet*.)

After writing some thirty-seven plays (the exact number is something which scholars argue about), Shakespeare retired to his native Stratford, wealthy and respected. He died on his birthday, in 1616.

His plays

Shakespeare's plays were not all published in his lifetime. None of them comes to us exactly as he wrote it.

In Elizabethan times, plays were not regarded as either literature or good reading matter. They were written at speed (often by more than one writer), performed perhaps ten or twelve times, and then discarded. Fourteen of Shakespeare's plays were first printed in Quarto (17cm × 21cm) volumes, not all with his name as the author. Some were authorized (the 'good' Quartos) and probably were printed from prompt copies provided by the theatre. Others were pirated (the 'bad' Quartos) by booksellers who may have employed shorthand writers, or bought actors' copies after the run of the play had ended.

In 1623, seven years after Shakespeare's death, John Hemming and Henry Condell (fellow-actors and shareholders in The King's Men) published a collected edition of Shakespeare's works – thirty-six plays in all – in a Folio (21cm × 34cm) edition. From their introduction it would seem that they used Shakespeare's original manuscripts ('we have scarce received from him a blot in his papers') but the Folio volumes that still survive are not all exactly alike, nor are the plays printed as we know them today, with act and scene divisions and stage-directions.

A modern edition of a Shakespeare play is the result of a great deal of scholarly research and editorial skill over several centuries. The aim is always to publish a text (based on the good and bad Quartos and the Folio editions) that most closely resembles what Shakespeare intended. Misprints have added to the problems, so some words and lines are pure guesswork. This explains why some versions of Shakespeare's plays differ from others.

His theatre

The first purpose-built playhouse in Elizabethan London, constructed in 1576, was *The Theatre*. Its co-founders were John Brayne, an investor, and James Burbage, a carpenter turned actor. Like the six or seven 'public' (or outdoor) theatres which followed it over the next thirty years, it was situated outside the city, to avoid conflict with the authorities. They disapproved of players and playgoing, partly on moral and political grounds, and partly because of the danger of spreading the plague. (There were two major epidemics during Shakespeare's lifetime, and on each occasion the theatres were closed for lengthy periods.)

The Theatre was a financial success, and Shakespeare's company performed there until 1598, when a dispute over the lease of the land forced Burbage to take down the building. It was re-created in Southwark, as *The Globe*, with Shakespeare and several of his fellow-actors as the principal shareholders.

By modern standards, *The Globe* was small. Externally, the octagonal building measured less than thirty metres across, but in spite of this it could accommodate an audience of between two and three thousand people. (The largest of the three theatres at the National Theatre complex in London today seats 1160.)

Performances were advertised by means of playbills posted around the city, and they took place during the hours of daylight when the weather was suitable. A flag flew to show that all was well, to save playgoers a wasted journey.

At the entrance, a doorkeeper collected one penny (about 60p in modern money) for admission to the 'pit' – a name taken from the

Interior of the Swan Theatre – from a pen and ink drawing made in 1596 (Mansell Collection)

old inn-yards, where bear-baiting and cock-fighting were popular sports. This was the minimum charge for seeing a play. The 'groundlings', as they were called, simply stood around the three sides of the stage, in the open air. Those who were better off could pay extra for a seat under cover. Stairs led from the pit to three tiers of galleries round the walls. The higher one went, the more one paid. The best seats cost one shilling, (or £6 today). In theatres owned by speculators like Francis Langley and Philip Henslowe, half the gallery takings went to the landlord.

A full house might consist of 800 groundlings and 1500 in the galleries, with a dozen more exclusive seats on the stage itself for the gentry. A new play might run for between six and sixteen performances; the average was about ten. As there were no breaks between scenes, and no intervals, most plays could be performed in two hours. A trumpet sounded three times before the play began.

The acting company assembled in the Tiring House at the rear of the stage. This was where they 'attired' (or dressed) themselves: not in costumes representing the period of the play, but in Elizabethan doublet and hose. All performances were therefore in modern dress, though no expense was spared to make the stage costumes lavish. The entire company was male. By law actresses were not allowed, and female roles were performed by boys.

Access to the stage from the Tiring House was through two doors, one on each side of the stage. Because there was no front curtain, every entrance had to have its corresponding exit, so an actor killed on stage had to be carried off. There was no scenery: the audience used its imagination, guided by the spoken word. Storms and night scenes might well be performed on sunny days in mid-afternoon; the Elizabethan playgoer relied entirely on the playwrights' descriptive skills to establish the dramatic atmosphere.

Once on stage, the actors and their expensive clothes were protected from sudden showers by a canopy, the underside of which was painted blue, and spangled with stars to represent the heavens. A trapdoor in the stage made ghostly entrances and the grave-digging scene in *Hamlet* possible. Behind the main stage, in between the two entrance doors, there was a curtained area, concealing a small inner stage, useful for bedroom scenes. Above this was a balcony, which served for castle walls (as in *Henry V*) or a domestic balcony (as in the famous scene in *Romeo and Juliet*).

The acting style in Elizabethan times was probably more declamatory than we favour today, but the close proximity of the audience also made a degree of intimacy possible. In those days soliloquies and asides seemed quite natural. Act and scene divisions did not exist (those in printed versions of the play today have been added by editors), but Shakespeare often indicates a scene-ending by a rhyming couplet.

A company such as The King's Men at *The Globe* would consist of around twenty-five actors, half of whom might be shareholders, and the rest part-timers engaged for a particular play. Amongst the shareholders in *The Globe* were several specialists – William Kempe, for example, was a renowned comedian and Robert Armin was a singer and dancer. Playwrights wrote parts to suit the actors who were available, and devised ways of overcoming the absence of women. Shakespeare often has his heroines dress as young men, and physical contact between lovers was formal compared with the realism we expect today.

His verse

Shakespeare wrote his plays mostly in blank verse: that is, unrhymed lines consisting of ten syllables, alternately stressed and unstressed. The technical term for this form is the 'iambic pentameter'. When Shakespeare first began to write for the stage, it was fashionable to maintain this regular beat from the first line of the play till the last.

Shakespeare conformed at first, and then experimented. Some of his early plays contain whole scenes in rhyming couplets – in *Romeo and Juliet*, for example, there is extensive use of rhyme, and as if to show his versatility, Shakespeare even inserts a sonnet into the dialogue.

But as he matured, he sought greater freedom of expression than rhyme allowed. Rhyme is still used to indicate a scene-ending, or to stress lines which he wishes the audience to remember. Generally, though, Shakespeare moved towards the rhythms of everyday speech. This gave him many dramatic advantages, which he fully and subtly exploits in terms of atmosphere, character, emotion, stress and pace.

It is Shakespeare's poetic imagery, however, that most distinguishes his verse from that of lesser playwrights. It enables him to stretch the imagination, express complex thought-patterns in memorable language, and convey a number of associated ideas in a compressed and economical form. A study of Shakespeare's imagery – especially in his later plays – is often the key to a full understanding of his meaning and purposes.

At the other extreme is prose. Shakespeare normally reserves it for servants, clowns, commoners, and pedestrian matters such as lists, messages and letters.

King Lear

Date

The play was entered in the Stationer's Register in November 1607, having been performed before King James in December 1606. It was probably written during the previous year, 1605.

Sources

The main plot of *King Lear* can be traced to several sources: *The Chronicles of England, Scotland and Ireland* by Ralph Holinshed (first published in 1577 and re-issued in 1587), which tells the story of 'Lear the Sonne of Baldud' and his three daughters 'Gonorilla, Regan and Cordeilla'; John Higgins' narrative poem in *The Mirror of Magistrates* (1574 edition) which is written from the viewpoint of 'Cordila'; an old play called *The True Chronicle History of King Leir* (known to have been performed in 1594, and written at least six years earlier); and Book Two of Edmund Spenser's *The Faerie Queene* (1590).

The Gloucester sub-plot may have been suggested by an episode in Sir Philip Sidney's *Arcadia* (1590) in which the King of Paphlagonia, blinded by 'a hard-hearted sonne of his', seeks a rock from which to 'cast himselfe headlong to death', led by his loyal son 'poorly arayed and extreamely weather-beaten'.

Shakespeare always restructured and developed his source material, and though these texts (and possibly others) were part of his initial working equipment, *King Lear* bears only a token resemblance to the older stories which he worked upon: for example, in Holinshed and the old chronicle play, Lear and the French army are victorious, and in neither does the King go mad.

Text

King Lear was first published in a Quarto version, in 1608. It was reprinted in 1619, when it was spuriously dated 1608: publishers in Elizabethan times often passed off reprints in this fraudulent way. Shakespeare was not involved in either publication. The play next appeared in the Folio edition of 1623. Hemming and Condell, the editors, are thought to have used a manuscript copy or theatre prompt-book, together with the first Quarto, in compiling their text.

The Quarto omits about 100 lines that appear in the Folio. The Folio omits about 300 lines that are printed in the Quartos. No definitive text therefore exists; all editors must use discretion in preparing the play for publication. This explains why editions often differ from each other.

King Lear

Original text and modern version

The characters

Lear   King of Britain
King of France
Duke of Burgundy
Duke of Cornwall   Regan's husband
Duke of Albany   Goneril's husband
Earl of Kent
Earl of Gloucester
Edgar   Gloucester's legitimate son
Edmund   Gloucester's bastard son
Curan   a courtier
Old Man   Gloucester's tenant
Doctor
Fool
Oswald   Goneril's steward
A Captain   employed by Edmund
Gentleman   in the service of Cordelia
Herald
Servants   to Cornwall
Goneril
Regan   } Lear's daughters
Cordelia
Knights   attending on Lear; **Officers, Messengers, Soldiers**
and **Attendants**

Act one

Scene 1

King Lear's Palace. Enter **Kent, Gloucester, and Edmund**

Kent I thought the King had more affected the Duke of
Albany than Cornwall.

Gloucester It did always seem so to us: but now, in the
division of the kingdom, it appears not which of the Dukes
5 he values most; for equalities are so weighed that curiosity
in neither can make choice of either's moiety.

Kent Is not this your son, my lord?

Gloucester His breeding, sir, hath been at my charge. I
have so often blushed to acknowledge him, that now I am
10 brazed to it.

Kent I cannot conceive you.

Gloucester Sir, this young fellow's mother could;
whereupon she grew round-wombed, and had, indeed, sir,
a son for her cradle ere she had a husband for her bed. Do
15 you smell a fault?

Kent I cannot wish the fault undone, the issue of it being so
proper.

Gloucester But I have a son, sir, by order of law, some year
elder than this, who yet is no dearer in my account: though
20 this knave came something saucily to the world before he
was sent for, yet was his mother fair; there was good sport
at his making, and the whoreson must be acknowledged.
Do you know this noble gentleman, Edmund?

20

Act one

Scene 1

King Lear's palace. Enter the **Earl of Kent**, *followed by the* **Earl of Gloucester** *and his illegitimate son* **Edmund**. *They are discussing court matters*

Kent   I thought the King favoured the Duke of Albany more than the Duke of Cornwall?

Gloucester   It always seemed so to us. But now he has divided up his kingdom, it isn't clear which of the Dukes he values most. Their shares are so equal that neither is to be preferred to the other.

Kent   [*Indicating* **Edmund**] Isn't this your son, my lord?

Gloucester   I fathered him, sir. I've so often been embarrassed to admit he's mine that now I'm hardened to it.

Kent   I cannot conceive why.

Gloucester   Sir, this young fellow's mother could! So she got pregnant, and had a son for her cradle before she had a husband for her bed. Do you detect a fault?

Kent   I cannot wish the fault undone, the result of it being so handsome!

Gloucester   But I have a legitimate son, sir, about a year older than this one, though I don't make any distinction in his favour. [*Nodding towards* **Edmund**] Though this villain was cheeky enough to be born before he was sent for, there's no denying his mother was beautiful. We had a good time begetting him, so the rascal can't be disowned. Do you know this noble gentleman, Edmund?

21

Edmund   No, my lord.

25 **Gloucester**   My Lord of Kent. Remember him hereafter as
my honourable friend.

Edmund   My services to your lordship.

Kent   I must love you, and sue to know you better.

Edmund   Sir, I shall study deserving.

30 **Gloucester**   He hath been out nine years, and away he shall
again. The King is coming.

[*Sennet. Enter* **King Lear, Cornwall, Albany, Goneril,
Regan, Cordelia,** *and Attendants*]

Lear   Attend the Lords of France and Burgundy, Gloucester.

Gloucester   I shall, my Liege.

[*Exeunt* **Gloucester** *and* **Edmund**]

Lear   Meantime, we shall express our darker purpose.
35   Give me the map there. Know that we have divided
In three our kingdom; and 'tis our fast intent
To shake all cares and business from our age,
Conferring them on younger strengths, while we
Unburdened crawl toward death. Our son of Cornwall,
40   And you, our no less loving son of Albany,
We have this hour a constant will to publish
Our daughters' several dowers, that future strife
May be prevented now. The princes, France and
        Burgundy,
Great rivals in our youngest daughter's love,
45   Long in our court have made their amorous sojourn,
And here are to be answered. Tell me, my daughters –
Since now we will divest us both of rule,

22

Edmund   No, my lord.

Gloucester   [*introducing him formally*] The Lord of Kent.
Regard him always as my honourable friend.

Edmund   [*bowing*] At your service, my lord.

Kent   My love to you: I'd like to know you better.

Edmund   Sir, I'll try to be worthy of your interest.

Gloucester   He's been soldiering abroad these last nine years,
and he'll be off again soon. [*The sound of trumpets is heard*]
The King is coming.

[*A servant enters carrying a coronet, followed by* **King Lear**;
the Dukes of **Albany** *and* **Cornwall**; *their wives* **Goneril** *and*
Regan, *two daughters of the King*; **Cordelia**, *Lear's youngest
daughter; and members of the court*]

Lear   Bring in the Lords of France and Burgundy, Gloucester.

Gloucester   I shall, my liege. [*He goes, followed by* **Edmund**]

Lear   Meanwhile we'll reveal our plan. Give me that map,
there. [**Servants** *hand him a large map of Britain. He
addresses the court*] Be it known that we have divided our
kingdom into three parts; and it is our firm intention to
shake off all cares and responsibilities in our old age, and to
confer them on younger shoulders while we, freed of our
burdens, crawl towards death. Our son-in-law Cornwall, and
you, our no less loving son-in-law Albany: we have resolved
at this juncture to make public the various doweries of our
daughters, so that future strife can be prevented now. The
King of France and the Duke of Burgundy – keen rivals for
the hand of our youngest daughter – have for a long time
resided at our court as suitors, and they are to have their
answer here. [*To* **Goneril**, **Regan** *and* **Cordelia**] Tell me, my
daughters – since we shall now divest us of our throne, our

23

Interest of territory, cares of state –
Which of you shall we say doth love us most?
50 That we our largest bounty may extend
Where nature doth with merit challenge. Goneril,
Our eldest-born, speak first.

Goneril   Sir, I love you more than words can wield the
matter;
Dearer than eye-sight, space and liberty;
55 Beyond what can be valued rich or rare;
No less than life, with grace, health, beauty, honour;
As much as child e'er loved, or father found;
A love that makes breath poor and speech unable;
Beyond all manner of so much I love you.

Cordelia   [*Aside*] What shall Cordelia speak? Love, and be
60 silent.

Lear   Of all these bounds, even from this line to this,
With shadowy forests and with champains riched,
With plenteous rivers and wide-skirted meads,
We make thee lady; to thine and Albany's issues
65 Be this perpetual. What says our second daughter
Our dearest Regan, wife of Cornwall? Speak.

Regan   I am made of that self metal as my sister,
And prize me at her worth. In my true heart
I find she names my very deed of love;
70 Only she comes too short: that I profess
Myself an enemy to all other joys
Which the most precious square of sense possesses,
And find I am alone felicitate
In your dear highness' love.

Cordelia   [*Aside*]   Then poor Cordelia!
75 And yet not so; since I am sure my love's
More ponderous than my tongue.

24

territorial possessions and our administrative
responsibilities – which of you shall we say is the one who
loves us most? Then we can bestow our greatest generosity
where natural affection most merits it. Goneril, our eldest
child, speak first.

Goneril   Sir, I love you more than words can express: dearer
than eyesight, freedom or independence; more than what is
utterly priceless or rare; no less than life itself when it has
dignity, health, beauty and honour; as much as a child ever
loved or a father ever enjoyed affection; a love that makes
words weak and speech inadequate. Beyond all such
comparisons I love you.

Cordelia   [*aside*] What shall Cordelia say? Just love, and be
silent . . .

Lear   [*indicating the boundaries of* **Goneril**'s *legacy on the
map*] All this region – from this line here to this – rich with
shady forests, fertile plains, teeming rivers and broad
meadows, we give you to rule. This is for you and your
husband Albany's descendants forever. [*He turns to* **Regan**]
What has our second daughter to say, our dearest Regan,
wife of the Duke of Cornwall? Speak.

Regan   I am made of the selfsame metal as my sister, so value
me as you have done her. From the bottom of my heart, I
find she describes my own love precisely, except that she
understates it. No other pleasure appeals to me: my
happiness is solely in the enjoyment of your love.

Cordelia   [*To herself*] Poor Cordelia, then! But not really so,
because I'm sure my love is greater than my tongue can
express.

25

Lear   To thee and thine, hereditary ever,
Remain this ample third of our fair kingdom,
No less in space, validity, and pleasure,
80   Than that conferred on Goneril. Now, our joy,
Although our last, not least; to whose young love
The vines of France and milk of Burgundy
Strive to be interessed; what can you say to draw
A third more opulent than your sisters? Speak.

85 **Cordelia**   Nothing, my lord.

Lear   Nothing?

Cordelia   Nothing.

Lear   Nothing will come of nothing: speak again.

Cordelia   Unhappy that I am, I cannot heave
90   My heart into my mouth: I love your majesty
According to my bond; no more nor less.

Lear   How, how, Cordelia! Mend your speech a little,
Lest it may mar your fortunes.

Cordelia   Good my lord,
You have begot me, bred me, loved me: I
95   Return those duties back as are right fit,
Obey you, love you, and most honour you.
Why have my sisters husbands, if they say
They love you all? Happily, when I shall wed,
That lord whose hand must take my plight shall carry
100   Half my love with him, half my care and duty:
Sure I shall never marry like my sisters,
To love my father all.

Lear   But goes thy heart with this?

Cordelia   Ay, my good lord.

Lear   So young, and so untender?

26

Lear   [*to* **Regan**] To you and yours, in perpetuity, is bestowed this extensive third of our fine kingdom: no smaller, less valuable or pleasurable than that conferred on Goneril. [*Turning to* **Cordelia**] Now our joy; last-born but not least; for whose young love the vineyards of France and the pastures of Burgundy compete. What can you say to attract a third share more valuable than that of your sisters? Speak.

Cordelia   Nothing, my lord.

Lear   Nothing?

Cordelia   Nothing.

Lear   Nothing begets nothing. Speak again.

Cordelia   Wretched as I am, I can't express in words what's in my heart. I love your majesty according to my duty as a daughter. No more, no less.

Lear   [*his anger rising*] What, what Cordelia? Speak more tactfully, lest you spoil your chances!

Cordelia   My good lord: you have fathered me, brought me up and loved me. I return those duties accordingly: I obey you, love you, and honour you most. Why have my sisters got husbands, if they say they love you absolutely? Be assured that when I wed, the man who has my hand in marriage will have half my love, half my care and duty. Certainly I'll never marry like my sisters, loving my father so totally.

Lear   Is this spoken from the heart?

Cordelia   Yes, my good lord.

Lear   So young, yet so hard-hearted?

105   **Cordelia**   So young, my lord, and true.

    Lear   Let it be so; thy truth then be thy dower:
       For, by the sacred radiance of the sun,
       The mysteries of Hecate and the night,
       By all the operation of the orbs
110   From whom we do exist and cease to be,
       Here I disclaim all my paternal care,
       Propinquity and property of blood,
       And as a stranger to my heart and me
       Hold thee from this for ever. The barbarous Scythian,
115   Or he that makes his generation messes
       To gorge his appetite, shall to my bosom
       Be as well neighboured, pitied, and relieved,
       As thou my sometime daughter.

    Kent   Good my liege –

    Lear   Peace, Kent!
120   Come not between the dragon and his wrath.
       I loved her most, and thought to set my rest
       On her kind nursery. Hence, and avoid my sight!
       So be my grave my peace, as here I give
       Her father's heart from her! Call France. Who stirs?
125   Call Burgundy. Cornwall and Albany,
       With my two daughters' dowers digest this third;
       Let pride, which she calls plainness, marry her.
       I do invest you jointly with my power,
       Pre-eminence, and all the large effects
130   That troop with majesty. Ourself, by monthly course,
       With reservation of an hundred knights
       By you to be sustained, shall our abode
       Make with you by due turn. Only we shall retain
       The name and all th'addition to a king;
135   The sway, revenue, execution of the rest,
       Beloved sons, be yours: which to confirm,
       This coronet part between you.

Cordelia   So young, my lord, and truthful.

Lear   Right, then: truth shall be your dowry! By the sun's
sacred beams, by the witch-queen's magic rites at night, by
all the stars that govern life and death: I here disclaim my
fatherly affection, my kinship, my blood relationship! For
evermore I shall regard you as a stranger to my heart and
me. Barbarians like the Scythians, or those who eat their
kinfolk when they're hungry, shall be as welcomed, pitied
and given succour as you, my *former* daughter!

Kent   Your majesty –

Lear   Silence, Kent! Don't come between the dragon and the
object of his wrath! I loved her most, and planned to live
with her in my retirement. Go, get out of my sight! Death is
my only consolation, since here I give away a father's love!
Call the King of France. Quick now! Call Burgundy! Cornwall
and Albany. To my two daughters' dowries add this third
[*pointing to* **Cordelia**'s *territory on the map*]. Let
pride – which she calls frankness – get her a husband. I
invest you jointly with my power, my absolute authority, and
all the ceremonial that goes with kingship. We shall live with
you alternately on a monthly basis, retaining the right to
have a hundred knights maintained at your expense. We'll
simply retain the title and all the ceremonies due to a king.
Policy, taxation, and all administrative matters, beloved
sons, will be yours. In confirmation, this coronet is divided
between you. [*The* **Servant** *presents it to the* **Duke**]

Kent   Royal Lear,
Whom I have ever honoured as my King,
Loved as my father, as my master followed,
140   As my great patron thought on in my prayers, –

Lear   The bow is bent and drawn; make from the shaft.

Kent   Let it fall rather, though the fork invade
The region of my heart: be Kent unmannerly,
When Lear is mad. What would'st thou do, old man?
145   Think'st thou that duty shall have dread to speak
When power to flattery bows? To plainness honour's bound
When majesty falls to folly. Reserve thy state;
And, in thy best consideration, check
This hideous rashness: answer my life my judgment,
150   Thy youngest daughter does not love thee least;
Nor are those empty-hearted whose low sounds
Reverb no hollowness.

Lear   Kent on thy life, no more.

Kent   My life I never held but as a pawn
To wage against thine enemies; nor fear to lose it,
Thy safety being the motive.

155 **Lear**   Out of my sight!

Kent   See better, Lear; and let me still remain
The true blank of thine eye.

Lear   Now, by Apollo –

Kent   Now, by Apollo, King,
Thou swear'st thy Gods in vain.

Lear   Oh, vassal! Miscreant!

[*Laying his hand on his sword*]

160 **Alb., Corn.**   Dear sir, forbear.

30

Kent   Royal Lear, whom I've always honoured as my King, loved as if he were my father, followed as he is my master, mentioned in my prayers as my great patron –

Lear   The bow is bent and drawn: keep clear of the arrow!

Kent   Better to let it go, even though it pierces my heart! Kent must be discourteous when Lear is mad. What are you doing, old man? Do you think loyal men will fear to speak when those in power fall for flattery? Honour demands plain speaking when kings descend to folly. Keep your crown, and think again; let this appalling rashness go no further. I'll stake my life on it: your youngest daughter does not love you least, nor are they heartless whose low-key speeches contain no flattery.

Lear   Kent, upon your life – no more!

Kent   I never considered my life as more than a mere pawn, to be used against your enemies, nor do I fear losing it when your safety is the issue.

Lear   Out of my sight!

Kent   See better, Lear, and let me – as ever – be clear-sighted on your behalf!

Lear   Now, by Apollo – !

Kent   Now, by Apollo, King, you invoke your gods in vain!

Lear   Oh, you ruffian! Infidel! [*He puts his hand to his sword*]

Alb., Corn.   Good sir, be patient!

Kent   Do: kill thy physician, and the fee bestow
Upon the foul disease. Revoke thy gift;
Or, whilst I can vent clamour from my throat,
I'll tell thee thou dost evil.

Lear   Hear me, recreant!
165   On thine allegiance, hear me!
Since thou hast sought to make us break our vow,
Which we durst never yet, and with strained pride
To come betwixt our sentence and our power,
Which nor our nature nor our place can bear,
170   Our potency made good, take thy reward.
Five days we do allot thee for provision
To shield thee from disasters of the world;
And on the sixth to turn thy hated back
Upon our kingdom: if on the tenth day following
175   Thy banished trunk be found in our dominions,
The moment is thy death. Away! By Jupiter,
This shall not be revoked.

Kent   Fare thee well, King; sith thus thou wilt appear,
Freedom lives hence, and banishment is here.
[*To* **Cordelia**] The Gods to their dear shelter take thee,
180   maid,
That justly think'st and has most rightly said!
[*To* **Goneril** *and* **Regan**] And your large speeches may your
deeds approve,
That good effects may spring from words of love.
Thus Kent, oh princes! bids you all adieu;
185   He'll shape his old course in a country new.

[*Exit*]

[*Flourish. Re-enter* **Gloucester**, *with* **France, Burgundy,**
and Attendants]

Gloucester   Here's France and Burgundy, my noble lord.

Kent Yes, do: kill your doctor and give the fee to the foul
disease! Withdraw your gift, or while I've still got breath to
protest, I'll tell you that you're doing wrong!

Lear Listen, traitor! On your oath of allegiance, hear me!
Since you have tried to make us break our vow, which we
have never done before, and because you've attempted to
come between our sentence and our authority – which
neither our character nor our rank can tolerate – to confirm
our power, take your reward! We give you five days to
prepare yourself for the rigours of the world. On the sixth,
turn your hated back upon our kingdom. If on the tenth day
after that your banished body is to be found in our realm,
that moment is your death. Away! By Jupiter, this will not
be revoked!

Kent Farewell, King. Since that's how you want it, freedom
lives abroad, and banishment is here. [*To* **Cordelia**] The gods
protect you, maid. Your reasoning's right and you've said
what's true. [*To* **Goneril** *and* **Regan**] As for your grandiose
speeches, may your deeds live up to them! Then some good
might come from loving words. [*To the assembled* **Nobles**]
Thus, Princes, Kent bids you all farewell. He'll continue to
be his old self in a new country.

[*He goes*]

[*A flourish of trumpets heralds the entry of* **Gloucester**, *the*
King of France, *the* **Duke of Burgundy**, *and their* **Attendants**]

Gloucester Here are France and Burgundy, my lord.

Lear   My Lord of Burgundy,
We first address toward you, who with this king
Hath rivalled for our daughter. What, in the least,
190   Will you require in present dower with her,
Or cease your quest of love?

Burgundy   Most royal majesty,
I crave no more than hath your highness offered,
Nor will you tender less.

Lear   Right noble Burgundy,
When she was dear to us we did hold her so,
195   But now her price is fallen. Sir, there she stands:
If aught within that little-seeming substance,
Or all of it, with our displeasure pieced,
And nothing more, may fitly like your grace,
She's there, and she is yours.

Burgundy   I know no answer.

200 **Lear**   Will you, with those infirmities she owes,
Unfriended, new-adopted to our hate,
Dowered with our curse and strangered with our oath,
Take her, or leave her?

Burgundy   Pardon me, royal sir;
Election makes not up in such conditions.

205 **Lear**   Then leave her, sir; for, by the power that made me,
I tell you all her wealth. [*To* **France**] For you, great King,
I would not from your love make such a stray
To match you where I hate; therefore beseech you
T'avert your liking a more worthier way
210   Than on a wretch whom Nature is ashamed
Almost to acknowledge hers.

France   This is most strange,
That she, whom even but now was your best object,
The argument of your praise, balm of your age,

Lear   My Lord of Burgundy: we address you first. You have competed with this King for our daughter's hand. What is the minimum dowry you will require with her, without which you'd cease to be a suitor?

Burgundy   Most royal majesty: I beg no more than your highness has offered. Surely you would not suggest less?

Lear   Right noble Burgundy: when we loved her, we valued her accordingly. Now her price has fallen. Sir, there she stands. If anything in particular about that outspoken object, or all of it − complete with our displeasure, and nothing more − happens to suit your grace, she's there, and she is yours.

Burgundy   I don't know what to say.

Lear   Will you − with all her imperfections; friendless; our hatred freshly upon her; her dowry our curse; disowned by our vow − take her or leave her?

Burgundy   With respect, royal sir. Decisions are not made on terms like those.

Lear   Then leave her, sir, because by the gods that made me, I'm telling you that's all she's worth. [*To* **France**] As for you, great king, I wouldn't distance myself from your love by marrying you to one I hate. Therefore I entreat you to turn your affections in a worthier direction than on a wretch who behaves so unnaturally.

France   It's very strange that she − who just now was your most precious possession, the subject of your praise, the comfort of your old age, the best, the dearest − should

The best, the dearest, should in this trice of time
215 Commit a thing so monstrous, to dismantle
So many folds of favour. Sure, her offence
Must be of such unnatural degree
That monsters it, or your fore-vouched affection
Fall into taint; which to believe of her,
220 Must be a faith that reason without miracle
Should never plant in me.

Cordelia   I yet beseech your majesty –
If for I want that glib and oily art
To speak and purpose not, since what I well intend,
I'll do't before I speak – that you make known
225 It is no vicious blot, murder or foulness,
No unchaste action, or dishonoured step,
That hath deprived me of your grace and favour,
But even for want of that for which I am richer,
A still-soliciting eye, and such a tongue
230 That I am glad I have not, though not to have it
Hath lost me in your liking.

Lear   Better thou
Hadst not been born than not t'have pleased me better.

France Is it but this? A tardiness in nature
Which often leaves the history unspoke
235 That it intends to do? My Lord of Burgundy,
What say you to the lady? Love's not love
When it is mingled with regards that stand
Aloof from th'entire point. Will you have her?
She is herself a dowry.

Burgundy   Royal King,
240 Give but that portion which yourself proposed,
And here I take Cordelia by the hand,
Duchess of Burgundy.

Lear Nothing: I have sworn; I am firm.

36

suddenly commit something so monstrous as to destroy
such deep affection. Either her offence must be atrociously
unnatural, or else your former vows of love are suspect.
Short of a miraculous revelation, my reason would never
allow me to believe that of her.

Cordelia   I appeal to your majesty – in spite of lacking the glib
and oily art of making empty promises, preferring action
rather than words – to state publicly that it is no vicious
misbehaviour, murder or wickedness, no wantonness or
dishonourable action, that has deprived me of your grace
and favour. Rather it is for lacking what I'm better off
without: an eye for seeking favours, and the kind of tongue
I'm glad I haven't got, though not having it has ruined me in
your affection.

Lear   Better you had never been born than not to have pleased
me better.

France   Is this all? A natural reticence that often
unintentionally leaves inner thoughts unspoken? My Lord of
Burgundy, will you have the lady? Love is not true love when
it is subject to irrelevant conditions. Will you have her?
She's a dowry in herself.

Burgundy   Royal King, just give the dowry which you yourself
proposed, and I'll take Cordelia by the hand – Duchess of
Burgundy.

Lear   Nothing. I have made a vow. I am resolute.

Burgundy   I am sorry, then, you have so lost a father
That you must lose a husband.

245 **Cordelia**   Peace be with Burgundy!
Since that respect and fortunes are his love,
I shall not be his wife.

France   Fairest Cordelia, that art most rich, being poor;
Most choice, forsaken; and most loved, despised!
250 Thee and thy virtues here I seize upon:
Be it lawful I take up what's cast away.
Gods, gods! 'Tis strange that from their cold'st neglect
My love should kindle to inflamed respect.
Thy dowerless daughter, King, thrown to my chance,
255 Is queen of us, of ours, and our fair France.
Not all the dukes of waterish Burgundy
Can buy this unprized precious maid of me.
Bid them farewell, Cordelia, though unkind:
Thou losest here, a better where to find.

260 **Lear**   Thou hast her, France; let her be thine; for we
Have no such daughter, nor shall ever see
That face of hers again; therefore be gone
Without our grace, our love, our benison.
Come, noble Burgundy.

[*Flourish. Exeunt* **Lear, Burgundy, Cornwall, Albany,
Gloucester** *and Attendants*]

265 **France**   Bid farewell to your sisters.

Cordelia   The jewels of our father, with washed eyes
Cordelia leaves you: I know you what you are;
And like a sister am most loath to call
Your faults as they are named. Love well our father:
270 To your professed bosoms I commit him:
But yet, alas, stood I within his grace,

Burgundy   [*to* **Cordelia**] Then I am sorry: losing a father has
    lost you a husband.

Cordelia   [*wryly*] God bless Burgundy! Since he's in love with
    respectability and wealth, I shall not be his wife!

France   Fairest Cordelia, who is most precious, being poor;
    most exquisite, being forsaken; and most loved, being
    despised! You and your virtues I here claim. If it is lawful, I
    will take up what has been cast away. The gods, the gods!
    It's strange that their cold indifference should ignite my love!
    Your dowerless daughter, King, by good fortune mine, is
    Queen to me, of all I possess, and of fair France. Not all the
    dukes of wishy-washy Burgundy could buy this underrated
    but priceless maid from me. Bid them farewell Cordelia,
    unkind though they are. You lose here to gain more
    elsewhere.

Lear   You've got her, France. She's yours. We have no such
    daughter, nor shall we ever see that face of hers again.
    Therefore be gone: without our good wishes, our love, or
    our blessing. Come, noble Burgundy!

[**Lear** *departs, followed by* **Burgundy, Cornwall, Albany,
Gloucester** *and the Attendants*]

France   [*to* **Cordelia**] Say goodbye to your sisters.

Cordelia   My father's precious ones, Cordelia leaves in tears. I
    know you for what you are, but as your sister I am reluctant
    to expose you. Love our father well. I entrust him to your
    so-called care. However, if I were still in favour, I'd find him

I would prefer him to a better place.
So farewell to you both.

Regan   Prescribe not us our duty.

Goneril   Let your study
275   Be to content your lord, who hath received you
At fortune's alms; you have obedience scanted,
And well are worth the want that you have wanted.

Cordelia   Time shall unfold what plighted cunning hides;
Who covers faults, at last shame them derides.
Well may you prosper!

280   **France**   Come, my fair Cordelia.

[*Exeunt* **France** *and* **Cordelia**]

Goneril   Sister, it is not little I have to say of what most
nearly appertains to us both. I think our father will hence
to-night.

Regan   That's most certain, and with you; next month with
285   us.

Goneril   You see how full of changes his age is; the
observation we have made of it hath not been little: he
always loved our sister most; and with what poor judgment
he hath now cast her off appears too grossly.

290   **Regan**   'Tis the infirmity of his age; yet he hath ever but
slenderly known himself.

Goneril   The best and soundest of his time hath been but
rash; then must we look from his age, to receive not alone
the imperfections of long-engraffed condition, but
295   therewithal the unruly waywardness that infirm and
choleric years bring with them.

somewhere better to stay. So farewell to you both.

Regan   Don't tell us what to do!

Goneril   Concentrate on pleasing your husband, who took you when your luck was out. You have been less than obedient, and you well deserve what's happened to you.

Cordelia   Time will reveal what mischief you are up to. Tricksters get exposed in the end. Good luck to you.

France   Come, my fair Cordelia.

[**France** *and* **Cordelia** *leave*]

Goneril   Sister, I have a lot to say of mutual interest. I think our father will leave tonight.

Regan   That's for certain – and with you. Next month he'll stay with us.

Goneril   You see how fickle he can be in his old age. We've seen plenty of examples. He always loved our sister most. His poor judgment is very obvious from the way he now casts her off.

Regan   His age is the trouble. But then he has always lacked self-control.

Goneril   Even in his prime he was hot-headed. So we must expect not only his deep-rooted faults, but also the wilfulness that comes with crochety old age.

Regan   Such unconstant starts are we like to have from him as this of Kent's banishment.

Goneril   There is further compliment of leave-taking between
300   France and him. Pray you, let us hit together: if our father carry authority with such disposition as he bears, this last surrender of his will but offend us.

Regan   We shall further think of it.

Goneril   We must do something, and i'th'heat.

[*Exeunt*]

Scene 2

The Earl of Gloucester's Castle. Enter **Edmund,** *with a letter*

Edmund   Thou, Nature, art my goddess; to thy law
My services are bound. Wherefore should I
Stand in the plague of custom, and permit
The curiosity of nations to deprive me,
5   For that I am some twelve or fourteen moonshines
Lag of a brother? Why bastard? Wherefore base?
When my dimensions are as well compact,
My mind as generous, and my shape as true,
As honest madam's issue? Why brand they us
10   With base? with baseness? bastardy? base, base?
Who in the lusty stealth of nature take
More composition and fierce quality
Than doth, within a dull, stale, tired bed,
Go to the creating a whole tribe of fops,
15   Got 'tween asleep and wake? Well then,

Regan   We're likely to get more sudden whims like Kent's banishment.

Goneril   And there's the way he rudely took leave of France. Well then, let's work together. If our father continues to carry on like this, this recent abdication will be a nuisance to us.

Regan   We'll give it some more thought.

Goneril   We must *do* something before it's too late!

[*They go*]

Scene 2

The Earl of Gloucester's Castle. **Edmund** *enters, carrying a letter*

Edmund   Nature, you are my goddess! I obey your laws. Why should I be plagued by convention and let the narrow-mindedness of society keep me from my rights, just because I'm some twelve or fourteen months younger than my brother? Why am I 'bastard'? Why inferior? I'm as well-proportioned, my mind is as vigorous, my build as similar, as the married lady's offspring. Why do they brand us as inferior? With inferiority? Illegitimacy? Inferior, inferior? What, we – who get sounder constitutions and more guts from hot-blooded fornication than goes into the making of a whole tribe of idiots conceived between bedtime and morning in a dull, bored, tedious sort of bed?

Legitimate Edgar, I must have your land:
Our father's love is to the bastard Edmund
As to the legitimate. Fine word, 'legitimate'!
Well, my legitimate, if this letter speed,
20   And my invention thrive, Edmund the base
Shall top the legitimate. I grow, I prosper:
Now, gods, stand up for bastards!

[*Enter* **Gloucester**]

Gloucester   Kent banished thus! And France in choler
parted!
And the King gone tonight! Prescribed his power!
25   Confined to exhibition! All this done
Upon the gad! Edmund, how now! What news?

Edmund   So please your lordship, none.   [*Putting up the
letter*]

Gloucester   Why so earnestly seek you to put up that letter?

Edmund   I know no news, my lord.

30 **Gloucester**   What paper were you reading?

Edmund   Nothing, my lord.

Gloucester   No? What needed then that terrible dispatch of
it into your pocket? The quality of nothing hath not such
need to hide itself. Let's see: come; if it be nothing, I shall
35   not need spectacles.

Edmund   I beseech you, sir, pardon me; it is a letter from my
brother that I have not all o'erread, and for so much as I
have perused, I find it not fit for your o'erlooking.

Gloucester   Give me the letter, sir.

40 **Edmund**   I shall offend, either to detain or give it. The
contents, as in part I understand them, are to blame.

44

Well, then, legitimate Edgar, I must have your inheritance!
Our father loves the bastard Edmund as much as the
legitimate Edgar. Fine word, 'legitimate'! Well, my
legitimate, if this letter [*he flourishes it*] works properly, and
my plan prospers, Edmund the bastard will beat the
legitimate. I progress; I prosper. Now, gods – stand up for
bastards!

[*His father, the* **Earl of Gloucester**, *enters thinking aloud*]

Gloucester   Kent banished like that! And France has left in
anger! And the King departed last night, his power limited,
restricted to a token force! All this done on the spur of the
moment! [*He notices his son*] Greetings, Edmund. What
news?

Edmund   [*hiding his letter very obviously*] May it please your
lordship, none.

Gloucester   Why are you trying so hard to hide that letter?

Edmund   I've no news, my lord.

Gloucester   What was the document you were reading?

Edmund   Nothing, my lord.

Gloucester   No? Then why all the indecent haste to put it into
your pocket? What's 'nothing' has no such need to hide
itself. Let's see; come on; if it's nothing, I won't need
spectacles.

Edmund   I beg you, sir, excuse me: it's a letter from my
brother that I haven't finished reading, and from what I've
scanned, I believe it's not for your eyes.

Gloucester   Give me the letter, sir!

Edmund   I'll give offence whether I keep it or give it. The
contents, as far as I can follow them, are to blame.

Gloucester   Let's see, let's see.

Edmund   I hope, for my brother's justification, he wrote this but as an essay or taste of my virtue.

45 **Gloucester**   [*Reads*] *This policy and reverence of age makes the world bitter to the best of our times; keeps our fortunes from us till our oldness cannot relish them. I begin to find an idle and fond bondage in the oppression of aged tyranny, who sways, not as it hath power, but as it is suffered. Come to me,*
50 *that of this I may speak more. If our father would sleep till I waked him, you should enjoy half his revenue for ever, and live the beloved of your brother, Edgar. –*

Hum! Conspiracy! 'Sleep till I waked him, you should enjoy half his revenue.' My son Edgar! Had he a hand to
55 write this? A heart and brain to breed it in? When came you to this? Who brought it?

Edmund   It was not brought me, my lord; there's the cunning of it; I found it thrown in at the casement of my closet.

Gloucester   You know the character to be your brother's?

60 **Edmund**   If the matter were good, my lord, I durst swear it were his; but, in respect of that, I would fain think it were not.

Gloucester   It is his.

Edmund   It is his hand, my lord; but I hope his heart is not
65 in the contents.

Gloucester   Has he never before sounded you in this business?

Edmund   Never, my lord. But I have heard him oft maintain it to be fit that, sons at perfect age, and fathers declined,
70 the father should be as ward to the son, and the son manage his revenue.

46

Gloucester   Let's see, let's see!

Edmund   I hope – to make excuses for my brother – that he wrote this as a test or trial of my honesty.

Gloucester   [*reading aloud*] *This practice of reverencing old people makes the best years of our lives a misery. It keeps our legacies from us till we're too old to enjoy them. I'm beginning to feel that oppression by an aged tyrant is stupid and foolish slavery. It operates not through strength, but through the victim's willingness to suffer. Come and see me, so I can explain further. If our father would only sleep till I awakened him, you'd enjoy half his income forever – and be beloved of your brother, Edgar.* Hmm! Conspiracy! 'Sleep till I awakened him, you'd enjoy half his income . . .' My son Edgar! Could he have written this? Had he a heart and a brain to think it up? When did this come to you? Who brought it?

Edmund   It wasn't brought to me, my lord. There's the cunning of it. I found it thrown through the window of my bedroom.

Gloucester   You recognize the handwriting as your brother's?

Edmund   If the contents were acceptable, my lord, I'd swear it was his. But in connection with that [*he indicates the letter*] I'd prefer to think it wasn't.

Gloucester   It *is* his!

Edmund   It's his writing, my lord, but I hope his heart isn't in the contents.

Gloucester   Has he ever sounded you out on this business before?

Edmund   Never, my lord. But I've often heard him maintain it to be only right that once sons reach maturity and fathers are past their prime, the father should be in the custody of the son, and the son should manage his affairs.

47

Gloucester   O villain, villain! His very opinion in the letter!
Abhorred villain! Unnatural, detested, brutish villain!
Worse than brutish! Go, sirrah, seek him; I'll apprehend
75   him. Abominable villain! Where is he?

Edmund   I do not well know, my lord. If it shall please you
to suspend your indignation against my brother till you can
derive from him better testimony of his intent, you should
run a certain course; where, if you violently proceed against
80   him, mistaking his purpose, it would make a great gap in
your own honour, and shake in pieces the heart of his
obedience. I dare pawn down my life for him, that he hath
writ this to feel my affection to your honour, and to no
other pretence of danger.

85 **Gloucester**   Think you so?

Edmund   If your honour judge it meet, I will place you
where you shall hear us confer of this, and by an auricular
assurance have your satisfaction; and that without any
further delay than this very evening.

90 **Gloucester**   He cannot be such a monster.

Edmund   Nor is not, sure.

Gloucester   To his father, that so tenderly and entirely loves
him. Heaven and earth! Edmund, seek him out; wind me
into him, I pray you: frame the business after your own
95   wisdom. I would unstate myself to be in a due resolution.

Edmund   I will seek him, sir, presently; convey the business
as I shall find means, and acquaint you withal.

Gloucester   These late eclipses in the sun and moon portend
no good to us: though the wisdom of nature can reason it
100   thus and thus, yet nature finds itself scourged by the
sequent effects. Love cools, friendship falls off, brothers
divide: in cities, mutinies; in countries, discord; in palaces,

Gloucester Oh, the villain, the villain! That's exactly what he says in the letter! The disgusting villain! The unnatural, detestable, brutish villain! Worse than brutish! Go, sir, find him. I'll arrest him. The detestable villain! Where is he?

Edmund I don't really know, my lord. If you could contain your anger against my brother till you can extract from him a clearer indication of his intentions, you'd be better advised. On the other hand, if you react violently against him, mistaking his purpose, your own honour will be greatly damaged, and his loyalty shaken to the core. I'd stake my life on him: he has written this to test my love for your honour, and not with dangerous intent.

Gloucester Do you think so?

Edmund If your honour thinks it's a good idea, I'll place you where you can hear us discuss this, and by hearing for yourself you can settle your doubts this very evening at the latest.

Gloucester He can't be such a monster –

Edmund Nor is he, surely.

Gloucester – to his own father, who loves him so entirely and tenderly! Heaven and earth! Edmund, find him. Get his confidence, do. Use your discretion. I'd give my all to be assured of his innocence.

Edmund I'll look for him, sir, immediately; work things as best I can, and report back.

Gloucester These recent eclipses of the sun and moon are not good omens for us. Though man's reason can explain such things away, nonetheless mankind has to suffer the natural consequences. Love cools off. Friendship declines. Brothers are divided. In cities there are riots; in countries civil war; in

treason; and the bond cracked 'twixt son and father. This
villain of mine comes under the prediction; there's son
105   against father: the King falls from bias of nature; there's
father against child. We have seen the best of our time:
machinations, hollowness, treachery, and all ruinous
disorders follow us disquietly to our graves. Find out this
villain, Edmund; it shall lose thee nothing: do it carefully.
110   And the noble and true-hearted Kent banished! His offence,
honesty! 'Tis strange.

                                  [*Exit*]

Edmund   This is the excellent foppery of the world, that,
when we are sick in fortune, often the surfeit of our own
behaviour, we make guilty of our disasters the sun, the
115   moon, and stars; as if we were villains by necessity, fools by
heavenly compulsion; knaves, thieves, and treachers by
spherical predominance; drunkards, liars, and adulterers by
an enforced obedience of planetary influence; and all that we
are evil in, by a divine thrusting on. An admirable evasion
120   of whoremaster man, to lay his goatish disposition to the
charge of a star! My father compounded with my mother
under the dragon's tail, and my nativity was under Ursa
major; so that it follows I am rough and lecherous. Tut! I
should have been that I am had the maidenliest star in the
125   firmament twinkled on my bastardizing. Edgar –

[*Enter* **Edgar**]

Pat he comes, like the catastrophe of the old comedy: my
cue is villainous melancholy, with a sigh like Tom o'
Bedlam. Oh, these eclipses do portend these divisions.

Edgar   How now, brother Edmund! What serious
130   contemplation are you in?

palaces, treason; and the bond between son and father is broken. This villain of mine fits the pattern: there's son against father. The King goes against his natural instincts: there's father against child. We've had the best years: intrigue, insincerity, treachery and chaos follow us distressingly to our graves. Sound out this villain, Edmund, you'll lose nothing by it. Do it discreetly. And the noble and loyal Kent is banished: his offence, honesty! It's strange.

[*He goes*]

Edmund   How typically stupid: when things go wrong, often through our own fault, we blame our troubles on the sun, moon and stars! As though we are villains through no choice of our own; fools by order of heaven; knaves, thieves and traitors through the dominance of a planet at our births; drunkards, liars and adulterers by compulsion from the stars; and that all our evil acts come from divine provocation! An admirable alibi for lecherous man, to blame his randy disposition on a star! My father tumbled my mother under a waning moon and I was born under the Great Bear: so it follows that I'm rough and lecherous? Pah! I'd be what I am had the most chaste star in the firmament twinkled over my illegitimacy! Edgar –

[**Edgar** *enters*]

– and here he comes, as predictably as the ending of an old-fashioned play. My role requires Deep Melancholy – with a sigh like that of a lunatic beggar. [*He assumes a suitably solemn face and manner of speech*] Oh, these eclipses are premonitions of disorder . . . [*He hums to himself as if deep in philosophic thought*]

Edgar   Greetings, brother Edmund! What's the big problem on your mind?

51

Edmund   I am thinking, brother, of a prediction I read this other day, what should follow these eclipses.

Edgar   Do you busy yourself about that?

Edmund   I promise you the effects he writes of succeed
135   unhappily; as of unnaturalness between the child and the parent; death, dearth, dissolutions of ancient amities; divisions in state; menaces and maledictions against king and nobles; needless diffidences, banishment of friends, dissipation of cohorts, nuptial breaches, and I know not what.

140   **Edgar**   How long have you been a sectary astronomical?

Edmund   When saw you my father last?

Edgar   The night gone by.

Edmund   Spake you with him?

Edgar   Ay, two hours together.

145   **Edmund**   Parted you in good terms? Found you no displeasure in him by word nor countenance?

Edgar   None at all.

Edmund   Bethink yourself wherein you may have offended him; and at my entreaty forbear his presence until some
150   little time hath qualified the heat of his displeasure, which at this instant so rageth in him that with the mischief of your person it would scarcely allay.

Edgar   Some villain hath done me wrong.

Edmund   That's my fear. I pray you have a continent
155   forbearance till the speed of his rage goes slower; and as I say, retire with me to my lodging, from whence I will fitly bring you to hear my lord speak. Pray ye, go; there's my key. If you do stir abroad, go armed.

Edgar   Armed, brother!

Edmund   I'm thinking, brother, of a prediction I read the other day about what will follow from these eclipses.

Edgar   Do you worry about things like that?

Edmund   I assure you that the consequences he writes about turn out to be disagreeable: such as unnaturalness between child and parent; death, famine and the ending of longstanding friendships; disunity in countries; threats and curses against King and nobles; unfounded suspicions, the banishment of friends; desertion of troops; matrimonial strife; and I don't know what.

Edgar   How long have you been a student of astrology?

Edmund   When did you last see my father?

Edgar   Last night.

Edmund   Did you speak to him?

Edgar   Yes. Fully two hours.

Edmund   Did you part on friendly terms? Did he seem displeased by the way he spoke or looked?

Edgar   Not at all.

Edmund   Try to think how you may have offended him. Do me the favour of avoiding him till his temper has cooled. At the moment he's so furious that your turning up would hardly be the cure.

Edgar   Some villain has wronged me!

Edmund   That's what I fear. I advise you to keep at a discreet distance till he calms down; and as I say, come back with me to my place, where at an opportune time I'll let you overhear what my lord says. Please – go! There's my key. If you do go out, go armed.

Edgar   Armed, brother?

160 **Edmund**   Brother, I advise you to the best. I am no honest
man if there be any good meaning towards you; I have told
you what I have seen and heard; but faintly, nothing like
the image and horror of it; pray you, away.

Edgar   Shall I hear from you anon?

165 **Edmund**   I do serve you in this business.

[*Exit* **Edgar**]

A credulous father, and a brother noble,
Whose nature is so far from doing harms
That he suspects none; on whose foolish honesty
My practices ride easy! I see the business.
170   Let me, if not by birth, have lands by wit:
All with me's meet that I can fashion fit.

[*Exit*]

Scene 3

The Duke of Albany's palace. Enter **Goneril**, *and* **Oswald**, *her*
Steward

Goneril   Did my father strike my gentleman for chiding of
his Fool?

Oswald   Ay, madam.

Goneril   By day and night, he wrongs me; every hour
5   He flashes into one gross crime or other,
That sets us all at odds: I'll not endure it:
His knights grow riotous, and himself upbraids us

Edmund   Brother, I advise you for the best. Call me liar if there's a good word to be said for you. I've told you what I've seen and heard, but toned it down — nothing like the horrible reality. Please, go!

Edgar   Shall I hear from you soon?

Edmund   Leave everything to me. [**Edgar** *goes.* **Edmund** *laughs out loud*] A credulous father and a noble brother! He's so incapable of mischief himself that he suspects none. His foolish honesty is no match for my wiles. It's very simple: if I can't get property through inheritance, I'll get it by using my wits. Anything goes that suits my purposes.

[*He goes*]

Scene 3

The Duke of Albany's palace. Enter **Goneril** *and her steward* **Oswald**

Goneril   Did my father strike my officer for rebuking his Fool?

Oswald   Yes madam.

Goneril   He does me wrong by day and night. Not an hour passes without he commits one flagrant offence or another that has us all at loggerheads. I won't put up with it. His knights are getting riotous, and he himself scolds us about

On every trifle. When he returns from hunting
I will not speak with him; say I am sick:
10   If you come slack of former services,
You shall do well; the fault of it I'll answer.

Oswald   He's coming, madam; I hear him.

[*Horns within*]

Goneril   Put on what weary negligence you please,
You and your fellows; I'd have it come to question:
15   If he distaste it, let him to my sister,
Whose mind and mine, I know, in that are one,
Not to be over-ruled. Idle old man,
That still would manage those authorities
That he hath given away! Now, by my life,
20   Old fools are babes again, and must be used
With checks as flatteries, when they are seen abused.
Remember what I have said.

Oswald   Well, madam.

Goneril   And let his knights have colder looks among you;
What grows of it, no matter; advise your fellows so:
25   I would breed from hence occasions, and I shall,
That I may speak: I'll write straight to my sister
To hold my very course. Prepare for dinner.

[*Exeunt*]

every little thing. When he returns from hunting, I won't
speak to him. Say I'm sick. If you're less dutiful than
formerly, that will be quite all right. I'll take the
responsibility.

[*Hunting horns can be heard*]

Oswald   He's coming, madam. I can hear him.

Goneril   Be as offhand as you like, you and your colleagues. I
want to make an issue of it. If he doesn't like it, let him go
to my sister. She and I are of one mind, not to be beaten by
him. Silly old man, who wants to be in charge of what he's
given away! Upon my soul, old fools are babies again, and
must be rebuked when they act stupidly. Remember what
I've said.

Oswald   I will indeed, madam.

Goneril   Be cooler to his knights. Ignore the consequences.
Spread the word amongst your colleagues. I'll make capital
out of such incidents; I will, so I can speak out. I'll write to
my sister at once to do the same. Prepare for dinner.

[*They go*]

Scene 4

A hall in the same. Enter **Kent** *disguised*

Kent   If but as well I other accents borrow,
That can my speech defuse, my good intent
May carry through itself to that full issue
For which I razed my likeness. Now, banished Kent,
5   If thou canst serve where thou dost stand condemned,
So may it come, thy master, whom thou lovest,
Shall find thee full of labours.

[*Horns within. Enter* **Lear,** *Knights and Attendants*]

Lear   Let me not stay a jot for dinner: go, get it ready.

[*Exit an Attendant*]

How now! What art thou?

10 **Kent**   A man, sir.

Lear   What dost thou profess? What would'st thou with us?

Kent   I do profess to be no less than I seem; to serve him
truly that will put me in trust; to love him that is honest; to
converse with him that is wise, and says little; to fear
15   judgment; to fight when I cannot choose; and to eat no fish.

Lear   What art thou?

Kent   A very honest-hearted fellow, and as poor as the King.

Lear   If thou be'st as poor for a subject as he is for a King,
thou art poor enough. What would'st thou?

20 **Kent**   Service.

Lear   Who would'st thou serve?

Scene 4

Another room in the Palace. Enter **Kent**, *in disguise*

Kent   If I can also alter my voice, I may be able to carry out the worthy purpose which prompted my disguise. Well now, banished Kent, if you can serve where you stand condemned, it might well be that your master, whom you love, will discover you are a dedicated servant.

[*Hunting horns herald the entrance of the* **King** *and his Knights*]

Lear   [*to his Servant*] Don't keep me waiting for dinner! Go and get it ready. [*The Servant goes*] Well now, who are you?

Kent   A man, sir.

Lear   What's your profession? What's your business with us?

Kent   I profess to be no less than I appear to be; to serve any man loyally who'll trust me; to love the man who is honest; to consort with the man who is wise but says little; to fear being judged; to fight when I have no alternative; and to eat no fish.

Lear   What are you?

Kent   A very genuine fellow, and as poor as the King.

Lear   If you are as poor a subject as he is a King, that's pretty poor! What are you seeking?

Kent   Employment.

Lear   With whom?

Kent   You.

Lear   Dost thou know me, fellow?

Kent   No, sir; but you have that in your countenance which I
25   would fain call master.

Lear   What's that?

Kent   Authority.

Lear   What services canst thou do?

Kent   I can keep honest counsel, ride, run, mar a curious tale
30   in telling it, and deliver a plain message bluntly; that which
ordinary men are fit for, I am qualified in, and the best of
me is diligence.

Lear   How old art thou?

Kent   Not so young, sir, to love a woman for singing, nor so
35   old to dote on her for anything; I have years on my back
forty-eight.

Lear   Follow me; thou shalt serve me; if I like thee no worse
after dinner I will not part from thee yet. Dinner, ho!
Dinner! Where's my knave? My Fool? Go you and call my
40   Fool hither.

[*Exit an Attendant*]

[*Enter* **Oswald**]

You, you, sirrah, where's my daughter?

Oswald   So please you –

[*Exit*]

Lear   What says the fellow there? Call the clotpoll back.

[*Exit a* **Knight**]

Kent   You.

Lear   Do you know me, man?

Kent   No, sir, but there's something in your bearing that I respect.

Lear   What's that?

Kent   Authority.

Lear   What services can you perform?

Kent   I can keep a secret; ride; run; spoil a good story in the telling of it; and deliver a simple message bluntly. What ordinary men are fit for, I'm good at. My best quality is determination.

Lear   How old are you?

Kent   Not so young, sir, that I'd love a woman for singing, nor so old as to dote on her for anything. I'm forty-eight.

Lear   Follow me. You can be my servant. If I like you no worse after dinner, I'll take you on permanently. Dinner! Hey there! Dinner! Where's my knave? My Fool? [*To an Attendant*] Go and fetch my Fool.

[*The Attendant leaves.* **Oswald** *enters*]

You. You, fellow. Where's my daughter?

Oswald   [*brushing past him*] Excuse me – [*He goes*]

Lear   What did the fellow say? Call the blockhead back! [*A* **Knight** *goes in pursuit*] Where's my Fool, eh? I think the

Where's my Fool, ho? I think the world's asleep.

[*Re-enter* **Knight**]

45   How now! Where's that mongrel?

Knight   He says, my lord, your daughter is not well.

Lear   Why came not the slave back to me when I called him?

Knight   Sir, he answered me in the roundest manner, he
would not.

50   **Lear**   He would not!

Knight   My lord, I know not what the matter is; but, to my
judgment, your highness is not entertained with that
ceremonious affection as you were wont; there's a great
abatement of kindness appears as well in the general
55   dependants as in the Duke himself also and your daughter.

Lear   Ha! say'st thou so?

Knight   I beseech you, pardon me, my lord, if I be mistaken;
for my duty cannot be silent when I think your highness
wronged.

60   **Lear**   Thou but rememberest me of mine own conception: I
have perceived a most faint neglect of late; which I have
rather blamed as mine own jealous curiosity than as a very
pretence and purpose of unkindness: I will look further
into't. But where's my Fool? I have not seen him this two
65   days.

Knight   Since my young lady's going into France, sir, the
Fool hath much pined away.

Lear   No more of that; I have noted it well. Go you, and tell world's asleep. [*The* **Knight** *returns alone*] Well, where's that mongrel?

Knight   He says, my lord, that your daughter isn't well.

Lear   Why didn't the slave come back to me when I called him?

Knight   Sir, he answered in the rudest manner that he would not.

Lear   He would not?

Knight   My lord, I don't know why, but in my opinion your highness is not being treated with the same respectful ceremony as you are used to. There's a distinct unfriendliness amongst the staff, as well as in the Duke himself and your daughter.

Lear   Hm? Do you think so?

Knight   Please do forgive me, my lord, if I'm mistaken. My duty won't allow me to be silent when I think your highness is being wronged.

Lear   You are only reminding me of what I've noticed myself. I have observed a hint of neglect lately. I'd put it down to my own jealous sensitivity rather than a deliberate intention to be uncivil. I'll look further into it. But where's my Fool? I haven't seen him these last two days.

Knight   Since my young lady went to France, sir, the Fool has pined away considerably.

Lear   Enough of that. I've taken good note of it. [*To an* my daughter I would speak with her.

[*Exit an Attendant*]

70   Go you, call hither my Fool.

[*Exit an Attendant*]

[*Enter* **Oswald**]

Oh, you sir, you, come you hither, sir. Who am I, sir?

75 **Oswald**   My lady's father.

Lear   'My lady's father!' My lord's knave: you whoreson dog!
You slave! You cur!

Oswald   I am none of these, my lord; I beseech your pardon.

Lear   Do you bandy looks with me, you rascal?   [*Striking
him*]

Oswald   I'll not be struck, my lord.

Kent   Nor tripped neither, you base football player.   [*Trip-
ping up his heels*]

Lear   I thank thee, fellow; thou servest me, and I'll love thee.

80 **Kent**   Come, sir, arise, away! I'll teach you differences: away,
away! If you will measure your lubber's length again, tarry;
but away! Have you wisdom? [*Exit* **Oswald**] So.

Lear   Now, my friendly knave, I thank thee: there's earnest
of thy service.   [*Gives* **Kent** *money*].

[*Enter* **Fool**]

85 **Fool**   Let me hire him too: here's my coxcomb.   [*Offers* **Kent**
his cap]

Lear   How now, my pretty knave! How dost thou?

Attendant] Go and tell my daughter I want to speak to her.
[*The Attendant leaves. To another*] You, go and bring my
Fool here. [*The Attendant goes*]

[**Oswald** *enters*]

Oh, it's you sir. You. Come here, sir. Who am I, sir?

Oswald   My lady's father.

Lear   'My lady's father!' My lord's lackey, you lousy dog! You
wretch! You cur!

Oswald   I am none of these, my lord, I beg your pardon.

Lear   Do you exchange looks with me, you rascal? [*He strikes*
Oswald *angrily*]

Oswald   I won't be struck, my lord.

Kent   Or tripped, either, you contemptible lout? [**Oswald** *falls*
to the ground]

Lear   Thank you, fellow. You're my servant, and I'll see you all
right.

Kent   [*to* **Oswald**] Come on sir, get up and go! I'll teach you
your place! Be off with you: go! If you want to measure your
loutish length again, stay. But away with you! Use your
commonsense. [**Oswald** *runs off*] That's right.

Lear   Now my friendly fellow, thank you: there's something on
account. [*He gives* **Kent** *some money*]

[*The* **Fool** *enters*]

Fool   Let me hire him too: here's my coxcomb. [*He offers* **Kent**
his jester's cap which resembles a cock's comb in shape
and colour]

Lear   Hello, there, my pretty fellow! How are you?

Fool   Sirrah, you were best take my coxcomb.

Kent   Why, Fool?

Fool   Why, for taking one's part that's out of favour. Nay,
90   and thou canst not smile as the wind sits, thou'lt catch cold
shortly: there, take my coxcomb. Why, this fellow has
banished two on's daughters, and did the third a blessing
against his will: if thou follow him thou must needs wear
my coxcomb. How now, nuncle! Would I had two cox-
95   combs and two daughters!

Lear   Why, my boy?

Fool   If I gave them all my living, I'd keep my coxcombs
myself. There's mine; beg another of thy daughters.

Lear   Take heed, sirrah; the whip.

100   **Fool**   Truth's a dog must to kennel; he must be whipped out
when Lady the Brach may stand by the fire and stink.

Lear   A pestilent gall to me!

Fool   Sirrah, I'll teach thee a speech.

Lear   Do.

105   **Fool**   Mark it, nuncle:

Have more than thou showest,
Speak less than thou knowest,
Lend less than thou owest,
Ride more than thou goest,
110   *Learn more than thou trowest,*
Set less than thou throwest;
Leave thy drink and thy whore

Fool Sir, you had better have my coxcomb.

Kent Why, Fool?

Fool Why? For siding with someone who's out of favour. No, if you can't trim your sails to the wind, you'll be in trouble shortly. So there: take my coxcomb. Why, this fellow [*indicating* **Lear**] has alienated two of his daughters and done the third one a blessing without intending to. If you join his service, you'll have to wear my coxcomb. [*To* **Lear**] Greetings, uncle. I wish I had two coxcombs and two daughters.

Lear Why my boy?

Fool If I gave them all my possessions, I'd keep my coxcombs for myself. [*He offers his cap to* **Lear**] There's mine. Beg the second off your daughters.

Lear Watch it, now: you'll be whipped!

Fool Truth is a dog that's sent to its kennel. He gets whipped, whereas Lady the lapdog is allowed to stand in front of the fire, and stink.

Lear [*brooding*] It's quite insufferable!

Fool Sir, I'll tell you something.

Lear Do.

Fool Listen carefully, uncle:

> *Own more than you show,*
> *Don't tell all you know,*
> *Lend less than you've got,*
> *Ride more than you trot,*
> *Don't believe all you're told,*
> *Don't risk all your gold;*
> *Give up drink and your whores,*

> *And keep in-a-door,*
> *And thou shalt have more*
115   *Than two tens to a score.*

Kent   This is nothing, Fool.

Fool   Then 'tis like the breath of an unfee'd lawyer; you give
me nothing for't. Can you make no use of nothing, nuncle?

Lear   Why no, boy; nothing can be made out of nothing.

120   **Fool**   [*To* **Kent**] Prithee, tell him, so much the rent of his
land comes to: he will not believe a Fool.

Lear   A bitter Fool!

Fool   Dost thou know the difference, my boy, between a
bitter Fool and a sweet one?

125   **Lear**   No, lad; teach me.

Fool   *That lord that counselled thee*
> *To give away thy land,*
> *Come place him here by me,*
> *Do thou for him stand:*
130   *The sweet and bitter fool*
> *Will presently appear;*
> *The one in motley here,*
> *The other found out there.*

Lear   Dost thou call me fool, boy?

135   **Fool**   All thy other titles thou hast given away; that thou wast
born with.

Kent   This is not altogether fool, my lord.

Fool   No, faith, lords and great men will not let me; if I had

> *Don't stray out of doors,*
> *And you will have more*
> *Than two tens to the score.*

Kent This is a lot of nothing, Fool.

Fool Then it's like the advocacy of a lawyer working without a fee: you get it for nothing. Can't you make use of nothing, uncle?

Lear Why no, boy. Nothing can be made out of nothing.

Fool [*To* **Kent**] Do me a favour. Tell him that's what his income amounts to. He won't believe a Fool.

Lear A bitter Fool!

Fool [*to* **Lear**] Do you know the difference, my boy, between a bitter Fool and a sweet one?

Lear No lad, tell me.

Fool *Whoever counselled you*
> *To give away your land,*
> *Come place him here by me,*
>   *While you for him there stand:*
> *The sweet and bitter fool*
>   *Will instantly appear;*
> *The one in motley here –*
>   *The other standing there!*

[He points to **Lear** *as the bitter one]*

Lear Are you calling me a fool, boy?

Fool All your other titles you have given away. That one you were born with.

Kent He's not all fool, my lord.

Fool No, indeed. Lords and great men won't let me be. If I

140 a monopoly out, they would have part on't: and ladies too, they will not let me have all the fool to myself: they'll be snatching. Nuncle, give me an egg, and I'll give thee two crowns.

Lear   What two crowns shall they be?

Fool   Why, after I have cut the egg i'th'middle and eat up
145 the meat, the two crowns of the egg. When thou clovest thy crown i'th'middle, and gavest away both parts, thou borest thine ass on thy back o'er the dirt: thou hadst little wit in thy bald crown when thou gavest thy golden one away. If I speak like myself in this let him be whipped that first
150 finds it so.

> Fools had ne'er less grace in a year;
>   For wise men are grown foppish,
> And know not how their wits to wear,
>   Their manners are so apish.

155 **Lear**   When were you wont to be so full of songs, sirrah?

Fool   I have used it, nuncle, ever since thou madest thy daughters thy mothers; for when thou gavest them the rod and puttest down thine own breeches,

> Then they for sudden joy did weep,
160   And I for sorrow sung,
> That such a king should play bo-peep,
>   And go the fools among.

Prithee, nuncle, keep a schoolmaster than can teach thy Fool to lie: I would fain learn to lie.

165 **Lear**   And you lie, sirrah, we'll have you whipped.

Fool   I marvel what kin thou and thy daughters are: they'll have me whipped for speaking true, thou't have me whipped for lying; and sometimes I am whipped for holding my peace. I had rather be any kind o'thing than a fool; and had the monopoly, they'd want their share of the profits. And ladies, too: they wouldn't let me monopolize fooling. They like their banter. Uncle, give me an egg, and I'll give you two crowns.

Lear What two crowns would they be?

Fool Why, after I'd cut the egg down the middle, and eaten the yolk, the two halves of the eggshell! When you chopped your crown in two and gave both parts away, you were like the man in the fable who carried his ass on his back over the mire. You had little commonsense in that bald crown of yours when you gave your golden one away. If I'm speaking like a fool, whip the man who's responsible. [*He sings*]

> *Fools have never fared so ill;*
> *'Cos wise men have turned soppy.*
> *They don't know how to sell their skill,*
> *When it's not hard to copy.*

Lear Since when have you been so full of songs, eh?

Fool I've been in the mood, uncle, ever since you made your daughters your mothers. When you gave them a cane and dropped your trousers,

> *They suddenly both wept for joy,*
> *And I in sorrow sang,*
> *That such a King should play the fool,*
> *And join the foolish gang.*

Please, uncle, employ a schoolmaster to teach your Fool how to lie. I'd like to learn how to lie.

Lear If you lie, laddie, we'll have you whipped.

Fool I can't make out the relationship between you and your daughters. They'll have me whipped for speaking the truth; you'll have me whipped for lying. Sometimes I'm whipped for saying nothing at all. I'd rather be anything than a Fool.

170   yet I would not be thee, nuncle; thou hast pared thy wit
o'both sides, and left nothing i'th'middle: here comes one
o'the parings.

[*Enter* **Goneril**]

Lear How now, daughter! What makes that frontlet on? You
are too much of late i'th'frown.

175 **Fool** Thou was a pretty fellow when thou hadst no need to
care for her frowning; now thou art an O without a figure. I
am better than thou art now; I am a Fool, thou art nothing.
[*To* **Goneril**] Yes, forsooth, I will hold my tongue; so your
face bids me, though you say nothing.

180   *Mum, Mum:*
He that keeps nor crust nor crumb,
Weary of all, shall want some.

That's a shealed peascod. [Pointing to **Lear**]

Goneril Not only, sir, this your all-licensed Fool,
185   But other of your insolent retinue
Do hourly carp and quarrel, breaking forth
In rank and not-to-be-endured riots. Sir,
I had thought, by making this well known unto you,
To have found a safe redress; but now grow fearful,
190   By what yourself too late have spoke and done,
That you protect this course, and put it on
By your allowance; which if you should, the fault
Would not 'scape censure, nor the redresses sleep,
Which, in the tender of a wholesome weal,
195   Might in their working do you that offence,
Which else were shame, that then necessity
Will call discreet proceeding.

Fool For you know, nuncle,

The hedge-sparrow fed the cuckoo so long,

72

But I wouldn't be you, uncle. You have sliced your brains in
two and left nothing in the middle. Here comes one of the
halves.

[**Goneril** *enters*]

Lear   Well, now, daughter. Why the face? You frown too
much lately.

Fool   You were a lucky fellow when you didn't need to care
about her frowning. Now you are a nonentity. I'm better
than you are now. I'm a Fool. You are nothing. [*To* **Goneril**]
Yes indeed. I'll hold my tongue. That's what your face is
saying, though you haven't spoken.

> *Hush, hush:*
> *The man who gives away his all,*
> *May find his kindness turns to gall.*

[*pointing to* **Lear**] He's an empty pea-pod.

Goneril   Not merely, sir, your free-speaking Fool, but others
amongst your insolent followers are bickering and
quarrelling hour by hour, erupting into gross and intolerable
rioting. Sir, I thought that by bringing this to your notice I'd
get things put right. Now I'm beginning to fear – judging
from your slow response – that you are covering up this
behaviour, and encouraging it by your tolerance. If this is the
case, the offence would not go uncriticized. Nor would
disciplinary measures for the good of society be slow in
coming: much as they'll offend you, and might in other
circumstances seem humiliating, if it were not that
necessity justified them.

Fool   'Cos you know, uncle:

> *The hedge-sparrow fed the cuckoo for so long*

73

200   *That it had its head bit off by its young.*

So out went the candle, and we were left darkling.

Lear   Are you our daughter?

Goneril   I would you would make use of your good wisdom,
Whereof I know you are fraught; and put away
205   These dispositions which of late transport you
From what you rightly are.

Fool   May not an ass know when a cart draws the horse?
Whoop, Jug! I love thee.

Lear   Does any here know me? This is not Lear:
210   Does Lear walk thus? Speak thus? Where are his eyes?
Either his notion weakens, his discernings
Are lethargied – Ha! waking? 'tis not so.
Who is it that can tell me who I am?

Fool   Lear's shadow.

215 **Lear**   I would learn that; for by the marks of sovereignty,
knowledge and reason, I should be false persuaded I had
daughters.

Fool   Which they will make an obedient father.

Lear   Your name, fair gentlewoman?

220 **Goneril**   This admiration, sir, is much o'th' savour
Of other your new pranks. I do beseech you
To understand my purposes aright:
As you are old and reverend, you should be wise.
Here you do keep a hundred knights and squires;
225   Men so disordered, so deboshed, and bold,
That this our court, infected with their manners,
Shows like a riotous inn: epicurism and lust
Makes it more like a tavern or a brothel
Than a graced palace. The shame itself doth speak

That it had its head bitten off by its young.

So out went the light and we were in darkness!

Lear   [*to* **Goneril**] Are you really our daughter?

Goneril   I wish you would use your common sense – which I
know you possess – and that you would cast off these
temperamental moods which recently have changed your
personality.

Fool   Can't a fool tell when the cart draws the horse? Gee-up,
Joan! I love you!

Lear   Does anyone here recognize me? This can't be Lear.
Does Lear walk like this? Speak like this? Where are his
eyes? His brain is getting weak or his senses are sluggish.
What – awake? It can't be so. Is there anyone here who can
tell me who I am?

Fool   [*aside*] Lear's shadow . . .

Lear   [*not heeding the comment*] I'd really like to know,
because from the evidence of sanity, knowledge and reason
I'd be misled into believing I had daughters.

Fool   Who will make you into an obedient father . . .

Lear   [*to* **Goneril** *with heavy sarcasm*] Your name, fair lady?

Goneril   This play-acting, sir, is much in line with these other
new pranks of yours. I want you to understand me clearly.
As you are old and respected, you should be wise. Here you
keep a hundred knights and squires, men so disorderly, so
debauched and insolent, that our court-influenced by their
conduct – resembles a rowdy inn. Luxury–living and
pleasure-seeking make it more like a tavern or a brothel than
a respectable palace. It's so shameful as to demand instant

230   For instant remedy; be then desired
      By her, that else will take the thing she begs,
      A little to disquantity your train;
      And the remainders, that shall still depend,
      To be such men as may besort your age,
      Which know themselves and you.

235 **Lear**   Darkness and devils!
      Saddle my horses; call my train together.
      Degenerate bastard! I'll not trouble thee:
      Yet have I left a daughter.

      Goneril   You strike my people, and your disordered rabble
240   Make servants of their betters.

      [*Enter* **Albany**]

      Lear   Woe, that too late repents! Oh, sir, are you come?
      Is it your will? Speak, sir. Prepare my horses.
      Ingratitude, thou marble-hearted fiend,
      More hideous, when thou show'st thee in a child,
      Than the sea-monster.

245 **Albany**   Pray, sir, be patient.

      Lear   [*To* **Goneril**] Detested kite, thou liest!
      My train are men of choice and rarest parts,
      That all particulars of duty know,
      And in the most exact regard support
250   The worships of their name. Oh most small fault,
      How ugly didst thou in Cordelia show!
      Which, like an engine, wrenched my frame of nature
      From the fixed place, drew from my heart all love,
      And added to the gall. Oh Lear, Lear, Lear!
255   Beat at this gate, that let thy folly in,
      And thy dear judgment out! Go, go, my people.

                            [*Exeunt* **Kent** *and Knights*]

redress. Therefore, be requested by one who'll otherwise
take what she's politely asking for: reduce the size of your
retinue somewhat. And those who remain as your
attendants should be men appropriate to your age, who can
control themselves and you.

Lear   Hell and damnation! Saddle my horses! Call my troop
together! [*To* **Goneril**] You misbegotten bastard! I won't
trouble you. I still have one daughter left!

Goneril   You strike my servants, and your rowdy rabble order
their betters around.

[**Albany** *enters*]

Lear   Woe to him who repents too late! [*To* **Albany**] Oh, sir, so
you're here. Is this your doing? Answer me, sir! [*To his
servants*] Get my horses ready. Oh, ingratitude! You're a
fiend with a heart of stone, more hideous than any monster
of the sea when you reveal yourself in a child.

Albany   Really, sir, compose yourself!

Lear   [*To* **Goneril**] Vulture! You tell lies. My troops are men of
rare distinction, who know their duties, and are meticulous
in living up to their honourable reputations. Oh, how a
relatively small defect seemed repugnant in Cordelia! It
wrenched me apart as if I were on the rack, drew all my love
from my heart, and generated bitterness. Oh, Lear, Lear,
Lear! [*He slaps his forehead in despair*] Knock at this door
that let your folly in, and your discretion out! [*Gesturing to
his followers*] Go, go, my people. [**Kent** *and the Knights
leave*]

Albany   My lord, I am guiltless, as I am ignorant
Of what hath moved you.

Lear   It may be so, my lord.
Hear, Nature, hear! Dear Goddess, hear!
260   Suspend thy purpose, if thou didst intend
To make this creature fruitful!
Into her womb convey sterility!
Dry up in her the organs of increase,
And from her derogate body never spring
265   A babe to honour her! If she must teem,
Create her child of spleen, that it may live
And be a thwart disnatured torment to her!
Let it stamp wrinkles in her brow of youth,
With cadent tears fret channels in her cheeks,
270   Turn all her mother's pains and benefits
To laughter and contempt, that she may feel
How sharper than a serpent's tooth it is
To have a thankless child! Away, away!

                                                    [*Exit*]

Albany   Now, gods that we adore, whereof comes this?

275 **Goneril**   Never afflict yourself to know more of it:
But let his disposition have that scope
As dotage gives it.

     [*Enter* **Lear**]

Lear   What! fifty of my followers at a clap!
Within a fortnight!

Albany   What's the matter, sir?

Lear   I'll tell thee. [*To* **Goneril**] Life and death! I am
280   ashamed

Albany   My lord, I am as guiltless as I am ignorant of what has upset you.

Lear   Possibly so, my lord. [*He turns again to* **Goneril**] Hear, Nature, hear! Dear goddess, hear! If you intended her to be fertile, change your mind! Make her sterile! Dry up her womb, and may her despicable body never honour her with a baby! If she must breed, make her child all malice, so it will live to be a peevish, cold-hearted torment to her! May it put wrinkles in her young brow; may tears cut channels in her cheeks; all her maternal care turn into mockery and contempt; so that she realizes how sharper than a serpent's tooth it is to have an ungrateful child! Let's away, away . . . [*He rushes off, overcome with emotion*]

Albany   Now by all the gods, what started that?

Goneril   Don't bother yourself to find out. Let his old age have its fling.

[**Lear** *returns*]

Lear   What, fifty of my followers at a stroke? Within a fortnight?

Albany   How do you mean sir?

Lear   I'll tell you. [*To* **Goneril**] Life and death! I am ashamed

That thou hast power to shake my manhood thus,
That these hot tears, which break from me perforce,
Should make thee worth them. Blasts and fogs upon thee!
Th'untented woundings of a father's curse

285   Pierce every sense about thee! Old fond eyes,
Beweep this cause again, I'll pluck ye out,
And cast you, with the waters that you loose,
To temper clay. Yea, is't come to this?
Ha! Let it be so: I have another daughter,

290   Who, I am sure, is kind and comfortable:
When she shall hear this of thee, with her nails
She'll flay thy wolvish visage. Thou shalt find
That I'll resume the shape which thou dost think
I have cast off for ever.

[Exit]

295 **Goneril**   Do you mark that?

Albany   I cannot be so partial, Goneril,
To the great love I bear you, –

Goneril   Pray you, content. What, Oswald, ho!
[*To the* **Fool**] You, sir, more knave than fool, after your
master.

300 **Fool**   Nuncle Lear, Nuncle Lear! Tarry, take the Fool with
thee.

A fox, when one has caught her,
And such a daughter,
Should sure to the slaughter,
305   *If my cap would buy a halter;*
So the Fool follows after.

[Exit]

that you can shake my manly dignity like this, as though you are worthy of these hot tears that burst from me. Storms and fogs upon you! May the deep wounds of a father's curse pierce all your senses! Foolish old eyes, if you persist in weeping, I'll pluck you out, and trample you and your tears into the ground. Has it really come to this? Right. So be it. I have another daughter who I'm sure is kind and comforting. When she hears about you, she'll scratch your wolvish face with her nails. You'll discover that I'll resume the role that you think I've cast off forever.

[*He staggers off, overwhelmed*]

Goneril   Did you note that?

Albany   For all the great love I have for you, Goneril, I can't be so biased as –

Goneril   [*stopping him*] That's enough. [*Calling*] Oswald there! [*To the* **Fool**] You, sir – more rascal than fool – be off after your master.

Fool   Uncle Lear, Uncle Lear! Hold on, take the Fool with you!
   A fox, when one has caught her,
   And such a daughter,
   Should surely go for slaughter,
   If my cap would buy a halter.
   So the Fool chases after . . .

[*He runs off in pursuit of* **Lear**]

Goneril   This man hath had good counsel. A hundred
knights!
'Tis politic and safe to let him keep
At point a hundred knights; yes, that on every dream,
310   Each buzz, each fancy, each complaint, dislike,
He may enguard his dotage with their powers,
And hold our lives in mercy. Oswald, I say!

Albany   Well, you may fear too far.

Goneril   Safer than trust too far.
Let me still take away the harms I fear,
315   Not fear still to be taken: I know his heart.
What he hath uttered I have writ my sister;
If she sustain him and his hundred knights,
When I have showed th'unfitness –

[*Enter* **Oswald**]

                                   How now, Oswald!
What, have you writ that letter to my sister?

320 **Oswald**   Ay, madam.

Goneril   Take you some company, and away to horse:
Inform her full of my particular fear;
And thereto add such reasons of your own
As may compact it more. Get you gone,
And hasten your return.

                                   [*Exit* **Oswald**]

325   No, no, my lord,
This milky gentleness and course of yours
Though I condemn not, yet, under pardon,
You are much more attasked for want of wisdom
Than praised for harmful mildness.

330 **Albany**   How far your eyes may pierce I cannot tell:
Striving to better, oft we mar what's well.

Goneril   This man [*she means her father*] has been well
advised. A hundred knights! [*Sarcastically*] It's sensible and
safe to let him keep a hundred fully armed knights! Yes – so
that after every wild dream, each rumour, each fantasy,
each complaint or dislike, he can back up his senile ways
with their strikepower, and put our lives in jeopardy.
Oswald, I say!

Albany   Well, you may be worrying too much.

Goneril   That's safer than trusting too much. I'd rather
eliminate the dangers that worry me than live continually in
fear. I know his character. I've written to my sister reporting
what he has said. If she accommodates him and his hundred
knights after I've explained the undesirability –

[**Oswald** *returns*]

Well, Oswald: have you written that letter to my sister?

Oswald   Yes, madam.

Goneril   Take some companions with you and ride off. Inform
her fully of my personal fear. Add such reasons of your own
as may make it more convincing. Be off with you and return
quickly.

[**Oswald** *goes*]

This very tolerant attitude of yours, though I don't condemn
it, yet – if I may say so – you are much more criticized for
your naivety than praised for your dangerous mildness.

Albany   How far you are right I don't know. Sometimes things
are best left alone . . .

Goneril   Nay, then –

Albany   Well, well; th'event.

[*Exeunt*]

Scene 5

Court before the same. Enter **Lear, Kent,** *and* **Fool**

Lear   Go you before to Gloucester with these letters.
Acquaint my daughter no further with anything you know
than comes from her demand out of the letter. If your
diligence be not speedy I shall be there afore you.

5 **Kent**   I will not sleep, my lord, till I have delivered your
letter.

[*Exit*]

Fool   If a man's brains were in's heels, were't not in danger
of kibes?

Lear   Ay, boy.

10 **Fool**   Then, I prithee, be merry; thy wit shall not go
slipshod.

Lear   Ha, ha, ha!

Fool   Shalt see thy other daughter will use thee kindly; for
though she's as like this as a crab's like an apple, yet I can
15   tell what I can tell.

Lear   What canst tell, boy?

Goneril   So –

Albany   Well, well. Let us see what happens.

[They go]

Scene 5

A room in the Duke of Albany's palace. Enter **Lear**, **Kent**, *and the* **Fool**

Lear   [*to* **Kent**] Go ahead to Gloucester with this letter. Tell my daughter only what's needed to answer questions arising from the letter. If you're not quick, I'll be there before you.

Kent   I will not sleep, my Lord, till I've delivered your letter. [*He goes*]

Fool   If a man's brains were in his heels, wouldn't they be in danger of blisters?

Lear   Yes, boy.

Fool   Then cheer up. You'll never need to wear soft slippers with your intelligence . . .

Lear   Ha, ha, ha!

Fool   You'll see your other daughter will treat you just as kindly. Because though she's as like this one [*jerking his thumb in the direction of* **Goneril**] as a crab-apple is to an apple, yet I can tell what I can tell.

Lear   What *can* you tell, boy?

Fool   She will taste as like this as a crab does to a crab.
Thou canst tell why one's nose stands i'th'middle on's face?

Lear   No.

20 **Fool**   Why, to keep one's eyes on either side's nose, that
what a man cannot smell out, he may spy into.

Lear   I did her wrong, –

Fool   Canst tell how an oyster makes his shell?

Lear   No.

25 **Fool**   Nor I neither; but I can tell why a snail has a house.

Lear   Why?

Fool   Why, to put's head in; not to give it away to his
daughters, and leave his horns without a case.

Lear   I will forget my nature. So kind a father! Be my horses
30 ready?

Fool   Thy asses are gone about 'em. The reason why the
seven stars are no more than seven is a pretty reason.

Lear   Because they are not eight?

Fool   Yes, indeed: thou would'st make a good Fool.

35 **Lear**   To take't again perforce! Monster ingratitude!

Fool   If thou wert my Fool, nuncle, I'd have thee beaten for
being old before thy time.

Lear   How's that?

Fool   Thou should'st not have been old till thou hadst been
40 wise.

Lear   Oh! let me not be mad, not mad, sweet heaven;
Keep me in temper; I would not be mad!

Fool   The taste will be the same. You know why one's nose is in the middle of one's face?

Lear   No.

Fool   Why, to keep one's eyes on either side of one's nose. Then what a man can't smell out, he can look into.

Lear   I wronged her . . .

Fool   Do you know how an oyster makes its shell?

Lear   No.

Fool   I don't either. But I can say why a snail has a house.

Lear   Why?

Fool   To put his head in, of course, not to give it away to his daughters, and leave himself exposed.

Lear   I'll forget what's in my nature. Me, so kind a father! Are my horses ready?

Fool   Your asses are preparing them. The reason why the Seven Stars are only seven is a good one . . .

Lear   Because they aren't eight?

Fool   Yes, indeed. You'd make a good Fool!

Lear   To take it all back again! Monstrous ingratitude!

Fool   If you were my Fool, uncle, I'd have you beaten for being old too soon.

Lear   How do you mean?

Fool   You shouldn't have got old till you'd acquired some sense.

Lear   Oh, don't let me go mad; not mad, sweet heaven! Keep me sane. I don't want to be mad!

[*Enter* **Gentleman**]

How now! Are the horses ready?

Gentleman   Ready, my lord.

45 **Lear**   Come, boy.

Fool   *She that's a maid now, and laughs at my departure,*
Shall not be a maid long, unless things be cut shorter.

[*Exeunt*]

[*A* **Gentleman** *enters*]

Well, are the horses ready?

Gentleman   Ready, my lord.

Lear   [*to the* **Fool**] Come on, boy . . .

Fool   [*to the audience*]

> *The virgin of today, who laughs at my departure*
> *Won't be one much longer, unless some thing's cut*
>   *shorter.*

[*They go*]

Act two

Scene 1

The Castle of the Earl of Gloucester. Enter **Edmund** *and* **Curan**, *meeting*

5 **Edmund** Save thee, Curan.

Curan And you, sir. I have been with your father, and given him notice that the Duke of Cornwall and Regan his Duchess will be here with him this night.

Edmund How comes that?

10 **Curan** Nay, I know not. You have heard of the news abroad? I mean the whispered ones, for they are yet but ear-kissing arguments.

Edmund Not I: pray you, what are they?

Curan Have you heard of no likely wars toward, 'twixt the Dukes of Cornwall and Albany?

Edmund Not a word.

Curan You may do then, in time. Fare you well, sir.

[*Exit*]

Edmund The Duke be here to-night! The better! Best!
15   This weaves itself perforce into my business.
    My father hath set guard to take my brother;
    And I have one thing, of a queasy question,
    Which I must act. Briefness and Fortune, work!
    Brother, a word; descend: brother, I say!

[*Enter* **Edgar**]

Act two

Scene 1

Inside the castle of the Earl of Gloucester. **Edmund** *enters and meets* **Curan**, *a courtier*

Edmund   God be with you, Curan.

Curan   And you, sir. I've been with your father, and informed him that the Duke of Cornwall, and his Duchess Regan, will be here with him tonight.

Edmund   How has that come about?

Curan   I don't know. You've heard the latest? I mean the rumours, since at the moment they're only idle gossip.

Edmund   No, I haven't. What are they?

Curan   Haven't you heard of the impending wars between the Dukes of Cornwall and Albany?

Edmund   Not a word.

Curan   You probably will soon. Fare you well sir.

[*He goes*]

Edmund   The Duke coming here tonight! So much the better! Marvellous! This fits in with my scheme. My father has hidden himself to overhear my brother and I've got some tricky and dirty work to do. Speed and good fortune, come to my aid! [*He calls up the adjacent stairs*] Brother, a word with you! Come down! Brother, I say!

[**Edgar** *descends*]

20   My father watches: Oh sir, fly this place;
      Intelligence is given where you are hid;
      You have now the good advantage of the night.
      Have you not spoken 'gainst the Duke of Cornwall?
      He's coming hither, now, i'th'night, i'th'haste,
25   And Regan with him; have you nothing said
      Upon his party 'gainst the Duke of Albany?
      Advise yourself.

Edgar   I am sure on't, not a word.

Edmund   I hear my father coming; pardon me;
      In cunning I must draw my sword upon you;
30   Draw; seem to defend yourself; now quit you well.
      Yield; come before my father. Light, ho! here!
      Fly, brother. Torches! Torches! So, farewell.

                                        [*Exit* **Edgar**]

      Some blood drawn on me would beget opinion
      Of my more fierce endeavour: I have seen drunkards
35   Do more than this in sport. Father! Father!
      Stop, stop! No help?

      [*Enter* **Gloucester**, *and Servants with torches*]

Gloucester   Now, Edmund, where's the villain?

Edmund   Here stood he in the dark, his sharp sword out,
      Mumbling of wicked charms, conjuring the moon
      To stand auspicious mistress.

Gloucester   But where is he?

Edmund   Look, sir, I bleed.

40 **Gloucester**   Where is the villain, Edmund?

Edmund   Fled this way, sir, when by no means he could –

[*To the audience*] My father is watching. [*Whispering to* **Edgar***, and assuming an agitated manner*] Sir – run away! Your hiding-place has been discovered. You have the advantage of night cover. Have you been speaking out against the Duke of Cornwall? He's coming here now, overnight, in great haste, and Regan is with him. Have you said something supportive of his case against the Duke of Albany? Think hard.

Edgar   I'm sure of it. Not a word.

Edmund   I can hear my father coming. Excuse me: I must pretend to draw my sword upon you. [*He does so*] Draw yours. Make as if to defend yourself. [**Edgar***, bewildered, does as he is told*] Do your best. [*Speaking out loud for* **Gloucester** *to hear*] Surrender! Come to my father! Light there! [*Whispering*] Run, brother. [*Aloud*] Torches, torches! [*Pushing* **Edgar** *out*] So, farewell. [**Edgar** *runs off*] Some blood on me would be convincing evidence of my tough struggle. [*He cuts his arm*] I've seen drunkards do more than this in fun. [*Calling pathetically*] Father, father! [*After* **Edgar**] Stop, stop! Will no one help?

[**Gloucester** *enters with servants and torches*]

Gloucester   Now, Edmund, where's the villain?

Edmund   He was standing here in the dark, his sharp sword drawn, mumbling wicked spells, and making incantations to the moon to seek her favour.

Gloucester   But where is he?

Edmund   [*playing for time*] Look sir, I'm bleeding.

Gloucester   Where *is* the villain Edmund?

Edmund   [*pointing*] He fled this way, sir, when he was quite unable –

93

Gloucester   [*To Servants*] Pursue him ho! Go after. 'By no
means' what?

Edmund   Persuade me to the murder of your lordship;
45   But that I told him, the revenging Gods
'Gainst parricides did all the thunder bend;
Spoke with how manifold and strong a bond
The child was bound to th'father; sir, in fine,
Seeing how loathly opposite I stood
50   To his unnatural purpose, in fell motion,
With his prepared sword he charges home
My unprovided body, lanced mine arm:
But when he saw my best alarumed spirits
Bold in the quarrel's right, roused to th'encounter,
55   Or whether gasted by the noise I made,
Full suddenly he fled.

Gloucester   Let him fly far:
Not in this land shall he remain uncaught;
And found – dispatch. The noble Duke my master,
My worthy arch and patron, comes to-night:
60   By his authority I will proclaim it,
That he which finds him shall deserve our thanks,
Bringing the murderous coward to the stake;
He that conceals him, death.

Edmund   When I dissuaded him from his intent,
65   And found him pight to do it, with curst speech
I threatened to discover him: he replied,
'Thou unpossessing bastard! Dost thou think,
If I would stand against thee, would the reposal
Of any trust, virtue, or worth in thee
70   Make thy words faithed? No: what I should deny –
As this I would; ay, though thou didst produce
My very character – I'd turn it all
To thy suggestion, plot, and damned practice:
And thou must make a dullard of the world,

Gloucester   Follow him, quick! Go after him! [*Servants rush off in pursuit*] 'Quite unable' to do what?

Edmund   Persuade me to murder your lordship. And I told him the vengeful gods deal ruthlessly with parricides. I spoke about how the bond between father and son was complex and strong. Sir, in short, seeing how bitterly opposed I was to his unnatural plan, with a deadly thrust he lunged at my defenceless body with his naked sword and wounded my arm. But when he saw my energetic response to the challenge, inspired by the justice of the cause – or perhaps aghast at the noise I made – he suddenly ran off.

Gloucester   No matter how far he goes, there's nowhere in this land where he can stay free. Once found, kill him. The noble Duke, my master and chief patron, comes here tonight. With his authority I'll announce that whoever finds him will be rewarded for bringing the murderous coward to his execution. For anyone who hides him, death!

Edmund   When I tried to dissuade him from his plan, and found he was determined to proceed, with angry words I threatened to expose him. He replied, 'You poverty-stricken bastard! Do you think anyone would believe a word you said if I spoke to the contrary? No. I'd deny it all – indeed I would, even if you produced my own handwriting – and say it was your scheme, plot and treacherous proposal. People would have to be very stupid not to see that the profits from

75   If they not thought the profits of my death
        Were very pregnant and potential spirits
        To make thee seek it.'

    Gloucester   Oh strange and fastened villain!
        Would he deny his letter, said he? I never got him.

    [*Tucket within*]

        Hark! the Duke's trumpets. I know not why he comes.
80   All ports I'll bar; the villain shall not 'scape;
        The Duke must grant me that: besides his picture
        I will send far and near, that all the kingdom
        May have due note of him; and of my land,
        Loyal and natural boy, I'll work the means
85   To make thee capable.

        [*Enter* **Cornwall, Regan,** *and Attendants*]

    Cornwall   How now, my noble friend! Since I came hither
        Which I can call but now, I have heard strange news.

    Regan   If it be true, all vengeance comes too short
        Which can pursue th'offender. How dost, my lord?

90 **Gloucester**   Oh, madam, my old heart is cracked, it's cracked.

    Regan   What! did my father's godson seek your life?
        He whom my father named, your Edgar?

    Gloucester   Oh, lady, lady, shame would have it hid.

    Regan   Was he not companion with the riotous knights
95   That tended upon my father?

    Gloucester   I know not, madam; 'tis too bad, too bad.

    Edmund   Yes, madam, he was of that consort.

    Regan   No marvel then though he were ill affected;
        'Tis they have put him on the old man's death,

96

my death give you an obvious and powerful motive for
seeking it.'

Gloucester   Oh, the unnatural, the inveterate villain! He'd deny
his letter, did he say? He's no child of mine.

[*The* **Duke of Cornwall***'s trumpet-call is heard*]

Listen! The Duke's trumpets. I don't know why he's come.
I'll block all seaports. The villain won't escape. The Duke
must grant me that. Also, I'll send a picture of him far and
wide so that all the kingdom will take note of him. And I'll
devise a way of your inheriting my lands, you loyal and true
son.

[**Cornwall**, **Regan** *and their Attendants enter*]

Cornwall   Greetings, my noble friend! Since I arrived just
now, I've heard strange news.

Regan   If it's true, no vengeance is adequate in pursuit of the
offender. How are you, my lord?

Gloucester   Oh, madam, my old heart is broken. It's broken!

Regan   What, did my father's godson seek your life? The one
my father named: your Edgar?

Gloucester   Oh, lady, lady. Shame would have it hidden.

Regan   Wasn't he a companion of the riotous knights who
served my father?

Gloucester   I don't know, madam. It's too awful. Too awful.

Edmund   Yes, madam, he was one of that lot.

Regan   No wonder, then, that he was so disloyal. *They've*
incited him to plan the old man's death, so that he can

100   To have th'expense and waste of his revenues.
      I have this present evening from my sister
      Been well informed of them, and with such cautions
      That if they come to sojourn at my house,
      I'll not be there.

      Cornwall   Nor I, assure thee, Regan.
105   Edmund, I hear that you have shown your father
      A child-like office.

      Edmund   It was my duty, sir.

      Gloucester He did bewray his practice; and received
      This hurt you see, striving to apprehend him.

      Cornwall Is he pursued?

      Gloucester   Ay, my good lord.

110   **Cornwall** If he be taken he shall never more
      Be feared of doing harm; make your own purpose,
      How in my strength you please. For you, Edmund,
      Whose virtue and obedience doth this instant
      So much commend itself, you shall be ours:
115   Natures of such deep trust we shall much need;
      You we first seize on.

      Edmund   I shall serve you, sir,
      Truly, however else.

      Gloucester   For him I thank your grace.

      Cornwall You know not why we came to visit you –

      Regan Thus out of season, threading dark-eyed night:
120   Occasions, noble Gloucester, of some prize,
      Wherein we must have use of your advice.
      Our father he hath writ, so hath our sister,
      Of differences, which I best thought it fit
      To answer from our home; the several messengers

squander his wealth. Just this very evening I've been told
about them by my sister, with such warnings that if they
come to stay at my house, I won't be there.

Cornwall   Nor I, Regan, that's for sure. Edmund, I hear you
have behaved like a good son to your father.

Edmund   It was my duty sir.

Gloucester   He revealed his plot, and received the wound you
see while trying to arrest him.

Cornwall   Is he being pursued?

Gloucester   Yes, my good lord.

Cornwall   If he's captured, never fear his doing harm again.
Make your own plans, using my resources as you please. As
for you, Edmund, whose virtuous loyalty is so commendable
at this present time: you shall be one of us. Trustworthy
natures such as yours we have great need of. We seize upon
your services.

Edmund   [*bowing*] I shall serve you truly, sir, whatever else.

Gloucester   On his behalf I thank your grace.

Cornwall   You don't know why we came to visit you –

Regan   – so unexpectedly, travelling through the darkness of
the night. Business of some importance, Gloucester,
requiring your advice. Our father has written to us – and so
has our sister – about certain quarrels. I thought it best to
answer him away from home. The messengers are waiting

125   From hence attend dispatch. Our good old friend,
        Lay comforts to your bosom, and bestow
        Your needful counsel to our business,
        Which craves the instant use.

Gloucester   I serve you, madam.
        Your graces are right welcome.

                                    [*Flourish. Exeunt*]

Scene 2

Before Gloucester's Castle. Enter **Kent** *and* **Oswald,** *severally*

Oswald   Good dawning to thee, friend: art of this house?

Kent   Ay.

Oswald   Where may we set our horses?

Kent   I'th'mire.

5 **Oswald**   Prithee, if thou lovest me, tell me.

Kent   I love thee not.

Oswald   Why, then I care not for thee.

Kent   If I had thee in Lipsbury pinfold, I would make thee
        care for me.

10 **Oswald**   Why dost thou use me thus? I know thee not.

Kent   Fellow, I know thee.

Oswald   What dost thou know me for?

Kent   A knave, a rascal, an eater of broken meats; a base, to be dispatched. Our good old friend, be of good cheer, and give us your much-needed advice about these matters, which require instant action.

Gloucester   Your servant, madam. Your graces are most welcome.

[*Trumpets sound as they leave*]

Scene 2

Outside Gloucester's castle. **Kent** *and* **Oswald** *meet. Dawn has not yet broken*

Oswald   Good morning to you, friend. Are you a servant here?

Kent   Yes.

Oswald   Where may we put our horses?

Kent   In the mud.

Oswald   Please, if you love me, tell me.

Kent   I don't love you.

Oswald   Well, then, I don't much care for you.

Kent   Any more of your lip, and I'll make you care.

Oswald   Why the abuse? I don't know you.

Kent   I know you, man.

Oswald   What do you know of me?

Kent   You're a rogue, a rascal, a scrap-food guzzler. A low,

15   proud, shallow, beggarly, three-suited, hundred-pound,
      filthy worsted-stocking knave; a lily-livered, action-taking,
      whoreson, glass-gazing, super-serviceable, finical rogue;
      one-trunk-inheriting slave; one that wouldst be a bawd in way
      of good service, and art nothing but the composition of a
      knave, beggar, coward, pandar, and the son and heir of a
20   mongrel bitch: one whom I will beat into clamorous whining
      if thou deniest the least syllable of thy addition.

Oswald   Why, what a monstrous fellow art thou, thus to rail
on one that is neither known of thee nor knows thee!

Kent   What a brazen-faced varlet art thou, to deny thou
25   knowest me! Is it two days since I tripped up thy heels and
      beat thee before the King? Draw, you rogue; for though it be
      night, yet the moon shines: I'll make a sop o'th'moonshine of
      you. You whoreson cullionly barber-monger, draw.

Oswald   Away! I have nothing to do with thee.

30 **Kent**   Draw, you rascal; you come with letters against the
      King, and take vanity the puppet's part against the royalty of
      her father. Draw, you rogue, or I'll so carbonado your
      shanks: draw, you rascal; come your ways.

Oswald   Help, ho! Murder! Help!

35 **Kent**   Strike, you slave; stand, rogue, stand; you neat slave,
      strike.

Oswald   Help, ho! Murder! Murder!

[*Enter* **Edmund,** *with his rapier drawn*]

Edmund   How now! What's the matter? Part!

40 **Kent**   With you, goodman boy, if you please: come, I'll flesh ye;
      come on, young master.

proud, shallow, beggarly, scruffy, upstart of a dirty, shabby, mincing rogue. A down-and-out slave. A man who'd be a pimp to get a good job, and who's nothing but a mixture of knave, beggar, coward, ponce, and the son-and-heir of a mongrel bitch. A fellow I'll beat till he shrieks if he denies one syllable of what I've said!

Oswald   Why, what a terrible fellow you are, to curse someone who is neither known to you, nor knows you!

Kent   What a hard-faced rascal you are, to deny you know me! Is it two days since I tripped you up in front of the King? Draw your sword, you rogue, 'cos though it may be night, the moon's shining. I'll mop up the moonlight with you! [*He draws*] You lousy, rascally poser! Draw!

Oswald   Go away! I'll have nothing to do with you!

Kent   Draw, you rascal! You're here with letters critical of the King, and you side with Lady Stuck-Up against her royal father. Draw, you rogue, or I'll give you a real roasting! Draw, you rascal! Come on!

Oswald   Help! Murder! Help!

Kent   Fight, you coward! Stand your ground, you rogue! You swanky coward, fight! [*He beats* **Oswald** *with the flat of his sword*]

Oswald   Help! Murder! Murder!

[**Edmund** *enters with his rapier drawn*]

Edmund   Hey, what's all this about? Break!

Kent   About you, young shaver, if you like! Come on, I'll initiate you! Come on, laddie! [*He challenges* **Edmund** *too*]

[*Enter* **Cornwall, Regan, Gloucester,** *and Servants*]

Gloucester   Weapons! Arms! What's the matter here?

Cornwall   Keep peace, upon your lives. He dies that strikes
again. What is the matter?

Regan   The messengers from our sister and the King.

45 **Cornwall**   What is your difference? Speak.

Oswald   I am scarce in breath, my lord.

Kent   No marvel, you have so bestirred your valour. You
cowardly rascal, nature disclaims in thee: a tailor made thee.

Cornwall   Thou art a strange fellow; a tailor make a man?

50 **Kent**   A tailor, sir: a stone-cutter or a painter could not have
made him so ill, though they had been but two years
o'th'trade.

Cornwall   Speak yet, how grew your quarrel?

Oswald   This ancient ruffian, sir, whose life I have spared at
55   suit of his grey beard –

Kent   Thou whoreson zed! Thou unnecessary letter! My lord,
if you will give me leave, I will tread this unbolted villain
into mortar, and daub the wall of a jakes with him. Spare my
grey beard, you wagtail?

60 **Cornwall**   Peace, sirrah! You beastly knave, know you no
reverence?

Kent   Yes, sir; but anger hath a privilege.

Cornwall   Why art thou angry?

Kent   That such a slave as this should wear a sword,
65   Who wears no honesty. Such smiling rogues as these,
Like rats, oft bite the the holy cords a-twain

[**Cornwall** *enters, with* **Regan**, **Gloucester** *and Servants*]

Gloucester   Weapons! Fighting! What's all this?

Cornwall   No more, upon your lives: the next to strike dies!
  What's the matter?

Regan   They are the messengers from our sister and the King.

Cornwall   What's the quarrel? Speak.

Oswald   I'm out of breath, my lord.

Kent   No wonder; your courage is out of condition. You
  cowardly rascal, you're not natural. Some tailor stitched you
  together.

Cornwall   You're an odd fellow. A tailor make a man?

Kent   Yes, a tailor, sir. A stone-cutter or a painter couldn't
  have done such a botched job, even if they'd only been
  working for a couple of years.

Cornwall   So tell me, how did your quarrel start?

Oswald   This ancient ruffian, sir, whose life I have spared on
  account of his grey beard –

Kent   You useless wretch! You good-for-nothing! My lord,
  with your permission I'll grind this coarse villain into mortar,
  and plaster the wall of a lavatory with him. Spare my grey
  beard, you bower-and-scraper?

Cornwall   Quiet, man! You uncouth hooligan: have you no
  respect?

Kent   Yes, sir. But anger takes precedent.

Cornwall   Why are you so angry?

Kent   Because such a wretch as this should display a sword
  but not show any honesty. Smiling rogues such as these
  often gnaw like rats through bonds of love that are too tight

Which are too intrince t'unloose; smooth every passion
That in the natures of their lords rebel;
Bring oil to fire, snow to their colder moods;
70   Renege, affirm, and turn their halcyon beaks
With every gale and vary of their masters,
Knowing nought, like dogs, but following.
A plague upon your epileptic visage!
Smile you my speeches, as I were a fool?
75   Goose, if I had you upon Sarum plain,
I'd drive ye cackling home to Camelot.

Cornwall   What, art thou mad, old fellow?

Gloucester   How fell you out? Say that.

Kent   No contraries hold more antipathy
80   Than I and such a knave.

Cornwall   Why dost thou call him knave? What is his fault?

Kent   His countenance likes me not.

Cornwall   No more, perchance, does mine, nor his, nor hers.

Kent   Sir, 'tis my occupation to be plain:
85   I have seen better faces in my time
Than stands on any shoulder that I see
Before me at this instant.

Cornwall   This is some fellow,
Who, having been praised for bluntness, doth affect
A saucy roughness, and constrains the garb
90   Quite from his nature: he cannot flatter, he,
An honest mind and plain, he must speak truth:
And they will take it, so; if not, he's plain.
These kind of knaves I know, which in this plainness
Harbour more craft and more corrupter ends
95   Than twenty silly ducking observants,
That stretch their duties nicely.

to be undone by other means. They satisfy the lusts of their debauched masters. They add fuel to anger; they bring chill to moods of dejection; they deny, they affirm, and turn with the wind according to their masters' moods – knowing nothing but how to follow, like dogs. Damn your twitching face! Are you laughing at me, as if I were a fool? You goose, if you were on Salisbury Plain I'd make you cackle your way back home to Winchester.

Cornwall   What, are you mad, old fellow?

Gloucester   How did you come to quarrel? Explain that.

Kent   No two men hate each other more than I and that rogue.

Cornwall   Why do you call him a rogue? What has he done wrong?

Kent   I don't like his face.

Cornwall   Or mine, or his, or hers, probably.

Kent   Sir, I'm a plain man. I *have* seen better faces in my time than I see now.

Cornwall   This is a fellow who, having been praised for bluntness, has assumed a cheeky impertinence; but he mis-uses It. [*Sarcastically*] Oh no, he can't flatter. Not him! He has a plain, honest mind. He has to speak the truth. If people will take it, fine. If not, it's just his way. I know these rogues. Behind this bluntness they conceal more craftiness, and have corrupter purposes, than twenty grovelling bootlickers who never put a foot wrong.

Kent   Sir, in good sooth, in sincere verity,
    Under th'allowance of your great aspect,
    Whose influence, like the wreath of radiant fire
    On flickering Phoebus' front –

100 **Cornwall**   What mean'st by this?

Kent   To go out of my dialect, which you discommend so
much. I know, sir, I am no flatterer: he that beguiled you in
a plain accent was a plain knave; which for my part I will not
be, though I should win your displeasure to entreat me to't.

105 **Cornwall**   What was the offence you gave him?

Oswald   I never gave him any:
    It pleased the King his master very late
    To strike at me, upon his misconstruction;
    When he, compact, and flattering his displeasure,
110   Tripped me behind; being down, insulted, railed,
    And put upon him such a deal of man,
    That worthied him, got praises of the King
    For him attempting who was self-subdued;
    And, in the fleshment of this dread exploit,
    Drew on me here again.

115 **Kent**   None of these rogues and cowards
    But Ajax is their fool.

Cornwall   Fetch forth the stocks!
    You stubborn ancient knave, you reverend braggart,
    We'll teach you.

Kent   Sir, I am too old to learn.
    Call not your stocks for me; I serve the King,
120   On whose employment I was sent to you;
    You shall do small respect, show too bold malice
    Against the grace and person of my master,
    Stocking his messenger.

Kent   [*mockingly over-polite*] Sir, in all good faith; in sincere truthfulness; with the gracious approval of your mightiness, whose power – like the great ball of fire round the sun –

Cornwall   [*interrupting*] What's your game?

Kent   [*reverting to normality*] To change my manner of speech, which you disapprove of so much: I know, sir, that I'm no flatterer. The man who tricked you with plain-speaking was a plain rogue. That I'll never be, even if you begged me, and I risked your displeasure by turning you down.

Cornwall   [*to* Oswald] What offence did you give him?

Oswald   I didn't give him any. Recently, through a misunderstanding, his master the King chose to strike me. Then, backing his majesty up and pandering to his anger, he tripped me from behind. While I was down, he insulted me, abused me, and made himself out to be such a hero that he got credit from it, and was praised by the King for tackling a man who was offering no aggression. And, inspired by this amazing achievement, he drew on me here again.

Kent   All rogues and cowards think the noble Ajax is a fool compared with them.

Cornwall   Bring the stocks here! You fierce old rogue, you elderly braggart! We'll teach you!

Kent   Sir, I'm too old to learn. Don't call your stocks for me. I serve the King, on whose business I was sent to you. In stocking his messenger, you would be showing scant respect, insulting the King personally, and his office.

Cornwall   Fetch forth the stocks!
As I have life and honour, there shall he sit till noon.

125   **Regan**   Till noon! Till night, my lord; and all night too.

Kent   Why, madam, if I were your father's dog,
You should not use me so.

Regan   Sir, being his knave, I will.

Cornwall   This is a fellow of the self-same colour
Our sister speaks of. Come, bring away the stocks.

[*Stocks brought out*]

130   **Gloucester**   Let me beseech your grace not to do so.
His fault is much, and the good King his master
Will check him for't: your purposed low correction
Is such as basest and contemned'st wretches
For pilferings and most common trespasses
135   Are punished with: the King must take it ill,
That he, so slightly valued in his messenger,
Should have him thus restrained.

Cornwall   I'll answer that.

Regan   My sister may receive it much more worse
To have her gentleman abused, assaulted,
140   For following her affairs. Put in his legs.

[**Kent** *is put in the stocks*]

Cornwall   Come, my lord, away.

[*Exeunt all but* **Gloucester** *and* **Kent**]

Gloucester   I am sorry for thee, friend; 'tis the Duke's
pleasure,

Cornwall   Bring the stocks! Upon my life and honour, he'll sit there till noon.

Regan   Till noon? Till night, my lord, and all night too.

Kent   Why, madam, if I were your father's dog you wouldn't treat me like that.

Regan   Sir, you being his lackey, I will.

Cornwall   This is a fellow of the very sort our sister wrote about. Come, bring along the stocks.

[*They are carried in*]

Gloucester   Let me plead with your grace not to do this. He's greatly at fault, and the good King, his master, will rebuke him for it. Your proposed undignified punishment is the sort that the most disreputable and scorned of wretches are punished with, for petty pilfering and minor misdemeanours. The King won't take kindly to having his messenger shackled like this.

Cornwall   I'll answer for that.

Regan   My sister might be far more offended, having her servant abused and assaulted for carrying out her business. Put his legs in.

[**Kent** *is put in the stocks*]

Cornwall   Let's go, my lord.

[*All but* **Gloucester** *and* **Kent** *leave*]

Gloucester   I'm sorry for you friend. It's the Duke's whim. As

Whose disposition, all the world well knows,
Will not be rubbed nor stopped: I'll entreat for thee.

145 **Kent**   Pray, do not, sir. I have watched and travelled hard;
Some time I shall sleep out, the rest I'll whistle.
A good man's fortune may grow out at heels:
Give you good morrow!

Gloucester   The Duke's to blame in this; 'twill be ill taken.

[*Exit*]

150 **Kent**   Good King, that must approve the common saw,
Thou out of heaven's benediction comest
To the warm sun!
Approach, thou beacon to this under globe,
That by thy comfortable beams I may
155 Peruse this letter. Nothing almost sees miracles,
But misery: I know 'tis from Cordelia,
Who hath most fortunately been informed
Of my obscured course; and shall find time
From this enormous state, seeking to give
160 Losses their remedies. All weary and o'erwatched,
Take vantage, heavy eyes, not to behold
This shameful lodging.
Fortune, good night; smile once more; turn thy wheel!

[*He sleeps*]

all the world well knows, his temperament will brook no
restraint or impediment. I'll plead for you.

Kent   Please don't sir. I've gone without sleep and travelled
rough. I'll sleep away some of the time; the rest I'll whistle.
A good man's fortunes can get down at heel. Good day to
you!

Gloucester   The Duke's at fault in this. It will be taken badly.

[*He goes*]

Kent   Good King, who should have heeded the old proverb:
you've gone from the frying pan into the fire! Come, torch of
this world, so that I can read this letter by your comforting
beams! Miracles are mostly related to misery; I know this is
from Cordelia, who fortunately has been informed of my
disguise. She will find an opportune time to put things right
in this lawless state. Take this opportunity, heavy eyes — all
weary and fatigued — not to look upon these shameful
stocks. Goodnight, Fortune! Smile once more: then turn
your wheel!

[*He sleeps*]

Scene 3

A wood. Enter **Edgar**

Edgar   I heard myself proclaimed;
And by the happy hollow of a tree
Escaped the hunt. No port is free; no place,
That guard, and most unusual vigilance,
5   Does not attend my taking. Whiles I may 'scape,
I will preserve myself; and am bethought
To take the basest and most poorest shape
That ever penury, in contempt of man,
Brought near to beast; my face I'll grime with filth,
10   Blanket my loins, elf all my hairs in knots,
And with presented nakedness outface
The winds and persecutions of the sky.
The country gives me proof and precedent
Of Bedlam beggars, who, with roaring voices,
15   Strike in their numbed and mortified bare arms
Pins, wooden pricks, nails, sprigs of rosemary;
And with this horrible object, from low farms,
Poor pelting villages, sheep-cotes, and mills,
Sometime with lunatic bans, sometime with prayers,
20   Enforce their charity. Poor Turlygod! Poor Tom!
That's something yet: Edgar I nothing am.

[*Exit*]

Scene 3

A wood. **Edgar** *enters*

Edgar   I heard myself proclaimed an outlaw. By hiding in the
   convenient hollow of a tree, I escaped the hunt. No seaport
   is free. There's nowhere that isn't tightly guarded in order to
   capture me. While I can still escape, I'll protect myself. I
   intend to assume the role of the lowest and poorest man
   that poverty at its most degrading ever dragged down to the
   level of a beast. I'll begrime my face with filth, wear a
   loin-cloth, matt all my hair in knots and brave the winds and
   sufferings of the elements in the full exposure of my
   nakedness. There are many examples around the
   countryside of lunatic beggars who, with roaring voices,
   stick pins, wooden skewers, nails and sprigs of rosemary in
   their cold and numbed bare arms. Using this horrible
   spectacle they extort charity from humble farms, poor
   poverty-stricken villages, sheepfarms and mills, sometimes
   with lunatic curses, sometimes with prayers. [*He speaks like
   a Bedlam Beggar*] Poor Turlygod! Poor Tom! [*In his normal
   voice*] That's my new life. Edgar is a thing of the past.

[*He goes*]

Scene 4

Before Gloucester's Castle. **Kent** *in the stocks. Enter* **Lear, Fool** *and a* **Gentleman**

Lear   'Tis strange that they should so depart from home,
And not send back my messenger.

Gentleman   As I learned,
The night before there was no purpose in them
Of this remove.

Kent   Hail to thee, noble master!

5 **Lear**   Ha!
Mak'st thou this shame thy pastime?

Kent   No, my lord.

Fool   Ha, ha! He wears cruel garters. Horses are tied by the
heads, dogs and bears by the neck, monkeys by the loins,
and men by the legs: when a man's over-lusty at legs then
10   he wears wooden nether-stocks.

Lear   What's he that hath so much thy place mistook
To set thee here?

Kent   It is both he and she,
Your son and daughter.

Lear   No.

15 **Kent**   Yes.

Lear   No, I say.

Kent   I say, yea.

Lear   No, no; they would not.

Kent   Yes, yes, they have.

Scene 4

Outside Gloucester's castle. **Kent** *is in the stocks.* **Lear**, *the*
   Fool *and a* **Gentleman** *enter*

Lear   It's strange that they should leave home like that, and
   not send back my messenger.

Gentleman   I heard that the night before they had no intention
   of going.

Kent   Greetings, noble master!

Lear   What, Is this sort of disgrace a hobby with you?

Kent   No, my lord.

Fool   Ha, ha, he's wearing shoddy garters! Horses are tied by
   their heads, dogs and bears by the neck, monkeys by the
   waist, and men by the legs. When a man gets too frisky,
   then he has to wear wooden stockings.

Lear   Who has so mistaken your status that he has placed you
   here?

Kent   It's both 'he' and 'she': your son-in-law and daughter.

Lear   No.

Kent   Yes.

Lear   No, I say!

Kent   I say yes.

Lear   No, no. They would not!

Kent   Yes, yes. They have.

20 **Lear**   By Jupiter, I swear, no.

Kent   By Juno, I swear, ay.

Lear   They durst not do't.
They could not, would not do't; 'tis worse than murder,
To do upon respect such violent outrage.
Resolve me, with all modest haste, which way
25 Thou might'st deserve, or they impose, this usage,
Coming from us.

Kent   My lord, when at their home
I did commend your highness' letters to them,
Ere I was risen from the place that showed
My duty kneeling, came there a reeking post,
30 Stewed in his haste, half breathless, panting forth
From Goneril his mistress salutations;
Delivered letters, spite of intermission,
Which presently they read: on whose contents
They summoned up their meiny, straight took horse;
35 Commanded me to follow, and attend
The leisure of their answer; gave me cold looks:
And meeting here the other messenger,
Whose welcome, I perceived, had poisoned mine,
Being the very fellow which of late
40 Displayed so saucily against your highness,
Having more man than wit about me, drew:
He raised the house with loud and coward cries.
Your son and daughter found this trespass worth
The shame which here it suffers.

45 **Fool**   Winter's not gone yet, if the wild-geese fly that way.

Fathers that wear rags
    Do make their children blind,
But fathers that bear bags
    Shall see their children kind.
50 *Fortune, that arrant whore,*
Ne'er turns the key to the poor.

Lear   By Jupiter, I swear no!

Kent   By Juno, I swear yes.

Lear   They wouldn't dare do it. They could not – would not – do it! It's worse than murder to do such a violent outrage against the King's officer. Tell me quickly how you could have deserved – or they imposed – this treatment, coming as you did from me.

Kent   My lord, when I delivered your highness's letters to them at their home, I'd no sooner risen from my bow than a sweating courier, anxious in his haste, half breathless, came panting greetings from his mistress Goneril. He delivered letters, ignoring the fact that he was interrupting me, which they read at once. On noting the contents, they summoned their servants and immediately took to their horses. They ordered me to follow and await an answer at their leisure. They gave me cold looks. So when I met the other messenger here – whose welcome I realized had poisoned mine – and observing he was the very same fellow who had recently behaved so cheekily before your highness, having more courage than sense, I drew my sword. He awakened the servants with his loud and cowardly cries. Your son-in-law and daughter found this offence worthy of the shame I'm now suffering.

Fool   Winter isn't over while there are wild geese about like that!

> *Fathers who've no money*
> *Have children who ignore 'em.*
> *But fathers who are rich*
> *Have children who adore 'em.*
> *Luck, that shameless whore,*
> *Never helps the poor.*

But for all this thou shalt have as many dolours for thy
daughters as thou canst tell in a year.

Lear   Oh! how this mother swells up toward my heart;
55   Hysterica passio! Down, thou climbing sorrow,
Thy element's below. Where is this daughter?

Kent   With the Earl, sir; here within.

Lear   Follow me not; stay here.

[*Exit*]

Gentleman   Made you no more offence but what you
60   speak of?

Kent   None. How chance the King comes with so small a
number?

Fool   And thou hadst been set i'th'stocks for that question,
thou'dst well deserved it.

Kent   Why, Fool?

65 **Fool**   We'll set thee to school to an ant, to teach thee there's
no labouring i'th'winter. All that follow their noses are led
by their eyes but blind men; and there's not a nose among
twenty but can smell him that's stinking. Let go thy hold
when a great wheel runs down a hill, lest it break thy neck
70   with following; but the great one that goes upward, let him
draw thee after. When a wise man gives thee better
counsel, give me mine again: I would have none but knaves
follow it, since a Fool gives it.

> *That sir which serves and seeks for gain,*
75   *And follows but for form,*
> *Will pack when it begins to rain,*
> *And leave thee in the storm.*
> *But I will tarry; the Fool will stay,*
> *And let the wise man fly:*

So, you'll have more in-come from your daughters than you can cope with in one year.

Lear   Oh, how this smothering feeling spreads up towards my heart! [*He opens his collar*] The choking disease! Stay down, you spreading sorrow, keep your lowly place! Where is this daughter?

Kent   With the Earl, sir, indoors.

Lear   Don't follow me. Stay here.

[*He rushes off*]

Gentleman   Did you really give no more offence than that?

Kent   None. How come the King has so few with him?

Fool   If you'd been put in the stocks for that question, you would have well deserved it.

Kent   Why, Fool?

Fool   You must learn from the ant: there's nothing to be gained from toiling on behalf of a lost cause. All who follow their noses are guided by their eyes, except blind men, and most of *them* can smell a man who's had his day. When a huge wheel runs down a hill, don't hold on to it in case you break your neck trying to keep up with it. When it's going upwards, let it pull you with it. When a wise man gives you better advice, return mine. It's really only for knaves, since it's given by a Fool.

> The man who works in hope of gain,
>   And has no sense of loyalty,
> Will quit when fortune's on the wane,
>   And leave you in calamity.
> But I won't leave. The Fool will stay,
>   And let the wise man go;

80   *The knave turns Fool that runs away;*
                The Fool no knave, perdy.

Kent   Where learned you this, Fool?

Fool   Not i'th'stocks, fool.

[*Re-enter* **Lear,** *with* **Gloucester**]

Lear   Deny to speak with me? They are sick? They are
           weary?
85   They have travelled all the night? Mere fetches,
           The images of revolt and flying off.
           Fetch me a better answer.

Gloucester   My dear lord,
           You know the fiery quality of the Duke;
           How unremovable and fixed he is
90   In his own course.

Lear   Vengeance! Plague! Death! Confusion!
           Fiery! What quality? Why, Gloucester, Gloucester,
           I'd speak with the Duke of Cornwall and his wife.

Gloucester   Well, my good lord, I have informed them so.

95 **Lear**   Informed them! Dost thou understand me, man?

Gloucester   Ay, my good lord.

Lear   The King would speak with Cornwall; the dear father
           Would with his daughter speak, commands her service:
           Are they informed of this? My breath and blood!
100   Fiery! The fiery Duke! Tell the hot Duke that –
           No, but not yet; may be he is not well:
           Infirmity doth still neglect all office
           Whereto our health is bound; we are not ourselves
           When nature, being oppressed, commands the mind
105   To suffer with the body. I'll forbear;

> *The knave turns Fool who runs away;*
> *This Fool's no knave, you know.*

Kent   Where did you learn this, Fool?

Fool   Not in the stocks, fool.

[**Lear** *returns with* **Gloucester**]

Lear   Refused to speak to me! They are sick? They are tired?
They've travelled overnight? Mere excuses: yes, the
symbols of revolt and desertion! Bring me a better answer.

Gloucester   My dear lord, you know the fiery temperament of
the Duke; how obstinate and determined he is in having his
own way.

Lear   Vengeance! Plague! Death! Confusion! Fiery? What
'temperament'? Why, Gloucester, Gloucester, I want to
speak to the Duke of Cornwall and his wife . . .

Gloucester   Well, my good lord, I have informed them so.

Lear   'Informed' them! Do you understand me, man?

Gloucester   Yes, my good lord.

Lear   The King wishes to speak to Cornwall . . . The dear
father wants to speak to his daughter, commands her
obedience! Are they informed of this? My breath and blood!
Fiery? The fiery Duke? Tell the hot-tempered Duke
that – [*He stops short*] No, but not yet. Perhaps he isn't
well. Illness does cause neglect of the duties we perform
when we are fit. We are not ourselves when illness causes
the mind to suffer as well as the body. I'll restrain myself. I

And am fallen out with my more headier will,
To take the indisposed and sickly fit
For the sound man. Death on my state! Wherefore
Should he sit here? This act persuades me
110   That this remotion of the Duke and her
Is practice only. Give me my servant forth.
Go and tell the Duke and's wife I'd speak with them,
Now, presently: bid them come forth and hear me,
Or at their chamber-door I'll beat the drum
115   Till it cry sleep to death.

Gloucester I would have all well betwixt you.

[*Exit*]

Lear Oh, me! My heart, my rising heart! But, down!

Fool Cry to it, nuncle, as the cockney did to the eels when
she put 'em i'th'paste alive; she knapped 'em o'th'coxcombs
120   with a stick, and cried, 'Down, wantons, down!' 'Twas her
brother that, in pure kindness to his horse, buttered his
hay.

[*Re-enter* **Gloucester**, *with* **Cornwall**, **Regan**, *and Servants*]

Lear Good morrow to you both.

Cornwall   Hail to your Grace!

[**Kent** *is set at liberty*]

Regan I am glad to see your Highness.

125 **Lear** Regan, I think you are; I know what reason
I have to think so: if thou shouldst not be glad,
I would divorce me from thy mother's tomb,
Sepulchring an adultress. [*To* **Kent**] Oh, are you free?

won't think what's done in sickness represents the healthy
man. [*He looks at* **Kent** *in the stocks and flares up again*]
Death to my royal power! Why should he be sitting here?
This deed convinces me that this remoteness of the Duke
and her is pure deceit. I want my servant out of the stocks!
Go and tell the Duke and his wife that I want to speak to
them. Now. At once! Tell them to come out and hear me, or
I'll beat a drum at their bedroom door till they think they'll
never sleep again!

Gloucester   I'd like all to be well between you.

[*He goes*]

Lear   [*holding his chest*] Oh, me! My heart is rising. But, down!

Fool   Give it its orders, uncle, like the cockney-woman did the
eels, when she put them in the fish-paste alive! She rapped
them over the head with a stick, and cried 'Down, you randy
lot, down!' It was her brother who, out of pure kindness to
his horse, put butter on his hay.

[**Gloucester** *returns, with* **Cornwall, Regan** *and Servants*]

Lear   Good morning to you both.

Cornwall   Hail to your grace!

[**Kent** *is set free*]

Regan   I am glad to see your highness.

Lear   Regan, I believe you are. I well know the reason for
thinking so. If you were not glad, I would denounce the
grave of your mother, because it would be the tomb of an
adulteress. [*To* **Kent**] Oh, are you free? We'll discuss that

130   Some other time for that. [*Exit* **Kent**] Beloved Regan.
        Thy sister's naught: Oh Regan! She hath tied
        Sharp-toothed unkindness, like a vulture, here.
        I can scarce speak to thee; thou'lt not believe
        With how depraved a quality – Oh, Regan!

Regan   I pray you, sir, take patience. I have hope
135   You less know how to value her desert
        Than she to scant her duty.

Lear   Say? How is that?

Regan   I cannot think my sister in the least
        Would fail her obligation. If, sir, perchance
        She have restrained the riots of your followers,
140   'Tis on such ground, and to such wholesome end,
        As clears her from all blame.

Lear   My curses on her!

Regan   Oh, sir! You are old;
        Nature in you stands on the very verge
        Of her confine: you should be ruled and led
145   By some discretion that discerns your state
        Better than you yourself. Therefore I pray you
        That to our sister you do make return;
        Say you have wronged her.

Lear   Ask her forgiveness?
        Do you but mark how this becomes the house:
150   'Dear daughter, I confess that I am old;
        Age is unnecessary: on my knees I beg
        That you'll vouchsafe me raiment, bed, and food.'

Regan   Good sir, no more; these are unsightly tricks.
        Return you to my sister.

Lear   Never, Regan.
155   She hath abated me of half my train;

126

some other time. [**Kent** *leaves*] Beloved Regan, your sister is
wicked. Oh, Regan, her sharp-toothed unkindness has
stabbed at my heart like a vulture that's been tied there. I
can hardly speak to you. You won't believe the depraved
manner with which – [*He chokes*] Oh, Regan!

Regan   Really, sir, have patience. I hope it's you undervaluing
her, not she falling short of her duty.

Lear   What did you say? How do you mean?

Regan   I can't believe my sister would fail in her obligation to
you in the least. If, sir, she has indeed checked the rioting of
your followers, it would be on such grounds, and to such a
desirable end, as to clear her from all blame.

Lear   My curses on her!

Regan   Oh, sir, you are old. You are at the end of your life. You
should be governed and led by some wiser person who
knows you better than you do yourself. Therefore I suggest
you return to our sister. Tell her you have wronged her.

Lear   Ask her forgiveness? How becoming this would be to
royalty! 'Dear daughter, I admit that I am old. Old people are
a nuisance. On my knees I beg you to grant me clothes, bed
and food'. [*He kneels to drive his point home*]

Regan   Good sir, no more of this. These are unseemly tricks.
Go and return to my sister.

Lear   [*rising*] Never, Regan. She has deprived me of half my

Looked black upon me; struck me with her tongue,
Most serpent-like, upon the very heart.
All the stored vengeances of heaven fall
On her ingrateful top! Strike her young bones,
You taking airs, with lameness!

160 **Cornwall**   Fie, sir, fie!

Lear   You nimble lightnings, dart your blinding flames
Into her scornful eyes! Infect her beauty,
You fen-sucked fogs, drawn by the powerful sun,
To fall and blast her pride!

165 **Regan**   Oh the blest Gods! So will you wish on me,
When the rash mood is on.

Lear   No, Regan, thou shalt never have my curse:
Thy tender-hefted nature shall not give
Thee o'er to harshness: her eyes are fierce, but thine
170 Do comfort and not burn. 'Tis not in thee
To grudge my pleasures, to cut off my train,
To bandy hasty words, to scant my sizes,
And, in conclusion to oppose the bolt
Against my coming in: thou better know'st
175 The offices of nature, bond of childhood,
Effects of courtesy, dues of gratitude;
Thy half o'th'kingdom hast thou not forgot,
Wherein I thee endowed.

Regan   Good sir, to the purpose.

Lear   Who put my man i'th'stocks? [*Tucket within*]

Cornwall   What trumpet's that?

180 **Regan**   I know't, my sister's: this approves her letter,
That she would soon be here.

[*Enter* **Oswald**]

                              Is your lady come?

retinue, given me black looks, and lashed me with her tongue most viciously. May the entire stock of heaven's vengeances drop on her ungrateful head! Strike her unborn children with lameness, you corrupting winds!

Cornwall   Come, sir, come!

Lear   Swift-moving lightning, aim your blinding flames into her eyes! Infect her beauty, you fogs sucked up from the fens by the heat of the powerful sun, and make her ugly!

Regan   Oh, the blessed gods! That's what you'll wish on me when you're in one of your rash moods!

Lear   No, Regan, I will never curse you. Your tender-hearted nature couldn't turn to harshness. Her eyes are fierce, but yours are comforting, and don't smoulder. It's not in your nature to begrudge me my pleasures, to reduce my retinue, to exchange hasty words, to cut down my allowances, and finally to lock me out. You know your natural duties; the obligations of child to parent; the ways of good manners; the responsibilities of gratitude. You haven't forgotten the half of the kingdom that I gave to you.

Regan   Good sir. Get to the point.

Lear   Who put my man in the stocks? [*A trumpet sounds*]

Cornwall   Whose trumpet is that?

Regan   I recognize it: my sister's. This confirms her letter, that she'd be here soon.

   [**Oswald** *enters*]

   Has your lady arrived?

Lear   This is a slave, whose easy-borrowed pride
Dwells in the fickle grace of her he follows.
Out, varlet, from my sight!

Cornwall   What means your grace?

185   **Lear**   Who stocked my servant? Regan, I have good hope
Thou didst not know on't. Who comes here?

[*Enter* **Goneril**]

                                 Oh heavens
If you do love old men, if your sweet sway
Allow obedience, if you yourselves are old,
Make it your cause; send down and take my part!
190   [*To* **Goneril**] Art not ashamed to look upon this beard?
Oh Regan, will you take her by the hand?

Goneril   Why not by th'hand, sir? How have I offended?
All's not offence that indiscretion finds
And dotage terms so.

Lear   Oh sides, you are too tough!
195   Will you yet hold? How came my man i'th'stocks?

Cornwall   I set him there, sir; but his own disorders
Deserved much less advancement.

Lear   You! Did you?

Regan   I pray you, father, being weak, seem so.
If, till the expiration of your month,
200   You will return and sojourn with my sister,
Dismissing half your train, come then to me:
I am now from home, and out of that provision
Which shall be needful for your entertainment.

Lear   Return to her? And fifty men dismissed?
205   No, rather I abjure all roofs, and choose
To wage against the enmity o'th'air;

130

Lear   [*glowering at* **Oswald**] This is the wretch whose
impudence depends on the fickle patronage of his mistress.
Get out of my sight, rascal!

Cornwall   What does your grace mean?

Lear   Who put my servant in the stocks? Regan, I trust you
didn't know about it. [**Goneril** *approaches*] Who comes
here? Oh, the gods: if you love old men; if your gracious
power approves of obedience; if you yourselves are old;
make this an issue. Intercede, and take up my cause! [*To*
Goneril] Are you not ashamed to look upon this beard? [*The
sisters embrace*] Oh, Regan, will you hold her hand?

Goneril   Why not my hand, sir? What have I done wrong? All is
not 'offence' simply because it's so-called by the
irresponsible and those in their dotage.

Lear   [*holding his heart*] Is there no release? [*To* **Cornwall**]
How did my man come to be in the stocks?

Cornwall   *I* put him there, sir. His misconduct merited worse.

Lear   You! Did you?

Regan   Really, father, be your age. If you will return with my
sister and stay with her till the end of your month –
dismissing half your retinue – you can then come to me. I
am away from home now, and unable to provide properly for
your entertainment.

Lear   Return to her? With fifty men dismissed? No! Instead, I
reject all shelter, and choose to fight the elements, befriend

131

To be a comrade with the wolf and owl,
Necessity's sharp pinch! Return with her!
Why, the hot-blooded France, that dowerless took
210 Our youngest born, I could as well be brought
To knee his throne, and, squire-like, pension beg
To keep base life afoot. Return with her!
Persuade me rather to be slave and sumpter
To this detested groom. [*Pointing at* **Oswald**]

Goneril   At your choice, sir.

215 **Lear** I prithee, daughter, do not make me mad:
I will not trouble thee, my child; farewell.
We'll no more meet, no more see one another;
But yet thou art my flesh, my blood, my daughter;
Or rather a disease that's in my flesh,
220 Which I must needs call mine: thou art a boil,
A plague-sore, or embossed carbuncle,
In my corrupted blood. But I'll not chide thee;
Let shame come when it will, I do not call it;
I do not bid the thunder-bearer shoot,
225 Nor tell tales of thee to high-judging Jove.
Mend when thou canst; be better at thy leisure;
I can be patient; I can stay with Regan,
I and my hundred knights.

Regan   Not altogether so;
I looked not for you yet, nor am provided
230 For your fit welcome. Give ear, sir, to my sister;
For those that mingle reason with your passion
Must be content to think you old, and so –
But she knows what she does.

Lear   Is this well spoken?

Regan I dare avouch it, sir: what, fifty followers?
235 Is it not well? What should you need of more?

the wolf and owl, suffer hardship! Return with her? Why, I could as well be made to kneel before the throne of passionate France, who took our youngest born without a dowry, and beg a pension from him, like some petty squire, to make ends meet. Return with her? I'd rather you persuaded me to be slave and drudge to this detested servant! [*He points at* **Oswald**]

Goneril   Please yourself, sir.

Lear   I beg you, daughter, do not make me mad. I won't trouble you, my child. Farewell. We'll meet no more. We'll see each other no more. [*His anger returns*] But then you *are* my flesh and blood, my daughter; or rather, a disease that's in my flesh, which is mine whether I like it or not. You're a boil, a plague-sore, a swollen tumour in my infected blood! [*Calm again*] But I won't curse you. Let shame choose its own time — I won't stir it up. I do not call on Jupiter for vengeance, nor tell tales about you to Jove, whose judgment is supreme. Reform when you can. Be better at your leisure. I can be patient. I can stay with Regan, I and my hundred knights.

Regan   Not quite. I wasn't expecting you yet, nor am I prepared for a fitting welcome. Listen to my sister, sir. Anyone considering your words dispassionately would conclude you are old, and therefore — but she knows what she is doing.

Lear   Is this well said?

Regan   It certainly is, sir. What, fifty followers? Isn't that plenty? Why should you need more? Yes, or so many, since

Yea, or so many, sith that both charge and danger
Speak 'gainst so great a number? How, in one house,
Should many people, under two commands,
Hold amity? 'Tis hard; almost impossible.

240   **Goneril**   Why might not you, my lord, receive attendance
From those that she calls servants, or from mine?

Regan   Why not, my lord? If then they chanced to slack you
We could control them. If you will come to me,
For now I spy a danger, I entreat you
245   To bring but five-and-twenty; to no more
Will I give place or notice.

Lear   I gave you all –

Regan   And in good time you gave it.

Lear   Made you my guardians, my depositaries,
But kept a reservation to be followed
250   With such a number. What, must I come to you
With five-and-twenty? Regan, said you so?

Regan   And speak't again, my lord; no more with me.

Lear   Those wicked creatures yet do look well-favoured
When others are more wicked; not being the worst
Stands in some rank of praise. [*To* **Goneril**] I'll go with
255   thee:
Thy fifty yet doth double five-and-twenty,
And thou art twice her love.

Goneril   Hear me, my lord.
What need you five-and-twenty, ten, or five,
To follow in a house where twice so many
Have a command to tend you?

260   **Regan**   What need one?

Lear   Oh reason not the need; our basest beggars

the expense and the danger both argue against so great a number? How, in one house, could so many people under two commands live in harmony? It's difficult. Almost impossible.

Goneril   Why couldn't you, my lord, be attended by *her* servants, or by mine?

Regan   Why not, my lord? If then they happened to become neglectful, we could pull them up. If you want to come to me, because now I spy a danger, I would ask you to bring only twenty-five. I'll accommodate and recognize no more.

Lear   I gave you everything . . .

Regan   And you took your time!

Lear   . . . made you my stewardesses and trustees, but with a proviso that I should have a retinue of such-a-number. What? Must I come to you with twenty-five? Regan, is that what you said?

Regan   And say it again, my lord. No more with me.

Lear   Some wicked creatures seem attractive when compared with others more wicked still. Not being the worst is some measure of praise. [*To* **Goneril**] I'll go with you. Your fifty is twice twenty-five, and your love is double hers.

Goneril   Listen to me, my lord. Why do you need twenty-five – ten – or five – to attend you, in a house where twice as many are at your service?

Regan   What need have you of one?

Lear   Oh, don't argue about 'need'! Our lowliest beggars have

Are in the poorest thing superfluous:
Allow not nature more than nature needs,
Man's life's as cheap as beast's. Thou art a lady;
265   If only to go warm were gorgeous,
Why, nature needs not what thou gorgeous wear'st,
Which scarcely keeps thee warm. But, for true need –
You heavens, give me that patience, patience I need! –
You see me here, you gods, a poor old man,
270   As full of grief as age; wretched in both!
If it be you that stirs these daughters' hearts
Against their father, fool me not so much
To bear it tamely; touch me with noble anger,
And let not women's weapons, water-drops,
275   Stain my man's cheeks! No, you unnatural hags,
I will have such revenges on you both
That all the world shall – I will do such things,
What they are, yet I know not, but they shall be
The terrors of the earth. You think I'll weep;
280 ·   No, I'll not weep:
I have full cause of weeping, but this heart
Shall break into a hundred thousand flaws
Or ere I'll weep. Oh Fool! I shall go mad.

[*Exeunt* **Lear, Gloucester, Gentleman** *and* **Fool.** *Storm and tempest*]

Cornwall   Let us withdraw, 'twill be a storm.

285 **Regan**   This house is little: the old man and's people
Cannot be well bestowed.

Goneril   'Tis his own blame; hath put himself from rest,
And must needs taste his folly.

Regan   For his particular, I'll receive him gladly,
But not one follower.

something they could do without. If you argue for the bare
necessities, then man's life would be no better than a
beast's. You are a lady: if being warm were the purpose of
being well-dressed, well then, there'd be no physical reason
for the fashionable clothes you are wearing, which hardly
keep you warm. Whereas true need – [*He breaks off*]
Heavens, give me patience, the patience I require! You see
me here, you gods, a poor old man, as full of grief as I am of
age; wretched in both respects! If you are responsible for
turning these daughters' hearts against their father, don't
make me such a fool as to bear it tamely! Inspire me with
noble anger, and don't let women's weapons – tears –
stain my man's cheeks! No, you unnatural hags; I'll have my
revenge on you both, so that all the world will – I'll do such
things, I can't say what at present, but they will be earth-
shattering! You think I'll cry? No, I won't cry. I've got every
reason to cry [*thunder claps are heard in the distance*], but
this heart of mine will break into a hundred thousand pieces
before I'll cry. Oh, Fool! I shall go mad! [*He staggers out,
followed by* **Gloucester**, *the* **Gentleman** *and the* **Fool**]

Cornwall   Let us go in. There's going to be a storm.

Regan   This is a small house. The old man and his retinue
can't be adequately lodged.

Goneril   It's his own fault. He's upset himself, and he must
suffer for his folly.

Regan   For himself, I'll take him gladly. But not one follower.

290 **Goneril**   So am I purposed.
   Where is my Lord of Gloucester?

Cornwall   Followed the old man forth. He is returned.

   [*Re-enter* **Gloucester**]

Gloucester   The King is in high rage.

Cornwall   Whither is he going?

Gloucester   He calls to horse; but will I know not whither.

295 **Cornwall**   'Tis best to give him way; he leads himself.

Goneril   My lord, entreat him by no means to stay.

Gloucester   Alack! The night comes on, and the bleak winds
   Do sorely ruffle; for many miles about
   There's scarce a bush.

Regan   Oh sir, to wilful men,
300   The injuries that they themselves procure
   Must be their schoolmasters. Shut up your doors;
   He is attended with a desperate train,
   And what they may incense him to, being apt
   To have his ear abused, wisdom bids fear.

305 **Cornwall**   Shut up your doors, my lord; 'tis a wild night.
   My Regan counsels well: come out o'th'storm.

                                        [*Exeunt*]

138

Goneril   That's my attitude. Where is my Lord of Gloucester?

Cornwall   He followed the old man out. He's back.

[**Gloucester** *enters*]

Gloucester   The King is in a terrible rage.

Cornwall   Where is he going?

Gloucester   He's summoned the horses. Where he's going, I don't know.

Cornwall   Best give him his own way. He's his own master.

Goneril   My lord, by no means plead with him to stay.

Gloucester   Alas, it's almost night, and the bleak winds are blustering fiercely. There's hardly a bush for miles around.

Regan   Oh, sir, wilful men can only learn by suffering from their own actions. Shut your doors. His attendants are a desperate lot, and it's only sensible to fear what they might provoke him into doing. He's apt to be misled.

Cornwall   Shut your doors, my lord. It's a wild night. My Regan's advice is sound. Come out of the storm.

[*They leave*]

Act three

Scene 1

A heath. A storm, with thunder and lightning. Enter **Kent** *and a* **Gentleman,** *meeting*

Kent Who's there, besides foul weather?

Gentleman One minded like the weather, most unquietly.

Kent I know you. Where's the King?

Gentleman Contending with the fretful elements;
5 Bids the wind blow the earth into the sea,
Or swell the curled waters 'bove the main,
That things might change or cease; tears his white hair,
Which the impetuous blasts, with eyeless rage,
Catch in their fury, and make nothing of;
10 Strives in his little world of man to out-scorn
The to-and-fro-conflicting wind and rain.
This night, wherein the cub-drawn bear would couch,
The lion and the belly-pinched wolf
Keep their fur dry, unbonneted he runs,
And bids what will take all.

15 **Kent**   But who is with him?

Gentleman None but the Fool, who labours to out-jest
His heart-struck injuries.

Kent   Sir, I do know you;
And dare, upon the warrant of my note,
Commend a dear thing to you. There is division,
20 Although as yet the face of it is covered
With mutual cunning, 'twixt Albany and Cornwall;

140

Act three

Scene 1

A heath during a violent storm. **Kent** *and a* **Gentleman** *meet*

Kent Who's there, besides foul weather?

Gentleman Someone as disturbed as the weather is.

Kent I know you. Where's the King?

Gentleman He's battling with the angry elements. He tells the wind to blow the earth into the sea, or raise the waves above the mainland, to bring chaos or destruction. He tears his white hair, which violent blasts, blind with rage, seize in their fury and treat with scant respect. He strives with his puny human frame to out-storm the wind and rain as it swirls to and fro in conflict. Tonight, when even the ferocious mother-bear takes cover, and the lion and the starving wolf keep their fur dry, he runs bareheaded, and cries out in reckless desperation.

Kent But who is with him?

Gentleman Only the Fool, who tries to joke away his master's heartfelt injuries.

Kent Sir, I know you, and on that account I'll risk entrusting something important to you. Although it's concealed by their craftiness, there is a rift between Albany and Cornwall.

Who have – as who have not, that their great stars
Throned and set high? – servants, who seem no less,
Which are to France the spies and speculations
25   Intelligent of our state; what hath been seen,
Either in snuffs and packings of the Dukes,
Or the hard rein which both of them have borne
Against the old kind King; or something deeper,
Whereof perchance these are but furnishings;
30   But, true it is, from France there comes a power
Into this scattered kingdom; who already,
Wise in our negligence, have secret feet
In some of our best ports, and are at point
To show their open banner. Now to you:
35   If on my credit you dare build so far
To make your speed to Dover, you shall find
Some that will thank you, making just report
Of how unnatural and bemadding sorrow
The King hath cause to plain.
40   I am a gentleman of blood and breeding,
And from some knowledge and assurance offer
This office to you.

Gentleman   I will talk further with you.

Kent   No, do not.
For confirmation that I am much more
45   Than my out-wall, open this purse, and take
What it contains. If you shall see Cordelia –
As fear not but you shall – show her this ring,
And she will tell you who that fellow is
That yet you do not know. Fie on this storm!
50   I will go seek the King.

Gentleman   Give me your hand. Have you no more to say?

Kent   Few words, but, to effect, more than all yet;
That, when we have found the King, in which your pain

They have servants – which great ones have not? – who seem genuine, but who are spies supplying information about our kingdom to the King of France: either concerning the quarrels and intrigues of the Dukes; or the tough way both have handled the old kind King; or something more profound, of which these are perhaps the outward manifestations. But the fact is that an army has arrived in this divided kingdom, from France. Taking advantage of our negligence, they have already established a secret foothold in some of our best ports, and are on the point of revealing themselves. Now, as for you, if you'll trust me to the extent of hastening to Dover, you'll find men there who'll thank you for delivering a true account of the unnatural and maddening sorrow which the King is suffering from. I am a gentleman of noble blood and good breeding, and I offer this commission to you on reliable information.

Gentleman   I'd like to talk about this more.

Kent   No, don't. For confirmation that I am more than my outward appearance suggests, open this purse and take what it contains. [*The* **Gentleman** *finds a ring inside*] If you should see Cordelia – and no doubt you will – show her this ring, and she will tell you who the fellow is who's now unknown to you. Damn this storm! I'll look for the King.

Gentleman   Give me your hand. Have you nothing to add?

Kent   Few words, but of prime importance. When we find the King – you go that way, and I'll go this – whoever sees him

That way, I'll this, he that first lights on him
55 Holla the other.

[*Exeunt severally*]

Scene 2

Another part of the heath. Storm still. Enter **Lear** *and* **Fool**

Lear   Blow, winds, and crack your cheeks! rage! blow!
You cataracts and hurricanoes, spout
Till you have drenched our steeples, drowned the cocks!
You sulphurous and thought-executing fires,
5 Vaunt-couriers of oak-cleaving thunderbolts,
Singe my white head! And thou, all-shaking thunder,
Strike flat the thick rotundity o'th'world!
Crack nature's moulds, all germens spill at once
That makes ingrateful man!

10 **Fool**   Oh nuncle, court holy-water in a dry house is better
than this rain-water out o'door. Good nuncle, in, and ask
thy daughters' blessing; here's a night pities neither wise
men nor fools.

Lear   Rumble thy bellyful! Spit, fire! Spout, rain!
15 Nor rain, wind, thunder, fire, are my daughters:
I tax you not, you elements, with unkindness;
I never gave you kingdom, called you children,
You owe me no subscription: then let fall
Your horrible pleasure; here I stand, your slave,
20 A poor, infirm, weak, and despised old man.
But yet I call you servile ministers,

first, shout to the other.

[*They leave separately*]

Scene 2

Another part of the heath. The storm still rages. **Lear** *and the* **Fool** *enter*

Lear   Blow, winds, and burst your cheeks! Rage! Blow! You floodgates and waterspouts: gush till you've drenched our church steeples and drowned the weathercocks! You searing and mind-dazzling flashes – forerunners of oak-splitting thunderbolts – singe my white beard! And you, all-shaking thunder: flatten the globe! Crack the moulds which Nature uses for replenishment! Destroy in an instant the seeds from which ungrateful man is born!

Fool   Oh, uncle, humble-pie in a house that's dry is better than a drenching out in the open. Good uncle, go in and ask a blessing from your daughters. This is a night fit for neither wise men nor fools.

Lear   Rumble your bellyful! Spit, fire! Spout, rain! Rain, wind, thunder, fire – they're not my daughters! I don't accuse you, you natural elements, of unkindness! I never gave you a kingdom, or called you children. You owe me no obligation. So enjoy yourselves: Here I stand, your victim – a poor, infirm, weak and despised old man! You're no better than servile lackeys if you'll conspire with two pernicious

145

That will with two pernicious daughters join
Your high-engendered battles 'gainst a head
So old and white as this. Oh, 'tis foul.

25 **Fool**   He that has a house to put's head in has a good head-
piece.

> The cod-piece that will house
>   Before the head has any,
> The head and he shall louse;
30 >   So beggars marry many.
> The man that makes his toe
>   What he his heart should make,
> Shall of a corn cry woe,
>   And turn his sleep to wake.

35   For there was never yet fair woman but she made mouths
in a glass.

[*Enter* **Kent**]

Lear   No, I will be the pattern of all patience;
I will say nothing.

Kent   Who's there?

40 **Fool**   Marry, here's grace and a cod-piece, that's a wise man
and a Fool.

Kent   Alas, sir, are you here? Things that love night
Love not such nights as these; the wrathful skies
Gallow the very wanderers of the dark,
45   And make them keep their caves. Since I was man
Such sheets of fire, such bursts of horrid thunder,
Such groans of roaring wind and rain, I never
Remember to have heard; man's nature cannot carry
Th'affliction nor the fear.

Lear   Let the great gods,

146

daughters to use your heavenly battalions against a head so
old and white as mine! Oh, it's despicable!

Fool   The man who has a house to put his head in has got a
hat with brains under it.

> The randy man who fornicates
>   And never saves a penny
> His life to lice he dedicates
>   So beggars marry many.

> The foolish man who cherishes
>   His toe more than his heart
> Will think from corns he perishes
>   And wake up with a start.

There never yet was a beautiful woman who didn't preen
herself in front of a mirror.

[**Kent** *enters*]

Lear   [*to himself*] No, I will be a model of patience. I'll say
nothing.

Kent   Who's there?

Fool   Well, here's graciousness and vulgarity. That is, a wise
man and a Fool.

Kent   Alas, sir, are you here? Even nocturnal things dislike
such nights as these. The angry skies terrify even the wild
animals and make them keep to their caves. I don't
remember having seen such sheets of fire, or heard such
peals of thunder, such groans of roaring wind and rain. Man
is not made to endure such suffering and fear.

Lear   Let the almighty gods, who are making this dreadful

50   That keep this dreadful pudder o'er our heads,
         Find out their enemies now. Tremble, thou wretch,
         That has within thee undivulged crimes,
         Unwhipped of justice; hide thee, thou bloody hand,
         Thou perjured, and thou simular man of virtue
55   That art incestuous; caitiff, to pieces shake,
         That under covert and convenient seeming
         Hast practised on man's life; close pent-up guilts
         Rive your concealing continents, and cry
         These dreadful summoners grace. I am a man
         More sinned against than sinning.

60 **Kent**   Alack, bare-headed!
         Gracious my lord, hard by here is a hovel;
         Some friendship will it lend you 'gainst the tempest;
         Repose you there while I to this hard house –
         More harder than the stones whereof 'tis raised,
65   Which even but now, demanding after you,
         Denied me to come in – return and force
         Their scanted courtesy.

     Lear   My wits begin to turn.
         Come on, my boy. How dost, my boy? Art cold?
         I am cold myself. Where is this straw, my fellow?
70   The art of our necessities is strange,
         And can make vile things precious. Come, your hovel.
         Poor Fool and knave, I have one part in my heart
         That's sorry yet for thee.

     Fool   *He that has and a little tiny wit,*
75   *With hey, ho, the wind and the rain,*
        Must make content with his fortunes fit,
        Though the rain it raineth every day.

     Lear   True, boy. Come, bring us to this hovel.

                                 [*Exeunt* **Lear** *and* **Kent**]

hubbub over our heads, identify their enemies now!
Tremble, you wretch, with your undiscovered crimes as yet
unpunished! Hide yourself, you murderer; you perjurer; you
incestuous humbug! Rogue, shiver yourself to pieces: under
cover of convenient hypocrisy you've tricked your way
through life! Well-hidden crimes, burst out from your
concealment, and plead for mercy from those dreadful
ministers of vengeance! [*Removing his hat to show he has
nothing to fear himself*] I am a man who's been more sinned
against than ever he has sinned.

Kent   Alas, bare-headed! My gracious lord, there is a shelter
close by here. It will afford you some friendly protection
against the tempest. Rest there, while I return to this cruel
house – whose stony-hearted occupants refused me
admittance when I asked for you – to force them to be civil.

Lear   My mind is going. [*To the* **Fool**] Come on, my boy. [*He
puts his arm round him*] How are you, my boy? Are you
cold? I'm cold myself. [*To* **Kent**] Where is this straw, my
fellow? Need transforms things strangely. It can make what's
paltry, precious. Come then, to your shelter. Poor Fool and
knave, there's one part of my heart that's sorry still for you.

Fool   *He whose brain is somewhat dim
          With hey, ho, the wind and the rain
          Must take what Fortune gives to him
          Though the rain keeps raining every day.*

Lear   True, boy. [*To* **Kent**] Come, take us to this shelter. [**Lear**
and **Kent** *go*]

Fool   This is a brave night to cool a courtezan.
80   I'll speak a prophecy ere I go:

> *When priests are more in word than matter;*
> *When brewers mar their malt with water;*
> *When nobles are their tailors' tutors;*
> *No heretics burned, but wenches' suitors;*
> 85   *When every case in law is right;*
> *No squire in debt, nor no poor knight;*
> *When slanders do not live in tongues;*
> *Nor cut-purses come not to throngs;*
> *When usurers tell their gold i'th'field;*
> 90   *And bawds and whores do churches build;*
> *Then shall the realm of Albion*
> *Come to great confusion:*
> *Then comes the time, who lives to see't,*
> *That going shall be used with feet.*

95   This prophecy Merlin shall make; for I live before his time.

[*Exit*]

Scene 3

Gloucester's Castle. Enter **Gloucester** *and* **Edmund,** *with lights.*

Gloucester   Alack, alack! Edmund, I like not this unnatural
dealing. When I desired their leave that I might pity him,
they took from me the use of mine own house; charged me,
on pain of perpetual displeasure, neither to speak of him,
5   entreat for him, or any way sustain him.

Fool   This is a fine night for cooling down a randy wench. I'll
speak a prophecy before I go:

> *When priests are theorists, not doers;*
> *When beer is watered by the brewers;*
> *When nobles teach their tailors stitches;*
> *And lusty lads don't suffer itches;*
> *When every case is right in law;*
> *No gentry-folk say they are poor;*
> *When tongues aren't used for dangerous tales;*
> *And thieves aren't caught and sent to jails;*
> *When moneylenders show their hoards;*
> *And churches are endowed by bawds;*
> *Then shall all the British nation*
> *Come to its humiliation.*
> *That's when, if you are still around,*
> *Feet will be used to walk on ground.*

Merlin the magician will make this prophecy one day. I was
born before his time . . .

[*He goes*]

Scene 3

A room in Gloucester's castle after dark. **Gloucester** *and*
Edmund *enter, carrying torches*

Gloucester   Alas, alas, Edmund. I don't like this unnatural
behaviour. When I asked their permission to take pity on
him, they commandeered my house, and ordered me – on
pain of their permanent displeasure – neither to speak of
him, plead for him, nor in any way sustain him.

Edmund   Most savage and unnatural!

Gloucester   Go to; say you nothing. There is division
between the Dukes, and a worse matter than that. I have
received a letter this night; 'tis dangerous to be spoken; I
10   have locked the letter in my closet. These injuries the King
now bears will be revenged home; there is part of a power
already footed; we must incline to the King. I will seek him
and privily relieve him; go you and maintain talk with the
Duke, that my charity be not of him perceived. If he ask
15   for me, I am ill and gone to bed. If I die for it, as no less is
threatened me, the King, my old master, must be relieved.
There is strange things toward, Edmund; pray you, be
careful.

[*Exit*]

Edmund   This courtesy, forbid thee, shall the Duke
20   Instantly know; and of that letter too:
This seems a fair deserving, and must draw me
That which my father loses: no less than all;
The younger rises when the old doth fall.

[*Exit*]

Scene 4

The heath. Before the hovel. Enter **Lear, Kent,** *and* **Fool**

Kent   Here is the place, my lord; good my lord, enter:
The tyranny of the open night's too rough
For nature to endure.

Edmund   How savage and unnatural!

Gloucester   Sh! Say nothing. The Dukes have quarrelled, and
something worse: I've had a letter about it tonight. It's too
dangerous to talk about; I've locked it in my bedroom. These
wrongs the King is suffering will be revenged to the full.
Part of an army has already landed. We must take the King's
side. I'll look for him and aid him secretly. Go and keep the
Duke talking, so that he won't observe my charity. If he asks
for me, say I'm ill and gone to bed. Even if I die for it – as
they've threatened me – the King my old master must be
given help. Strange things are about to happen, Edmund. Do
be careful.

[*He goes in search of* **Lear**]

Edmund   I'll tell the Duke at once about this kindness, which
you have been forbidden to do. And the letter, too. This
should be worth something to me, and must gain me what
my father will lose: nothing less than everything! The young
rise when the old fall.

[*He goes*]

Scene 4

The heath, in front of the shelter. **Lear** *enters, with* **Kent** *and
the* **Fool**

Kent   Here's the place, my lord. Good my lord, go in. The
suffering of a night out in the open is too much for flesh and
blood to endure.

153

Lear   Let me alone.

Kent   Good my lord, enter here.

Lear   Wilt break my heart?

5 **Kent**   I had rather break mine own. Good my lord, enter.

Lear   Thou think'st 'tis much that this contentious storm
Invades us to the skin: so 'tis to thee;
But where the greater malady is fixed,
The lesser is scarce felt. Thou'ldst shun a bear;
10   But if thy flight lay toward the roaring sea,
Thou'ldst meet the bear i'th'mouth. When the mind's free
The body's delicate; this tempest in my mind
Doth from my senses take all feeling else
Save what beats there – filial ingratitude!
15   Is it not as this mouth should tear this hand
For lifting food to't? But I will punish home:
No, I will weep no more. In such a night
To shut me out! Pour on; I will endure.
In such a night as this! Oh Regan, Goneril!
20   Your old kind father, whose frank heart gave all –
Oh, that way madness lies; let me shun that;
No more of that.

Kent   Good my lord, enter here.

Lear   Prithee, go in thyself; seek thine own ease:
This tempest will not give me leave to ponder
25   On things would hurt me more. But I'll go in.
[*To the* **Fool**] In, boy; go first. You houseless poverty –
Nay, get thee in. I'll pray, and then I'll sleep.

[**Fool** *goes in*]

Poor naked wretches, whereso'er you are,
That bide the pelting of this pitiless storm,
30   How shall your houseless heads and unfed sides,

[*The storm rages on unabated*]

Lear   Leave me alone.

Kent   Good my lord, go in.

Lear   Will you break my heart?

Kent   I'd rather break my own. Good my Lord, enter.

Lear   You think it's remarkable that this raging storm soaks us
to the skin. So it is, to you. But where there's a greater
suffering, the lesser is hardly felt. You'd avoid a bear; but if
your escape lay towards the roaring sea, you'd tackle the
bear face to face. When there's nothing on your mind, you
are conscious of your ailments; this tempest going on in my
mind obliterates all feeling other than what's tormenting
me – the ingratitude of my daughters! Isn't it equivalent to
my mouth biting my hand for lifting food to it? I'll punish
ruthlessly! No, I'll weep no more. To shut me out on a night
like this! [*To the rain*] Pour on – I can take it! [*To* **Kent**] On
such a night as this! Oh, Regan, Goneril! Your kind old father,
whose open-heartedness gave you all! Oh, that way leads to
madness! Let me avoid that! I mustn't think of that!

Kent   Good my lord, go in here.

Lear   Please go in yourself: seek some comfort. This tempest
prevents me from thinking about things that would hurt me
more. But I'll go in. [*To the* **Fool**] In, boy. Go first. [*He
returns to his thoughts*] You who are poor and
homeless – [*Noting the* **Fool** *is hesitant*] No – go in. I'll pray
and then I'll sleep. [*The* **Fool** *obeys*] Poor naked wretches,
wherever you are, that endure the pelting of this pitiless
storm: how shall your bare heads and bony bodies, your

155

Your looped and windowed raggedness, defend you
From seasons such as these? Oh I have ta'en
Too little care of this. Take physic, Pomp;
Expose thyself to feel what wretches feel,
35   That thou mayst shake the superflux to them,
And show the Heavens more just.

Edgar   [*Within*] Fathom and half, fathom and half!
Poor Tom!   [*The* **Fool** *runs out from the hovel*]

Fool   Come not in here, nuncle; here's a spirit.
40   Help me! Help me!

Kent   Give me thy hand. Who's there?

Fool   A spirit, a spirit: he says his name's poor Tom.

Kent   What art thou that dost grumble there i'th'straw?
Come forth.

[*Enter* **Edgar** *disguised as a madman*]

45 **Edgar**   Away! The foul fiend follows me! Through the sharp
hawthorn blows the cold winds. Hum! go to thy bed and
warm thee.

Lear   Didst thou give all to thy daughters?
And art thou come to this?

50 **Edgar**   Who gives any thing to poor Tom? Whom the foul
fiend hath led through fire and through flame, through ford
and whirlpool, o'er bog and quagmire; that hath laid knives
under his pillow, and halters in his pew; set ratsbane by his
porridge; made him proud of heart, to ride on a bay
55   trotting-horse over four inched bridges, to course his own
shadow for a traitor. Bless thy five wits! Tom's a-cold. Oh,
do de, do de, do de. Bless thee from whirlwinds, star-

tattered-and-torn raggedness, protect you from storms such as these? Oh, I've cared too little about this! Take a dose of this medicine, great ones! Expose yourself to feel what wretches feel, so that you can share their deprivations, and show that the gods are just!

Edgar   [*from inside, as if he's taking soundings from a sinking ship*] Fathom and a half! Fathom and a half! Poor Tom!

[*The* **Fool** *rushes out, terrified*]

Fool   Don't come in here, uncle. There's a ghost. Help me, help me!

Kent   Give me your hand. [*Calling inside*] Who's there?

Fool   A spirit, a spirit! He says his name's Poor Tom.

Kent   Who are you, grumbling there in the straw? Come out.

[**Edgar** *appears, disguised as a madman*]

Edgar   [*talking dementedly*] Go away! The foul fiend follows me! The cold winds blow through the prickly hawthorn bushes. Hmm. [*To* **Lear**] Go to your bed and get warm.

Lear   Did you give everything to your daughters? And have you come down to this?

Edgar   Who gives anything to Poor Tom? The foul fiend has led him through fire and through flame, through ford and whirlpool, over bog and quagmire. He's put knives under his pillow, and hung nooses from his balconies. He's put ratkiller by his soup; made him over-proud, riding a brown trotting-horse over narrow bridges, chasing his own shadow as if it were a traitor. Bless your five wits! Tom's cold. [*He shivers and stamps his feet, making noises to warm himself*] Oh, do-de, do-de, do-de! Bless you against whirlwinds,

blasting, and taking! Do poor Tom some charity, whom the
foul fiend vexes. There could I have him now, and there,
60   and there again, and there.

Lear What! Have his daughters brought him to this pass?
Could'st thou save nothing? Would'st thou give 'em all?

Fool Nay, he reserved a blanket, else we had been all
shamed.

65 **Lear** Now all the plagues that in the pendulous air
Hang fated o'er men's faults light on thy daughters!

Kent He hath no daughters, sir.

Lear Death, traitor! Nothing could have subdued nature
To such a lowness but his unkind daughters.
70   Is it the fashion that discarded fathers
Should have thus little mercy on their flesh?
Judicious punishment! 'Twas this flesh begot
Those pelican daughters.

Edgar Pillicock sat on Pillicock hill:
75   Alow, alow, loo, loo!

Fool This cold night will turn us all to fools and madmen.

Edgar Take heed o'th'foul fiend. Obey thy parents: keep thy
word justly; swear not; commit not with man's sworn spouse;
set not thy sweet heart on proud array. Tom's a-cold.

80 **Lear** What hast thou been?

Edgar A servingman, proud in heart and mind; that curled
my hair, wore gloves in my cap, served the lust of my

shooting stars and evil influences! Do Poor Tom a favour, who's tormented by the foul fiend. [*He swipes at an imaginary attacker*] I could catch him now – and there – and there again – and there!

[*The storm rages on*]

Lear What, have his daughters brought him to this? Could you save nothing? Did you give them everything?

Fool No. He kept a blanket, otherwise we'd all be embarrassed.

Lear May all the plagues that hover menacingly in the air over men's faults now descend upon your daughters!

Kent He has no daughters, sir.

Lear Death to you, traitor! Nothing could have brought him down to this but his unkind daughters! Is it the fashion now for discarded fathers to endure such sufferings of the flesh? How just the punishment! It was this very flesh that conceived those father-killing daughters!

Edgar [*reciting an old rhyme*] 'Pillycock sat on Pillycock Hill. [*the second line is 'If he's not gone, he sits there still,' but* **Edgar** *replaces it with howling noises*] Alow, alow! Loo! Loo!

Fool This cold night will turn us all into fools or madmen.

Edgar Beware of the foul fiend. Obey your parents. Tell no lies. Don't swear. Commit no adultery. Do not yearn for splendid clothes. [*He shudders*] Tom feels cold.

Lear What were you?

Edgar A lover, proud in heart and mind. I curled my hair, wore love-tokens in my hat, fulfilled the heart's desire of my loved

mistress' heart, and did the act of darkness with her; swore
as many oaths as I spake words, and broke them in the

85   sweet face of Heaven; one that slept in the contriving of
lust, and waked to do it. Wine loved I deeply, dice dearly,
and in woman out-paramoured the Turk: false of heart, light
of ear, bloody of hand; hog in sloth, fox in stealth, wolf in
greediness, dog in madness, lion in prey. Let not the

90   creaking of shoes nor the rustling of silks betray thy poor
heart to woman: keep thy foot out of brothels, thy hand out
of plackets, thy pen from lenders' books, and defy the foul
fiend. Still through the hawthorn blows the cold wind; says
suum, mun, hey no nonny. Dophin my boy, boy; sessa! let

95   him trot by.

Lear   Thou wert better in a grave than to answer with thy
uncovered body this extremity of the skies. Is man no more
than this? Consider him well. Thou owest the worm no
silk, the beast no hide, the sheep no wool, the cat no

100   perfume. Ha! here's three on's are sophisticated; thou art
the thing itself; unaccommodated man is no more but such a
poor, bare, forked animal as thou art. Off, off, you lendings!
Come; unbutton here.   [*Tearing off his clothes*]

Fool   Prithee, nuncle, be contented; 'tis a naughty night to

105   swim in. Now a little fire in a wide field were like an old
lecher's heart; a small spark, all the rest on's body cold.
Look! Here comes a walking fire.

[*Enter* **Gloucester** *with a torch*]

one and slept with her. I made vows with every word I
spoke, and broke them openly. My dreams were fantasies
of lust; I awoke to practise them. Wine I loved deeply;
gambling, dearly; as for women, I had more mistresses than
the Sultan of Turkey. I was deceitful; interested in scandal;
quick to draw blood; as lazy as a hog, stealthy as a fox,
greedy as a wolf, mad as a dog, ruthless as a lion. Don't be
turned on by fashion shoes or the sound of rustling silks.
Keep your feet out of brothels, your hand away from
petticoats, your signature from moneylender's ledgers, and
defy the foul fiend. The cold wind blows through the
hawthorn bushes: it says [*imitating the sound*] 'suum',
'mum', 'hey-no-nonny'. [*He seems to recognize a presence*]
The devil, my boy, boy! [*He puts his finger to his lips*] Sh! Let
him pass by.

[*The storm rages on*]

Lear   You'd be better off in your grave than trying to endure
this extreme weather in your nakedness. Is man no more
than this? [*To the* **Fool**] Note him well. [*To* **Edgar**] You're not
indebted to the silkworm for its silk; or the ox for its hide;
the sheep for its wool, or the civet cat for its perfume.
[*Pointing to himself,* **Edgar** *and the* **Fool**] We three are
tainted, but you are the genuine article! Basic man is only a
poor, bare, two-legged animal such as you are. [*He begins
to take off his clothes*] Off, off, you borrowings! Come,
unbutton here!

Fool   Please, uncle, don't do that! It's a wicked night to go
swimming in. [*He sees* **Gloucester** *approaching carrying a
torch*] Now a little fire in a big field is like the heart of an old
lecher: a small spark of life with all the rest of his body cold.
Look, here comes a walking fire!

[**Gloucester** *enters*]

Edgar   This is the foul fiend Flibbertigibbet: he begins at
curfew, and walks till the first cock; he gives the web and
110   the pin, squinies the eye, and makes the harelip; mildews
the white wheat, and hurts the poor creature of the earth.

> *Swithold footed thrice the old;*
> *He met the night-mare, and her nine-fold;*
> *Bid her alight,*
> *And her troth plight,*
115   > *And aroint thee, witch, aroint thee!*

Kent   How fares your grace?

Lear   What's he?

Kent   Who's there? What is't you seek?

Gloucester   What are you there? Your names?

120   **Edgar**   Poor Tom; that eats the swimming frog, the toad, the
tadpole, the wall-newt, and the water; that in the fury of his
heart, when the foul fiend rages, eats cow-dung for sallets;
swallows the old rat and the ditch-dog; drinks the green
mantle of the standing pool; who is whipped from tithing to
125   tithing, and stock-punished, and imprisoned; who hath had
three suits to his back, six shirts to his body,

> *Horse to ride, and weapons to wear,*
> *But mice and rats and such small deer,*
> *Have been Tom's food for seven long year.*

130   Beware my follower. Peace, Smulkin! Peace, thou fiend!

Gloucester   What, hath your grace no better company?

Edgar   The Prince of Darkness is a gentleman; Modo he's
called, and Mahu.

Gloucester   Our flesh and blood, my lord, is grown so vile,
135   That it doth hate what gets it.

Edgar   This is the foul fiend Flibbertigibbet; he begins at curfew-time, and walks about till midnight. He gives cataracts, squints eyes, and makes hare lips. He mildews the ripening wheat, and hurts the poor creatures of the earth.

> Saint Withold three times walked his land;
> He met a demon and her nine-fold band;
>   Her progress he stayed,
>   Her power he allayed,
> And 'Be off with you witch! Be off!'

Kent   How is your grace?

Lear   [peering in the dark] Who's he?

Kent   [to **Gloucester**] Who's there? What are you looking for?

Gloucester   Who are you, there? Your names?

Edgar   Poor Tom, who eats the swimming frog, the toad, the tadpole, the wall-newt and the water-newt. When the foul fiend rages, he eats cow-dung instead of salads; swallows dead rats and dead dogs; drinks the scum from standing ponds; is whipped from settlement to settlement, put in the stocks, imprisoned. He once had three suits and six shirts,

> A horse to ride and weapons to wear,
> But mice and rats and such small game,
> Have been Tom's food for seven long year.

Beware of my devil. [He talks to an invisible companion] Be quiet, Smulkin! Be quiet, you fiend!

Gloucester   What, has your grace no better company?

Edgar   The King of the Devils is a gentleman. He's called 'Modo', and 'Mahu'.

Gloucester   Humanity is so degraded, my lord, it hates its parents.

Edgar   Poor Tom's a-cold.

Gloucester   Go in with me. My duty cannot suffer
   T'obey in all your daughters' hard commands;
   Though their injunction be to bar my doors,
140   And let this tyrannous night take hold upon you,
   Yet I have ventured to come and seek you out
   And bring you where both fire and food is ready.

Lear   First let me talk with this philosopher.
   What is the cause of thunder?

145 **Kent**   Good my lord, take his offer; go into the house.

Lear   I'll talk a word with this same learned Theban.
   What is your study?

Edgar   How to prevent the fiend, and to kill vermin.

Lear   Let me ask you one word in private.

150 **Kent**   Importune him once more to go, my lord;
   His wits begin t'unsettle.

Gloucester   Canst thou blame him?
   His daughters seek his death. Ah, that good Kent;
   He said it would be thus, poor banished man!
   Thou say'st the King grows mad; I'll tell thee, friend,
155   I am almost mad myself. I had a son,
   Now outlawed from my blood; he sought my life,
   But lately, very late; I loved him, friend,
   No father his son dearer; truth to tell thee,
   The grief hath crazed my wits. What a night's this!
   I do beseech your grace –

160 **Lear**   Oh, cry you mercy, sir:
   Noble philosopher, your company.

Edgar   Tom's a-cold.

164

Edgar   Poor Tom is cold.

Gloucester   [*To* **Lear**] Come in with me. My sense of duty does not stretch so far as to obey all your daughters' harsh commands. Though their orders are to bar my doors and let this pitiless night have its way with you, I've nevertheless ventured to find you and bring you where warmth and food are ready.

Lear   First let me talk with this philosopher. [*To* **Edgar**] What is the cause of thunder?

Kent   Good my lord, take his offer. Go into the house.

Lear   I'll have a word with this learned professor. What is your subject?

Edgar   How to avoid the fiend, and to kill vermin.

Lear   Let me ask you one word in private.

Kent   Plead with him once more to go in, my lord. His mind is failing.

Gloucester   Can you blame him? [*Claps of thunder are heard overhead*] His daughters want him dead. Ah, that good Kent: he said it would be like this, the poor, banished man! You say the King is going insane. I'll tell you this, my friend: I'm almost mad myself. I had a son, now disowned. He sought my life, recently, very recently. I loved him, friend. No father loved his son more. To tell you the truth, the grief has touched my mind. What a night this is! [*To* **Lear**] I beg your grace –

Lear   Oh, I beg your pardon, sir. [*To* **Edgar**] Noble philosopher, do join us.

Edgar   Tom's cold.

Gloucester   In, fellow, there, into the hovel: keep thee warm.

Lear   Come, let's in all.

Kent   This way, my lord.

Lear   With him;
165   I will keep still with my philosopher.

Kent   Good my lord, soothe him; let him take the fellow.

Gloucester   Take him you on.

Kent   Sirrah, come on; go along with us.

Lear   Come, good Athenian.

170 **Gloucester**   No words, no words: hush.

Edgar   *Child Rowland to the dark tower came,*
               His word was still: Fie, foh, and fum,
               I smell the blood of a British man.

[*Exeunt*]

Scene 5

Gloucester's Castle. Enter **Cornwall** *and* **Edmund**

Cornwall   I will have my revenge ere I depart his house.

Edmund   How, my lord, I may be censured, that nature thus
gives way to loyalty, something fears me to think of.

Gloucester   In, fellow, there – into the shelter. Keep yourself warm.

Lear   Come, let's all go in.

Kent   This way, my lord.

Lear   [*his arm around* **Edgar**] With him: I want to be with my philosopher.

Kent   [*to* **Gloucester**] Good my lord, humour him. Let him take the fellow with him.

Gloucester   You take charge of him.

Kent   [*to* **Edgar**] Come on, go with us.

Lear   Come, good Athenian.

Gloucester   [*to* **Edgar**] Don't say anything, don't say anything. Sh!

Edgar   *Squire Roland to the dark tower came,*
His motto was: Fie, foh, and fum:
I smell the blood of a British man.

[*They enter the shelter*]

Scene 5

A room in Gloucester's castle. **Cornwall** *and* Edmund *enter.*
Cornwall *is waving a letter*

Cornwall   I'll have my revenge before I leave this house!

Edmund   What people will say about me, in putting loyalty before my feelings as a son, I fear to think.

167

Cornwall   I now perceive it was not altogether your brother's
5   evil disposition made him seek his death; but a provoking
merit, set a-work by a reprovable badness in himself.

Edmund   How malicious is my fortune, that I must repent to
be just! This is the letter he spoke of, which approves him
an intelligent party to the advantages of France. Oh,
10   heavens, that this treason were not, or not I the detector!

Cornwall   Go with me to the Duchess.

Edmund   If the matter of this paper be certain, you have
mighty business in hand.

Cornwall   True or false, it hath made thee Earl of
15   Gloucester. Seek out where thy father is, that he may be
ready for our apprehension.

Edmund   [*Aside*] If I find him comforting the King, it will
stuff his suspicion more fully. [*Aloud*] I will persever in
my course of loyalty, though the conflict be sore between
20   that and my blood.

Cornwall   I will lay trust upon thee; and thou shalt find a
dearer father in my love.

[*Exeunt*]

Scene 6

A chamber in a farmhouse adjoining the Castle. Enter
Gloucester *and* **Kent**

Gloucester   Here is better than the open air; take it
thankfully. I will piece out the comfort with what
addition I can: I will not be long from you.

Cornwall I see now that it wasn't just your brother's evil disposition that made him seek his father's death. He was provoked into it, helped by his evil nature.

Edmund How wickedly unfortunate that loyalty to my country should give me a feeling of guilt! This is the letter my father spoke of, which proves he is a spy acting on behalf of France. Oh, heavens! Would that this treason had never happened, and that I wasn't the one to discover it!

Cornwall Come with me to the Duchess.

Edmund If the contents of this letter are true, you have important work to do.

Cornwall True or false, it has made you the Earl of Gloucester. Find your father, so we can arrest him.

Edmund [*aside*] If I find him giving aid and comfort to the King, it will make the Duke even more suspicious. [*Aloud*] I shall continue in my loyal course, in spite of the painful conflict between duty and my feelings as a son.

Cornwall I have every confidence in you: and you'll find I'll make you a more loving father.

[*They go*]

Scene 6

A room in a farmhouse near the castle. **Gloucester** *and* **Kent** *enter*

Gloucester This is better than the open air. Be thankful for it. I'll try to make it more comfortable with what extras I can find. I won't be away long.

169

Kent   All the power of his wits have given way to his
5   impatience. The gods reward your kindness!

[*Exit* **Gloucester**]

[*Enter* **Lear, Edgar,** *and* **Fool**]

Edgar   Frateretto calls me, and tells me Nero is an angler in
the lake of darkness. Pray, innocent, and beware the foul
fiend.

Fool   Prithee, nuncle, tell me whether a madman be a
10   gentleman or a yeoman?

Lear   A king, a king!

Fool   No; he's a yeoman that has a gentleman to his son; for
he's a mad yeoman that sees his son a gentleman before
him.

15   **Lear**   To have a thousand with red burning spits
Come hissing in upon 'em –

Edgar   The foul fiend bites my back.

Fool   He's mad that trusts in the tameness of a wolf, a
horse's health, a boy's love, or a whore's oath.

20   **Lear**   It shall be done; I will arraign them straight. [*To*
Edgar] Come, sit thou here, most learned justicer; [*To the*
Fool] Thou, sapient sir, sit here. Now, you she foxes!

Edgar   Look where he stands and glares! Want'st thou eyes
at trial, madam?

Kent   His mind has completely gone under the stress. The gods reward your kindness!

[**Gloucester** *goes*]

[**Lear** *enters, with* **Edgar** *and the* **Fool**]

Edgar   Frateretto calls me, and tells me that Nero fishes in the Lake of Hell. [*To the* **Fool**] Pray, innocent one, and beware of the foul fiend!

Fool   Now, uncle, can you tell me whether a madman is a gentleman, or just someone who is rich?

Lear   A king, a king!

Fool   No. The rich man's son *becomes* a gentleman. Only a madman would have his son a gentleman before he's one himself!

Lear   [*brooding to himself about his ungrateful daughters*] To have a thousand devils armed with red-hot pokers come chasing after them . . .

Edgar   [*jerking about*] The foul fiend is biting my back!

Fool   Anyone's mad who trusts in the tameness of a wolf, or the health of a horse that's for sale, or a boy's love, or a whore's promise.

Lear   [*still in a world of his own*] It shall be done. I'll prosecute them immediately. [*To* **Edgar**] Come, sit you here, most learned judge. [*To the* **Fool**] You, wise sir, sit here. [*Rubbing his hands*] Now, you she foxes!

Edgar   [*pointing to* **Lear**] Look how he stands and glares! [*To the imaginary plaintiff*] Are you showing off in the witness-box, madam?   [*He breaks out into a romantic love-song*]

Come over the stream, Bessy, to me –

25   *Come o'er the bourn, Bessy, to me, –*

Fool   *Her boat hath a leek,*
           And she must not speak;
           Why she dares not come over to thee!

Edgar   The foul fiend haunts poor Tom in the voice of a
30   nightingale. Hoppedance cries in Tom's belly for two white
           herring. Croak not, black angel; I have no food for thee.

Kent   How do you, sir? Stand you not so amazed:
           Will you lie down and rest upon the cushions?

Lear   I'll see their trial first. Bring in their evidence.
35   [*To* **Edgar**] Thou robed man of justice, take thy place;
           [*To the* **Fool**] And thou, his yoke-fellow of equity,
           Bench by his side. [*To* **Kent**] You are o'th'commission,
           Sit you too.

Edgar   Let us deal justly.
40   *Sleepest or wakest thou, jolly shepherd?*
                   Thy sheep be in the corn;
               And for one blast of thy minikin mouth,
                   Thy sheep shall take no harm.

           Purr, the cat is grey.

45 **Lear**   Arraign her first; 'tis Goneril. I here take my oath
           before this honourable assembly, she kicked the poor King
           her father.

Fool   Come hither, mistress. Is your name Goneril?

Lear   She cannot deny it.

50 **Fool**   Cry you mercy, I took you for a joint-stool.

Lear   And here's another, whose warped looks proclaim
           What store her heart is made on. Stop her there!

Fool   [*joining in, picking up his words*]
    Her boat's got a leak,
    And she must not speak,
    Why she dares not come over to you!

Edgar   [*commenting on the quality of the* **Fool***'s singing voice*]
The foul fiend haunts Poor Tom, disguised as a nightingale.
[*He rubs his stomach*] Hoppedance is crying out in Tom's
belly for two pickled herrings. Stop your rumbling, black
angel: I've no food for you.

Kent   [*to* **Lear**] How are you, sir? Don't be dismayed. Will you
lie down and rest on these cushions?

Lear   I'll see their trial first. Bring in the witnesses. [*To* **Edgar**
who is scantily attired] Take your place, you man of justice,
in your robes. [*To the* **Fool**] And you, his learned colleague,
take your seat on the bench, at his side. [*To* **Kent**] You are
one of the magistrates. You must sit too.

Edgar   Let us handle the case justly.
    Are you sleeping or awake, jolly shepherd?
    Your sheep are in the corn.
    If you'd only give one little blast on your whistle
    Your sheep would come to no harm.

[*He makes a noise with his mouth*] Purr! [*Explaining*] The cat
is grey.

Lear   [*Pointing to an unoccupied seat*] Prosecute her first: it's
Goneril. I here take my oath before this honourable
assembly, that she kicked the poor King her father.

Fool   Come here, mistress. Is your name Goneril?

Lear   She can't deny it.

Fool   I beg your pardon. I mistook you for a stool!

Lear   And here's another one whose ugly looks reveal what
her heart is made of. [*He jumps up excitedly*] Stop her there!

Arms, arms, sword, fire! Corruption in the place!
False justicer, why hast thou let her 'scape?

55 **Edgar**   Bless thy five wits!

Kent   O pity! Sir, where is the patience now
That you so oft have boasted to retain?

Edgar   [*Aside*] My tears begin to take his part so much,
They mar my counterfeiting.

60 **Lear**   The little dogs and all,
Tray, Blanch, and Sweetheart, see, they bark at me.

Edgar   Tom will throw his head at them. Avaunt, you curs!

Be thy mouth or black or white,
Tooth that poisons if it bite;
65 Mastiff, greyhound, mongrel grim,
Hound or spaniel, brach or him,
Or bobtail tike or trundle-tail;
Tom will make him weep and wail:
For, with throwing thus my head,
70 Dogs leap the hatch, and all are fled.

Do de, de, de, Sessa! Come, march to wakes and fairs and
market-towns. Poor Tom, thy horn is dry.

Lear   Then let them anatomize Regan; see what breeds about
her heart. Is there any cause in nature that makes these
75 hard hearts? [*To* **Edgar**] You, sir, I entertain for one of my
hundred; only I do not like the fashion of your garments:
you will say they are Persian; but let them be changed.

Kent   Now, good my lord, lie here and rest awhile.

Lear   Make no noise, make no noise; draw the curtains: so, so.
80 We'll go to supper i'th'morning.

Fool   And I'll go to bed at noon.

174

Arms, arms, sword, fire! There's corruption here! [*To* **Edgar**]
False judge – why have you let her escape?

Edgar   Bless your five wits!

Kent   Oh, for pity! Sir, where now is the self-control you have
so often boasted of?

Edgar   [*aside, to himself*] My tears of sympathy for him are
beginning to ruin my disguise.

Lear   Even the little dogs – Tray, Blanch and Sweetheart –
see, they are barking at me!

Edgar   Tom will throw his head at them. Get away, you curs!

> *Whether your mouth is black or white,*
> *With teeth that poison if they bite,*
> *Mastiff, greyhound, mongrel grim,*
> *Hound or spaniel, her or him,*
> *Or bob-tail tike, or droopy-tail –*
> *Tom will make him weep and wail:*
> *'Cos, with throwing thus my head*
> *Dogs hurry out, and all are fled.*

Do de, de, de. Be quiet! Come, let's march to wakes and
fairs and market towns! Poor Tom, you're all dried up.

Lear   Let them take Regan to pieces, to see what's festering
around her heart. Is there any natural cause for these hard
hearts? [*To* **Edgar**] You, sir, I'll engage you as one of my
hundred knights, though I don't like the cut of your clothes.
You'll say they are Persian-style, but change them.

Kent   Now, good my lord, lie here and rest for a while.

Lear   [*as if at home in bed*] Make no noise, make no noise.
Draw the curtains. So, so. We'll have our supper in the
morning.

Fool   And I'll go to bed at noon.

[*Re-enter* **Gloucester**]

Gloucester   Come hither, friend: where is the King my
master?

Kent   Here, sir; but trouble him not, his wits are gone.

85 **Gloucester**   Good friend, I prithee, take him in thy arms;
I have o'erheard a plot of death upon him.
There is a litter ready; lay him in't,
And drive toward Dover, friend, where thou shalt meet
Both welcome and protection. Take up thy master:
90   If thou should'st dally half an hour, his life,
With thine, and all that offer to defend him,
Stand in assured loss. Take up, take up;
And follow me, that will to some provision
Give thee quick conduct.

Kent   Oppressed nature sleeps.
95   This rest might yet have balmed thy broken sinews
Which, if convenience will not allow,
Stand in hard cure. [*To the* **Fool**] Come, help to bear thy
master;
Thou must not stay behind.

Gloucester   Come, come, away.

[*Exeunt* **Kent**, **Gloucester**, *and the* **Fool**, *bearing off the* **King**]

Edgar   When we our betters see bearing our woes,
100   We scarcely think our miseries our foes.
Who alone suffers, suffers most i'th'mind,
Leaving free things and happy shows behind;
But then the mind much sufferance doth o'erskip,
When grief hath mates, and bearing fellowship.
105   How light and portable my pain seems now,
When that which makes me bend makes the King bow;

[**Gloucester** *returns*]

Gloucester   [*to* **Kent**] Come here, friend. Where is my master
the King?

Kent   Here, sir. But don't bother him. His mind has gone.

Gloucester   Good friend, I beg of you. Take him in your arms.
I've overheard a plot to kill him. There's a stretcher ready:
lay him on it, and drive towards Dover, friend, where you'll
meet both welcome and protection. Lift your master up. If
you dally half-an-hour, his life, and yours, and all who
support him, are certain to be lost. Take him up, take him
up, and follow me. I'll give you guidance and provisions.

Kent   Distress has induced sleep. This rest might have
soothed your tortured nerves. If circumstances won't allow
that, a cure will not be easy. [*To the* **Fool**] Come, help to
carry your master. You must not stay behind.

Gloucester   Come: come away.

[**Kent, Gloucester** *and the* **Fool** *leave, carrying* **Lear**]

Edgar   When we see our betters suffering from wretchedness,
our own miseries seem more bearable. The worst kind of
suffering is in the mind, when it ceases to be carefree and
happy. However, the mind is relieved of much suffering
when grief and adversity are shared. How tolerable my pain
seems now, when I see the King break beneath a burden

He childed as I fathered! Tom, away!
Mark the high noises, and thyself bewray
When false opinion, whose wrong thoughts defile thee,
110   In thy just proof repeals and reconciles thee.
What will hap more to-night, safe 'scape the King!
Lurk, lurk.

[*Exit*]

Scene 7

Gloucester's Castle. Enter **Cornwall, Regan, Goneril, Edmund,** *and Servants*

Cornwall   [*To* **Goneril**] Post speedily to my lord your
husband; show him this letter: the army of France is landed.
Seek out the traitor Gloucester.

[*Exeunt some of the Servants*]

Regan   Hang him instantly.

5 **Goneril**   Pluck out his eyes.

Cornwall   Leave him to my displeasure. Edmund, keep you
our sister company: the revenges we are bound to take upon
your traitorous father are not fit for your beholding. Advise
the Duke, where you are going, to a most festinate
10   preparation: we are bound to the like. Our posts shall be
swift and intelligent betwixt us. Farewell, dear sister;
farewell, my Lord of Gloucester.

that only puts a strain on me. He suffers from his children,
as I do from my father! Tom, away! Note how things are
amongst the great. Throw off your disguise when you are
cleared of the false charges that shame you, and you are
reconciled to your father. Whatever else happens tonight,
may the King make a safe escape! Meanwhile, stay in
hiding!

[*He goes*]

Scene 7

A room in Gloucester's castle. **Cornwall, Regan, Goneril,
Edmund** *and servants enter*

Cornwall   [*to* **Goneril**] Send a messenger quickly to my lord
your husband. Show him this letter. [*It is the one* **Gloucester**
mentioned in Act 3 Scene 3] The French army has landed.
Go and find the traitor Gloucester!

[*Several Servants leave*]

Regan   Hang him instantly!

Goneril   Blind him!

Cornwall   Leave him to my displeasure. Edmund, stay with our
sister Goneril. The revenge we are proposing to take on your
traitorous father is not fit for you to see. Tell the Duke,
when you see him, to prepare for war. We'll do the same.
Our messengers will keep us fully and swiftly informed. [*To*
Goneril] Farewell, dear sister. [*To* **Edmund**] Farewell, my
Lord of Gloucester.

179

ACT THREE   Scene 7

[*Enter* **Oswald**]

How now! Where's the King?

Oswald   My Lord of Gloucester hath conveyed him hence:
15   Some five or six and thirty of his knights,
        Hot questrists after him, met him at gate;
        Who, with some other of the Lord's dependants,
        Are gone with him toward Dover, where they boast
        To have well-armed friends.

20 **Cornwall**   Get horses for your mistress.

   Goneril   Farewell, sweet lord, and sister.

   Cornwall   Edmund, farewell.

                    [*Exeunt* **Goneril, Edmund,** *and* **Oswald**]

                         Go seek the traitor Gloucester,
        Pinion him like a thief, bring him before us.

                              [*Exeunt other Servants*]

25   Though well we may not pass upon his life
        Without the form of justice, yet our power
        Shall do a courtesy to our wrath, which men
        May blame but not control. Who's there? The traitor?

   [*Re-enter Servants, with* **Gloucester** *prisoner*]

   Regan   Ingrateful fox, 'tis he.

30 **Cornwall**   Bind fast his corky arms.

   Gloucester   What means your graces? Good my friends,
        consider
        You are my guests: do me no foul play, friends.

[**Oswald** *enters*]

Well, where's the King?

Oswald   My Lord of Gloucester has taken him away. Some
three dozen or so of his knights, eagerly searching for him,
met him at the castle gate. With some more of Lord
Gloucester's men, they have gone towards Dover, where
they claim they have well-armed friends.

Cornwall   Get horses for your mistress.

Goneril   Farewell, sweet lord, and sister.

Cornwall   Edmund, farewell.

[**Goneril, Edmund** *and* **Oswald** *leave*]

Go and find the traitor, Gloucester! Tie him up like a thief,
and bring him to us.

[*Several Servants respond*]

Though we can't condemn him to death without a trial, we
can indulge our anger. Men might deplore it, but not stop it.
Who's there? The traitor?

[*Several enter with* **Gloucester** *their prisoner*]

Regan   The ungrateful fox! It's him!

Cornwall   Tie his scraggy arms tight!

Gloucester   What do your graces mean? My dear friends,
remember you are my guests. Do me no injury, friends.

Cornwall   Bind him, I say.   [*Servants bind him*]

Regan   Hard, hard. Oh filthy traitor!

Gloucester   Unmerciful lady as you are, I'm none.

35 **Cornwall**   To this chair bind him. Villain, thou shalt find –

[**Regan** *plucks his beard*]

Gloucester   By the.kind gods, 'tis most ignobly done
To pluck me by the beard.

Regan   So white, and such a traitor!

Gloucester   Naughty lady,
These hairs, which thou dost ravish from my chin,
40   Will quicken, and accuse thee: I am your host:
With robbers' hands my hospitable favours
You should not ruffle thus. What will you do?

Cornwall   Come, sir, what letters had you late from France?

Regan   Be simple-answered, for we know the truth.

45 **Cornwall**   And what confederacy have you with the traitors
Late footed in the kingdom?

Regan   To whose hands
Have you sent the lunatic King? Speak.

Gloucester   I have a letter guessingly set down,
Which came from one that's of a neutral heart,
50   And not from one opposed.

Cornwall   Cunning.

Regan   And false.

Cornwall   Where hast thou sent the King?

Gloucester   To Dover.

Cornwall   Tie him, I say!

[*The Servants tie him up*]

Regan   Tight! Tight! Oh, you filthy traitor!

Gloucester   Merciless lady that you are, I'm not!

Cornwall   Bind him to this chair. Villain, you'll find –

[**Regan** *pulls* **Gloucester's** *beard*]

Gloucester   By the kind gods, it's extremely rude to pluck me by the beard!

Regan   [*Holding up some hair*] So white, and such a traitor!

Gloucester   Wicked lady, those hairs you've snatched from my chin will come to life and accuse you. I am your host and as such you shouldn't abuse my hospitality like robbers. What are you going to do?

Cornwall   Come, sir. What letters have you had recently from France?

Regan   A straight answer: we know the truth.

Cornwall   How have you conspired with the traitors who've landed recently in the Kingdom?

Regan   To whom have you sent the lunatic King? Speak!

Gloucester   I've had a vague sort of letter from a neutral source, not from an enemy.

Cornwall   Cunning!

Regan   And untrue!

Cornwall   Where have you sent the King?

Gloucester   To Dover.

Regan   Wherefore to Dover? Wast thou not charged at peril –

55 **Cornwall**   Wherefore to Dover? Let him answer that.

Gloucester   I am tied to the stake, and I must stand the
   course.

Regan   Wherefore to Dover?

Gloucester   Because I would not see
   Thy cruel nails pluck out his poor old eyes;
   Nor thy fierce sister in his anointed flesh
60   Stick boarish fangs. The sea, with such a storm
   As his bare head in hell-black night endured,
   Would have buoyed up, and quenched the stelled fires;
   Yet, poor old heart, he holp the heavens to rage.
   If wolves had at thy gate howled that stern time,
65   Thou should'st have said, 'Good porter, turn the key.'
   All cruels else subscribe: but I shall see
   The winged vengeance overtake such children.

Cornwall   See't shalt thou never. Fellows, hold the chair.
   Upon these eyes of thine I'll set my foot.

70 **Gloucester**   He that will think to live till he be old,
   Give me some help! Oh cruel! Oh you gods!

Regan   One side will mock another; the other too.

Cornwall   If you see vengeance, –

1st Servant   Hold your hand, my lord.
   I have served you ever since I was a child,
   But better service have I never done you
75   Than now to bid you hold.

Regan   How now, you dog!

1st Servant   If you did wear a beard upon your chin
   I'd shake it on this quarrel.

184

Regan   Why to Dover? Weren't you told under threat of
death –

Cornwall   Why to Dover? Let him answer that.

Gloucester   I'm tied to a stake like a bear. I must stand being
baited.

Regan   Why to Dover?

Gloucester   Because I couldn't see your cruel nails pluck out
his poor old eyes, nor your fierce sister's boarish fangs slash
his anointed flesh. Faced with a storm like the one his bare
head endured, during a night as black as hell, the sea itself
would have bobbed up and quenched the stars. Yet, poor
old heart, he helped the heavens to rage. If wolves had
howled at your gate at that ghastly time, you would have
said, 'Good porter, let them in.' All other cruel creatures
yield to compassion. I'll see that divine vengeance overtakes
such children as you!

Cornwall   See it you never shall. [*To the Servants*] You
fellows, hold the chair. I'll stamp my foot upon those eyes of
yours!

Gloucester   [*struggling*] Anyone who hopes to reach old age:
help me! [**Cornwall** *blinds* **Gloucester** *with his boot*] Oh,
cruel! Oh, gods!

Regan   One side will mock the other. The other, too!

Cornwall   [*raising his foot*] If you see vengeance –

1st Servant   Hold it, my lord. I've served you ever since I was
a child; but I've never served you better than I do now in
telling you to stop!

Regan   What, you dog!

1st Servant   If you were a man, I'd fight you over this!

185

80 **Regan**   What do you mean?

Cornwall   My villain!   [*They draw and fight*]

1st Servant   Nay then, come on, and take the chance of anger.

Regan   Give me thy sword. A peasant stand up thus!

[*Takes a sword and runs at him behind*]

1st Servant   Oh, I am slain. My lord, you have one eye left
85   To see some mischief on him. Oh!   [*Dies*]

Cornwall   Lest it see more, prevent it. Out, vile jelly!
     Where is thy lustre now?

Gloucester   All dark and comfortless. Where's my son
     Edmund?
     Edmund, enkindle all the sparks of nature
90   To quit this horrid act.

Regan   Out, treacherous villain!
     Thou call'st on him that hates thee; it was he
     That made the overture of thy treasons to us,
     Who is too good to pity thee.

95 **Gloucester**   Oh my follies! Then Edgar was abused.
     Kind gods, forgive me that, and prosper him!

Regan   Go thrust him out at gates, and let him smell
     His way to Dover.   [*Exit one with* **Gloucester**]
                         How is't, my lord. How look you?

Cornwall   I have received a hurt. Follow me, lady.
100   Turn out that eyeless villain; throw this slave
     Upon the dunghill. Regan, I bleed apace:
     Untimely comes this hurt. Give me your arm.

186

Regan   What do you mean?

Cornwall   Villain!

1st Servant   Right, then: come on. Take your chance against an angry man!

[*They fight*]

Regan   [*to another Servant*] Give me your sword. A peasant to presume like this? [*She runs him through from behind*]

1st Servant   Oh, you've killed me! My lord, you've one eye left to see him come to a bad end. Oh! [*He dies*]

Cornwall   In case it sees more, we'll prevent it. [*He gouges out* **Gloucester**'s *remaining eye*] Out, you vile piece of jelly! Where's your twinkle now?

Gloucester   [*groaning*] All's dark and comfortless. Where is my son, Edmund? Edmund, summon all the energy of nature to revenge this horrid act!

Regan   Pah! You treacherous villain! You are appealing to someone who hates you. It was Edmund who disclosed your treasons to us. He's too good to pity you.

Gloucester   Oh, my follies! Then Edgar was wronged. Kind gods, forgive me and make him prosper!

Regan   [*to a Servant*] Go and throw him out. Let him smell his way to Dover.

[**Gloucester** *is pushed out*]

How are you my lord? Are you all right?

Cornwall   I've been hurt. Follow me, lady. Turn that eyeless villain out. Throw this wretch on the dunghill. Regan, I'm bleeding badly. This wound has come at the wrong time. Give me your arm.

187

[*Exit* **Cornwall,** *led by* **Regan**]

2nd Servant   I'll never care what wickedness I do
If this man come to good.

3rd Servant   If she live long,
105   And in the end meet the old course of death,
Women will all turn monsters.

2nd Servant   Let's follow the old Earl, and get the Bedlam
To lead him where he would: his roguish madness
Allows itself to any thing.

110 **3rd Servant**   Go thou; I'll fetch some flax and whites of eggs
To apply to his bleeding face. Now, heaven help him!

[*Exeunt severally*]

[**Cornwall** *leaves supported by* **Regan**]

2nd Servant   I don't care what wickedness I do, if this man prospers!

3rd Servant   If she has a long life, and dies a natural death, all women will turn into monsters!

2nd Servant   Let's follow the old Earl, and get the madman to guide him wherever he wants to go. Nobody will criticize what a madman does.

3rd Servant   You go. I'll fetch some flax and whites of eggs to make a plaster for his bleeding face. Now, heaven help him!

[*They go separately*]

Act four

Scene 1

The heath. Enter **Edgar**

Edgar Yet better thus, and known to be contemned,
Than, still contemned and flattered, to be worst.
The lowest and most dejected thing of Fortune
Stands still in esperance, lives not in fear:
5 The lamentable change is from the best;
The worst returns to laughter. Welcome, then,
Thou unsubstantial air that I embrace:
The wretch that thou hast blown unto the worst
Owes nothing to thy blasts. But who comes here?

[*Enter* **Gloucester,** *led by an* **Old Man**]

10 My father, poorly led? World, world, oh, world!
But that thy strange mutations make us hate thee,
Life would not yield to age.

Old Man   Oh, my good lord!
I have been your tenant, and your father's tenant,
These fourscore years.

15 **Gloucester** Away, get thee away; good friend, be gone:
Thy comforts can do me no good at all;
Thee they may hurt.

Old Man   You cannot see your way.

Gloucester I have no way, and therefore want no eyes;
I stumbled when I saw. Full oft 'tis seen,
20 Our means secure us, and our mere defects
Prove our commodities. Oh! dear son Edgar,

190

Act four

Scene 1

The heath. **Edgar** *enters*

Edgar   It's better to be like this – openly despised – than what
is worse: scorned but deceived by flattery. The most
wretched and dejected victim of ill-fortune always has some
hope, and is proof against fear. What's more distressing is
to cease to enjoy life at its best; when things are at their
worst, they can only improve. Welcome, then, to the natural
elements that surround me. This man you've made so
wretched with your fierce winds owes you no thanks. But
who comes here?

[**Gloucester** *enters, led by an* **Old Man**]

My father, guided by a commoner? World, world, oh world!
It's hatred of your ups and downs that makes us reconciled
to death.

Old Man   [*to* Gloucester] Oh, my good lord! I've been your
tenant, and your father's tenant, these eighty years.

Gloucester   Away, go away. Good friend, be gone. Your help
can do me no good at all. It may do you some harm.

Old Man   You can't see your way.

Gloucester   I have no way, and therefore need no eyes. I
stumbled when I could see. Very often prosperity makes us
complacent, and adversity proves to be an asset. Oh, dear

The food of thy abused father's wrath;
Might I but live to see thee in my touch,
I'd say I had eyes again.

Old Man   How now! Who's there?

25 **Edgar**   [*Aside*] Oh gods! Who is't can say 'I am at the worst'?
I am worse than e'er I was.

Old Man   'Tis poor mad Tom.

Edgar   [*Aside*] And worse I may be yet; the worst is not
So long as we can say 'This is the worst.'

Old Man   Fellow, where goest?

Gloucester   Is it a beggar man?

30 **Old Man**   Madman and beggar too.

Gloucester   He has some reason, else he could not beg.
I'th'last night's storm I such a fellow saw,
Which made me think a man a worm. My son
Came then into my mind; and yet my mind
35 Was then scarce friends with him. I have heard more since:
As flies to wanton boys, are we to the gods;
They kill us for their sport.

Edgar   [*Aside*]   How should this be?
Bad is the trade that must play fool to sorrow,
Ang'ring itself and others. [*Aloud*] Bless thee, master!

Gloucester   Is that the naked fellow?

40 **Old Man**   Ay, my lord.

Gloucester   Then, prithee, get thee away. If, for my sake,
Thou wilt o'ertake us, hence a mile or twain,
I'th'way toward Dover, do it for ancient love;
And bring some covering for this naked soul,
Which I'll entreat to lead me.

son Edgar, the object of your deluded father's anger! If I
could only live to see you by touching you, I'd say I had my
eyes again.

Old Man   [*noticing* **Edgar**] Hello, who's there?

Edgar   [*aside*] Oh gods! Who can ever say 'I've hit the
bottom'? I'm worse than I was before.

Old Man   [*to* **Gloucester**] It's poor mad Tom.

Edgar   [*aside*] And worse may still be to come. 'The worst' is
no longer to be feared when we can say, 'This *is* the worst.'

Old Man   Fellow, where are you going?

Gloucester   Is it a beggar man?

Old Man   Lunatic and beggar, too.

Gloucester   He must have some intelligence, or he couldn't
beg. In last night's storm I saw such a fellow, which made
me think mankind's no better than a worm. My son then
came into my mind, though I was out of friends with him in
my thoughts. The gods treat us like naughty boys do flies;
they kill us for the fun of it.

Edgar   [*aside, commenting on his father's blindness*] What has
happened? It's a bad business having to joke with a man in
distress. Both parties resent it. [*Aloud*] Bless you, master.

Gloucester   Is that the naked fellow?

Old Man   Yes, my lord.

Gloucester   Then, please: go now. If, for my sake, you will
catch up with us a mile or two away from here — on the way
to Dover — do it for old time's sake. And bring some clothes
for this naked soul, who I shall ask to escort me.

45 **Old Man**   Alack, sir! He is mad.

Gloucester   'Tis the times' plague, when madmen lead the
        blind.
        Do as I bid thee, or rather do thy pleasure;
        Above the rest, be gone.

Old Man   I'll bring him the best 'parel that I have,
        Come on't what will.

                                                [*Exit*]

50 **Gloucester**   Sirrah, naked fellow –

Edgar   Poor Tom's a-cold. [*Aside*] I cannot daub it further.

Gloucester   Come hither, fellow.

Edgar   [*Aside*] And yet I must. Bless thy sweet eyes, they
        bleed.

55 **Gloucester**   Know'st thou the way to Dover?

Edgar   Both stile and gate, horse-way and foot-path. Poor
        Tom hath been scared out of his good wits: bless thee, good
        man's son, from the foul fiend! Five fiends have been in poor
        Tom at once; as Obidicut, of lust; Hoberdidance, prince of
60   dumbness; Mahu, of stealing; Modo, of murder;
        Flibbertigibbet, of mopping and mowing; who since possesses
        chambermaids and waiting-women. So, bless thee, master!

Gloucester   Here, take this purse, thou whom the heavens'
        plagues
        Have humbled to all strokes: that I am wretched
65   Makes thee the happier: heavens, deal so still!
        Let the superfluous and lust-dieted man,
        That slaves your ordinance, that will not see
        Because he does not feel, feel your power quickly;
        So distribution should undo excess,
70   And each man have enough. Dost thou know Dover?

194

Old Man   Alas, sir, he is mad . . .

Gloucester   It's a sign of the sick times, when the mad lead the blind. Do as I say, or rather as you feel inclined. Above all, go!

Old Man   I'll bring him the best clothes I've got, and take the consequences.

[*He goes*]

Gloucester   You there: the naked fellow!

Edgar   Poor Tom is cold. [*Aside*] I can't keep this up –

Gloucester   Come here, fellow.

Edgar   – but I must. [*Resuming his disguise*] Bless your sweet eyes. They are bleeding.

Gloucester   Do you know the way to Dover?

Edgar   Cross-country, bridle-path and footpath. Poor Tom has been scared out of his good wits. Bless you, laddie, from the foul fiend! Five devils have been in Poor Tom together: Obidicut, the lusty one; Hoberdidance, the prince of dumbness; Mahu, of stealing; Modo, of murder; Flibbertigibbet, of making strange faces. They've since possessed chambermaids and serving-women. So, bless you, master!

Gloucester   Here, take this purse, you who've become reconciled to Fortune's worst afflictions. My wretchedness makes you the better off. Heavens, stick to your policy! May the man who's well-heeled and over-indulgent – who abuses your kind favours – who refuses to see things because he does not feel them personally – quickly experience your power! Spreading things out would remedy excess. Every man would have enough. Do you know Dover?

195

Edgar   Ay, master.

Gloucester   There is a cliff, whose high and bending head
Looks fearfully in the confined deep;
Bring me but to the very brim of it,
75   And I'll repair the misery thou dost bear
With something rich about me; from that place
I shall no leading need.

Edgar   Give me thy arm:
Poor Tom shall lead thee.

[*Exeunt*]

Scene 2

Before the Duke of Albany's Palace. Enter **Goneril** *and*
Edmund

Goneril   Welcome, my lord; I marvel our mild husband
Not met us on the way.

[*Enter* **Oswald**]

                           Now, where's your master?

Oswald   Madam, within; but never man so changed.
I told him of the army that was landed;
5   He smiled at it: I told him you were coming;
His answer was 'The worse': of Gloucester's treachery,
And of the loyal service of his son,
When I informed him, then he called me sot,
And told me I had turned the wrong side out:
10   What most he should dislike seems pleasant to him;
What like, offensive.

196

Edgar   Yes, master.

Gloucester   There is a cliff whose great and brooding height
peers fearfully into the pounding sea below. Just take me to
the very edge of it, and I'll help to remedy your misery with
something valuable I'm carrying. From there I'll need no
guide.

Edgar   Give me your arm. Poor Tom will lead you.

[*They go*]

Scene 2

Near the Duke of Albany's palace. Enter **Goneril** *and* **Edmund**,
who have travelled from Gloucester's castle together

Goneril   Welcome, my lord. I'm amazed that my meek and mild
husband didn't meet us on the way.

[**Oswald** *enters*]

Where's your master?

Oswald   Madam, he's indoors. But never a man so changed. I
told him about the army that has landed; he smiled at it. I
told him you were coming. His answer was, 'So much the
worse.' When I informed him of Gloucester's treachery, and
of the loyal services of his son, he called me an idiot and
told me I'd got it wrong way round. What he ought to dislike
seems pleasant to him. What he should like, offensive.

Goneril   [*To* **Edmund**]   Then shall you go no further.
It is the cowish terror of his spirit
That dares not undertake; he'll not feel wrongs
15   Which tie him to an answer. Our wishes on the way
May prove effects. Back, Edmund, to my brother;
Hasten his musters and conduct his powers:
I must change arms at home, and give the distaff
Into my husband's hands. This trusty servant
20   Shall pass between us; ere long you are like to hear,
If you dare venture in your own behalf,
A mistress's command. Wear this; spare speech;
Decline your head: this kiss, if it durst speak,
Would stretch thy spirits up into the air.
25   Conceive, and fare thee well.

Edmund   Yours in the ranks of death.

Goneril   My most dear Gloucester!

[*Exit* **Edmund**]

Oh! the difference of man and man.
To thee a woman's services are due:
A fool usurps my bed.

Oswald   Madam, here comes my lord.

[*Exit*]

[*Enter* **Albany**]

Goneril   I have been worth the whistle.

30 **Albany**   O Goneril!
You are not worth the dust which the rude wind
Blows in your face. I fear your disposition:
That nature, which contemns its origin,
Cannot be bordered certain in itself;

Goneril   [*to* **Edmund**] Then you must go no further. He's too
   cowardly to take any action; he'll avoid provocation. The
   hopes we expressed on the way here may be fulfilled. Go
   back, Edmund, to my brother. Speed up recruitment and
   lead his army. I must change roles at home, and give my
   husband the embroidery to do. [*Pointing to* **Oswald**] This
   trusty servant will be our go-between. Soon you may well
   hear – if you're not afraid to do yourself some good – a
   certain command from your mistress . . . [**Edmund**'s *hand*
   goes to his dagger; he realizes **Goneril** *is hinting at the*
   murder of **Albany**] Wear this; there's no need to say
   anything. [*She puts a chain round his neck*] Lower your
   head. [*She kisses him*] This kiss, if it dared to speak, would
   rouse you . . . Keep me in your thoughts, and goodbye.

Edmund   Yours ever, until death!

Goneril   My dearest Gloucester!

   [**Edmund** *leaves*]

   Oh, the difference between one man and another! You
   deserve what a woman has to give. I have a fool for my
   bedfellow.

Oswald   Madam, here comes my lord.

                                                            [*He goes*]

   [**Albany** *enters*]

Goneril   So you've decided I'm worth looking for?

Albany   Oh, Goneril! You are not worth the dust that the harsh
   wind blows in your face! I distrust your character. A nature
   that can deny a parent cannot hold itself in check. As one

35   She that herself will sliver and disbranch
        From her material sap, perforce must wither
        And come to deadly use.

    Goneril   No more; the text is foolish.

    Albany   Wisdom and goodness to the vile seem vile;
40   Filths savour but themselves. What have you done?
        Tigers, not daughters, what have you performed?
        A father, and a gracious aged man,
        Whose reverence even the head-lugged bear would lick,
        Most barbarous, most degenerate, have you madded.
45   Could my good brother suffer you to do it?
        A man, a prince, by him so benefited!
        If that the heavens do not their visible spirits
        Send quickly down to tame these vile offences,
        It will come,
50   Humanity must perforce prey on itself,
        Like monsters of the deep.

    Goneril   Milk-livered man!
        That bear'st a cheek for blows, a head for wrongs;
        Who hast not in thy brows an eye discerning
        Thine honour from thy suffering; that not know'st
55   Fools do those villains pity who are punished
        Ere they have done their mischief. Where's thy drum;
        France spreads his banners in our noiseless land,
        With plumed helm thy state begins to threat,
        Whilst thou, a moral fool, sits still, and cries
        'Alack! why does he so?'

60 **Albany**   See thyself, devil!
        Proper deformity shows not in the fiend
        So horrid as in woman.

    Goneril   Oh, vain fool!

    Albany   Thou changed and self-covered thing, for shame, who has cut herself off from the main branch, you must of necessity wither and die.

Goneril   Say no more. Your sermon is a silly one.

Albany   Wisdom and goodness always seem vile to the vile. Filth is best appreciated by the filthy. What have you done? Tigers rather than daughters, what have you been up to? A father, and a gracious elderly man – that even a captive bear would lick with reverence – you have barbarously and degenerately made insane. How could my brother-in-law allow you to do it? A man – a prince – who owed so much to him! If the gods don't quickly intervene by sending down their agents to punish these vile offences, then surely men will start eating each other, like the monsters of the sea!

Goneril   You coward, you'll let anyone push you around! You can't distinguish between the tolerable and the insufferable. You don't realize that only fools pity villains who are punished before they get up to mischief. Where's your call to arms? The King of France raises his flags in our docile land; the threat of war hangs over your country while you, a moralizing fool, sit there and cry, 'Alas, why is he doing this?'

Albany   See yourself for what you are, devil! Depravity, bad enough when seen in the fiend, is even more horrid in a woman!

Goneril   You worthless idiot!

Albany   You transformed and self-deceiving thing, for shame!

Be-monster not thy feature. Were't my fitness
65   To let these hands obey my blood,
They are apt enough to dislocate and tear
Thy flesh and bones; howe'er thou art a fiend,
A woman's shape doth shield thee.

Goneril   Marry, your manhood mew –

[*Enter a* **Messenger**]

70 **Albany**   What news?

Messenger   Oh, my good lord, the Duke of Cornwall's dead;
Slain by his servant, going to put out
The other eye of Gloucester.

Albany   Gloucester's eyes!

Messenger   A servant that he bred, thrilled with remorse,
75   Opposed against the act, bending his sword
To his great master: who, thereat enraged,
Flew on him, and amongst them felled him dead;
But not without that harmful stroke, which since
Hath plucked him after.

Albany   This shows you are above,
80   You justicers, that these our nether crimes
So speedily can venge! But, oh, poor Gloucester!
Lost he his other eye?

Messenger   Both, both, my lord.
This letter, madam, craves a speedy answer;
'Tis from your sister.

Goneril [*Aside*]   One way I like this well;
85   But being widow, and my Gloucester with her,
May all the building in my fancy pluck
Upon my hateful life: another way,

Stop acting like a monster! If I were inclined to let my emotions govern my behaviour, these hands would tear your flesh and bones apart! Fiend though you are, your female form protects you.

Goneril   [*contemptuously*] You and your manhood! Pah!

[*A* **Messenger** *enters*]

Albany   What's your news?

Messenger   Oh, my good lord, the Duke of Cornwall is dead: killed by his servant as he was putting out Gloucester's other eye.

Albany   Gloucester's eyes!

Messenger   One of his servants, moved by compassion, made objection, raising his sword against his great master. Furious at this, he attacked him, and the man was struck dead; but not before sustaining a mortal wound that later took his life.

Albany   [*addressing the heavens*] This proves you are there above, you judges, in that our crimes down here below are so speedily revenged! But oh, poor Gloucester! Did he lose his other eye?

Messenger   Both, my lord, both. [*To* **Goneril**] This letter, madam, requires a speedy answer. It's from your sister.

Goneril   [*Aside*] In one sense, I like this. However, she being a widow and my Gloucester with her, all my dreams for the future could collapse in ruins. Looking at it another way, the

The news is not so tart. [*Aloud*] I'll read, and answer.

[*Exit*]

Albany   Where was his son when they did take his eyes?

Messenger   Come with my lady hither.

90 **Albany**   He is not here.

Messenger   No, my good lord; I met him back again.

Albany   Knows he the wickedness?

Messenger   Ay, my good lord; 'twas he informed against him,
And quit the house on purpose that their punishment
Might have the freer course.

95 **Albany**   Gloucester, I live
To thank thee for the love thou show'dst the King,
And to revenge thine eyes. Come hither, friend:
Tell me what more thou know'st.

[*Exeunt*]

Scene 3

The French Camp near Dover. Enter **Kent** *and a* **Gentleman**

Kent   Why the King of France is so suddenly gone back know
you the reason?

Gentleman   Something he left imperfect in the state, which
since his coming forth is thought of; which imports to the

news is not so grievous. [*Aloud*] I'll read it and answer it.

[*She goes*]

Albany   Where was his son when they blinded him?

Messenger   On his way here with my lady.

Albany   He isn't here.

Messenger   No, my good lord. I met him on his way back.

Albany   Does he know about the wickedness?

Messenger   Yes, my good lord. It was he who informed against him. He left the house on purpose so that they would have a free hand with their punishment.

Albany   Gloucester, I live to thank you for the love that you have shown the King, and to revenge your eyes! [*To the* **Messenger**] Come here, friend. Tell me what more you know.

[*They go*]

Scene 3

The French camp near Dover. Enter **Kent** *and a* **Gentleman**

Kent   Have you no idea why the King of France has returned so suddenly?

Gentleman   He remembered something he'd forgotten to do in his own kingdom which had such risky complications that

5   kingdom so much fear and danger that his personal return
       was most required and necessary.

   Kent   Who hath he left behind him general?

   Gentleman   The Marshal of France, Monsieur La Far.

   Kent   Did your letters pierce the Queen to any demonstration
10   of grief?

   Gentleman   Ay, sir; she took them, read them in my presence;
       And now and then an ample tear trilled down
       Her delicate cheek; it seemed she was a queen
       Over her passion; who, most rebel-like,
       Sought to be king o'er her.

15 **Kent**   Oh, then it moved her.

   Gentleman   Not to a rage; patience and sorrow strove
       Who should express her goodliest. You have seen
       Sunshine and rain at once; her smiles and tears
       Were like, a better way; those happy smilets
20   That played on her ripe lip seemed not to know
       What guests were in her eyes; which parted thence,
       As pearls from diamonds dropped. In brief,
       Sorrow would be a rarity most beloved,
       If all could so become it.

   Kent   Made she no verbal question?

25 **Gentleman**   Faith, once or twice she heaved the name of
          'father'
       Pantingly forth, as if it pressed her heart;
       Cried 'Sisters! sisters! Shame of ladies! sisters!
       Kent! father! sisters! What? i'th'storm! i'th'night?
       Let pity not believe it!' There she shook
30   The holy water from her heavenly eyes,
       And clamour moistened, then away she started
       To deal with grief alone.

his return was vital and necessary.

Kent Which general has he left in charge?

Gentleman The Marshal of France, Monsieur La Far.

Kent Did your letters cause the Queen to show any sign of grief?

Gentleman Yes, sir. She took them, and read them in my presence. Every now and then a large tear trickled down her soft cheek. She governed her emotions like a queen; they, like rebels, tried to play the superior role of king.

Kent Oh, then she was moved by it?

Gentleman Not to distraction. Self control vied with sorrow as to which should show most attractively in her face. You have seen sunshine and rain happen together. Her smiles and tears were similar, but more attractive. The happy little smiles that played on her ruby lips seemed unaware of the tears that lodged in her eyes. They fell like pearls dropping from diamonds. In short, sorrow would be a precious rarity if it were always as becoming as it was in her case.

Kent Did she ask no questions?

Gentleman Indeed, once or twice she gasped the name 'father' as if it pressed upon her heart. She cried, 'Sisters! Sisters! Disgrace to womanhood! Sisters! Kent! Father! Sisters! What – in the storm? At night? For pity's sake, it's unbelievable!' At that point she let her holy tears fall from her heavenly eyes. Then away she went, calmed by her outburst, to cope with her grief in private.

Kent   It is the stars,
The stars above us, govern our conditions;
Else one self mate and make could not beget
35   Such different issues. You spoke not with her since?

Gentleman   No.

Kent   Was this before the King returned?

Gentleman   No, since.

Kent   Well, sir, the poor distressed Lear's i'th' town;
Who sometime, in his better tune, remembers
40   What we are come about, and by no means
Will yield to see his daughter.

Gentleman   Why, good sir?

Kent   A sovereign shame so elbows him: his own unkindness,
That stripped her from his benediction, turned her
To foreign casualties, gave her dear rights
45   To his dog-hearted daughters, these things sting
His mind so venomously that burning shame
Detains him from Cordelia.

Gentleman   Alack, poor gentleman.

Kent   Of Albany's and Cornwall's powers you heard not?

Gentleman   'Tis so, they are afoot.

50   **Kent**   Well, sir, I'll bring you to our master Lear,
And leave you to attend him. Some dear cause
Will in concealment wrap me up awhile;
When I am known aright, you shall not grieve
Lending me this acquaintance. I pray you,
55   Go along with me.

                              [*Exeunt*]

Kent   It's the stars, the stars above us, who decide our
characters! Otherwise parents couldn't beget such different
children. You've not spoken to her since?

Gentleman   No.

Kent   Was this before the King returned to France?

Gentleman   No, after.

Kent   Well, sir, the poor distressed Lear has reached Dover.
Sometimes in his more lucid moments he remembers why
we are here, and won't in any circumstances consent to see
his daughter.

Gentleman   Why, sir?

Kent   An overpowering shame nudges his conscience. His
own unkindness – which lost her his blessing, turned her
out to live abroad as best she could, and gave her dowry to
his pitiless daughters – these things sting his mind so
poisonously that he's held back from meeting Cordelia by a
burning sense of shame.

Gentleman   Alas, poor gentleman!

Kent   You haven't heard anything of the armies of Albany and
Cornwall?

Gentleman   Yes. They are on the march.

Kent   Well, sir, I'll bring you to our master, Lear, and leave you
to look after him. Important business will keep me privately
occupied for some time. When I resume my real name, you
won't be sorry you associated with me like this. Please,
come with me.

[*They go*]

Scene 4

The same. Enter, with drum and colours, **Cordelia, Doctor,** *and Soldiers*

Cordelia   Alack, 'tis he: why, he was met even now
　　　As mad as the vexed sea; singing aloud;
　　　Crowned with rank fumiter and furrow-weeds,
　　　With hardocks, hemlock, nettles, cuckoo-flowers,
5　　Darnel, and all the idle weeds that grow
　　　In our sustaining corn. A century send forth;
　　　Search every acre in the high-grown field,
　　　And bring him to our eye.　　　　　　*[Exit an Officer]*
　　　　　　　　　　　What can man's wisdom
　　　In the restoring his bereaved sense?
10　He that helps him take all my outward worth.

Doctor   There is means, madam;
　　　Our foster-nurse of nature is repose,
　　　The which he lacks; that to provoke in him,
　　　Are many simples operative, whose power
　　　Will close the eye of anguish.

15 **Cordelia**　　　　　　　　　All blest secrets,
　　　All you unpublished virtues of the earth,
　　　Spring with my tears! Be aidant and remediate
　　　In the good man's distress! Seek, seek for him,
　　　Lest his ungoverned rage dissolve the life
　　　That wants the means to lead it.

　　　[Enter a **Messenger***]*

20　　　　　　　　　　　　　　News, madam;
　　　The British powers are marching hitherward.

Cordelia   'Tis known before; our preparation stands
　　　In expectation of them. Oh dear father!

Scene 4

The French Camp near Dover. **Cordelia** *enters with a* **Doctor** *and Soldiers*

Cordelia   Alas, it's him. He was found just now, as mad as the raging sea, singing aloud, with a crown of luxuriant fumitory and common weeds – burdocks, hemlock, nettles, cuckoo-flowers, coarse grasses, and all the worthless weeds that grow amongst our health-giving corn. Send out a troop of soldiers; search every acre in the fields of crops, and bring him to our sight.

[*An Officer leaves*]

What can man's learning do to restore his lost reason? I'd give all I possess to the man who can cure him.

Doctor   There is a way, madam. Sleep is nature's nourishment, which he lacks. To induce it, there are many effective medicinal herbs, with the power to put pain to sleep.

Cordelia   May all the blessed secrets and little-known remedies of the earth germinate with my tears! Be helpful and curative in the good man's distress! Look, look for him, in case in his frenzy he ends a life that lacks the means to survive.

[**Messenger** *enters*]

Messenger   News, madam. The British army is marching towards you.

Cordelia   We know that. We are ready for them. Oh, dear

It is thy business that I go about;
25   Therefore great France
My mourning and importuned tears hath pitied.
No blown ambition doth our arms incite,
But love, dear love, and our aged father's right.
Soon may I hear and see him!

[*Exeunt*]

Scene 5

Gloucester's Castle. Enter **Regan** *and* **Oswald**

Regan   But are my brother's powers set forth?

Oswald   Ay, madam.

Regan   Himself in person there?

Oswald   Madam, with much ado:
Your sister is the better soldier.

Regan   Lord Edmund spake not with your lord at home?

5 **Oswald**   No, madam.

Regan   What might import my sister's letter to him?

Oswald   I know not, lady.

Regan   Faith, he is posted hence on serious matter.
It was great ignorance, Gloucester's eyes being out,
10   To let him live; where he arrives he moves
All hearts against us. Edmund, I think, is gone,
In pity of his misery, to dispatch

father! It is *your* interests I'm pursuing. That's why my royal husband has pitied my sorrowful and pleading tears. We aren't roused to war by puffed-up ambition, but by love, dear love, and our father's rights. May I soon hear and see him!

[*They go*]

Scene 5

A room in Gloucester's castle. **Regan** *enters, followed by* **Oswald** *who is carrying a letter*

Regan   Have my brother-in-law's troops set out?

Oswald   Yes, madam.

Regan   Himself there in person?

Oswald   Madam, after a lot of fuss. Your sister is the better soldier.

Regan   Lord Edmund didn't speak to your lord at his home?

Oswald   No, madam.

Regan   What was behind my sister's letter to him?

Oswald   I don't know, lady.

Regan   Indeed, he has gone off on important business. It was stupid to let Gloucester live after he was blinded. Wherever he goes he turns all hearts against us. Edmund, I think, has gone to end his darkened life out of pity for his misery, as

213

His nighted life; moreover, to descry
The strength o'th'enemy.

15 **Oswald**   I needs must after him, madam, with my letter.

Regan   Our troops set forth to-morrow; stay with us,
The ways are dangerous.

Oswald   I may not, madam;
My lady charged my duty in this business.

Regan   Why should she write to Edmund? Might not you
20   Transport her purposes by word? Belike,
Some things – I know not what. I'll love thee much:
Let me unseal the letter.

Oswald   Madam, I had rather –

Regan   I know your lady does not love her husband;
I am sure of that: and at her late being here
25   She gave strange oeillades and most speaking looks
To noble Edmund. I know you are of her bosom.

Oswald   I, madam!

Regan   I speak in understanding; y'are, I know't:
Therefore I do advise you, take this note:
30   My lord is dead; Edmund and I have talked;
And more convenient is he for my hand
Than for your lady's. You may gather more.
If you do find him, pray you give him this,
And when your mistress hears thus much from you,
35   I pray desire her call her wisdom to her:
So, fare you well.
If you do chance to hear of that blind traitor,
Preferment falls on him that cuts him off.

Oswald   Would I could meet him, madam: I should show
What party I do follow.

well as to determine the strength of the enemy.

Oswald   I must go after him, madam, with my letter.

Regan   Our troops set out tomorrow. Stay with us. It's dangerous outside.

Oswald   I must not, madam. My lady put me on special trust with this business.

Regan   Why should she write to Edmund? Couldn't you convey her message by word of mouth? Probably somethings – [*She breaks off, not wishing to express her suspicion that* **Goneril** *and* **Edmund** *are lovers*] I don't know what . . . I'd very much appreciate it . . . Let me open the letter . . .

Oswald   Madam, I'd rather –

Regan   I know your lady doesn't love her husband. I'm sure of that. When she was here recently, she gave knowing and meaningful looks to noble Edmund. I know you have her confidence . . .

Oswald   I, madam?

Regan   I know what I'm talking about. You have, I know it. Therefore I advise you: take note of this. My lord is dead. Edmund and I have come to an understanding, and he's more available to me than he is to your lady. You know what I'm getting at. If you find him, give him this. [*She hands* **Oswald** *a ring*] And when your mistress hears what I've told you, I suggest you advise her to act sensibly. So, goodbye. If you happen to hear of that blind traitor, there's promotion for the one who ends his life.

Oswald   If only I could meet him, madam. I'd show where my loyalty lies.

40 **Regan**   Fare thee well.

                                                    [*Exeunt*]

Scene 6

The country near Dover. Enter **Gloucester** *and* **Edgar** *dressed like a peasant*

Gloucester   When shall I come to the top of that same hill?

Edgar   You do climb up it now; look how we labour.

Gloucester   Methinks the ground is even.

Edgar   Horrible steep:
Hark! Do you hear the sea?

Gloucester   No, truly.

5 **Edgar**   Why, then your other senses grow imperfect
By your eyes' anguish.

Gloucester   So may it be, indeed.
Methinks thy voice is altered, and thou speak'st
In better phrase and matter than thou didst.

Edgar   You're much deceived; in nothing am I changed
But in my garments.

10 **Gloucester**   Methinks you're better spoken.

Edgar   Come on, sir; here's the place: stand still. How fearful
And dizzy 'tis to cast one's eyes so low!
The crows and choughs that wing the midway air
Show scarce so gross as beetles; half way down

Regan   Fare you well.

[*They go*]

Scene 6

The countryside near Dover. **Gloucester** *enters, led by* **Edgar**
who is now dressed like a peasant

Gloucester   When shall I reach the top of the hill?

Edgar   You're climbing up it now. Notice how hard it's getting.

Gloucester   I think the ground is level.

Edgar   It's horribly steep. Listen! Do you hear the sea?

Gloucester   Frankly, no.

Edgar   Well then, your other senses are growing imperfect
through the pain in your eyes.

Gloucester   It might be so, indeed. I think your voice is altered,
and that you speak more coherently than you used to.

Edgar   You've got it wrong. I'm the same as before except for
my clothing.

Gloucester   I think you are better spoken.

Edgar   Come on, sir. Here's the place. Stand still. [*He has
stopped in the middle of a field, though he pretends he is at
the edge of a cliff*] How frightening and dizzy-making it is to
look so far down! The crows and jackdaws that fly at
middling height look hardly as big as beetles. Halfway down

15   Hangs one that gathers samphire, dreadful trade!
       Methinks he seems no bigger than his head.
       The fishermen that walk upon the beach
       Appear like mice, and yond tall anchoring bark
       Diminished to her cock; her cock a buoy
20   Almost too small for sight. The murmuring surge,
       That on the unnumbered idle pebble chafes,
       Cannot be heard so high. I'll look no more,
       Lest my brain turn, and the deficient sight
       Topple down headlong.

Gloucester   Set me where you stand.

25 **Edgar**   Give me your hand; you are now within a foot
       Of the extreme verge: for all beneath the moon
       Would I not leap upright.

Gloucester   Let go my hand.
       Here, friend, 's another purse; in it a jewel
       Well worth a poor man's taking: fairies and gods
30   Prosper it with thee! Go thou further off;
       Bid me farewell, and let me hear thee going.

Edgar   Now fare ye well, good sir.

Gloucester   With all my heart.

Edgar [*Aside*] Why I do trifle thus with his despair
       Is done to cure it.

35 **Gloucester** [*Kneeling*] Oh, you mighty gods!
       This world I do renounce, and in your sights
       Shake patiently my great affliction off;
       If I could bear it longer, and not fall
       To quarrel with your great opposeless wills,
40   My snuff and loathed part of nature should
       Burn itself out. If Edgar live, oh, bless him!
       Now, fellow, fare thee well.

there's a man gathering samphire. What a dreadful job! He
looks to me no bigger than his head. The fishermen walking
on the beach look like mice, and that tall ship at anchor over
there is reduced to the size of her tender, and her tender a
buoy almost too small to be seen. The murmuring waves,
that agitate the countless, useless pebbles, cannot be heard
from this height. I'll look no more, in case it turns my head,
and blurred sight makes me topple headlong down.

Gloucester   Put me where you are.

Edgar   Give me your hand. You are now within a foot of the
extreme edge. For all the world, I wouldn't jump up and
down.

Gloucester   Let go my hand. Here, friend, is another purse. In
it there's a jewel worth a lot to a poor man. May good
fortune see you enjoy it! Go further away. Say goodbye, and
let me hear you go.

Edgar   [*pretending to go*] Goodbye, good sir.

Gloucester   With all my heart.

Edgar   [*aside*] The reason I'm trifling with his misery like this is
to cure it.

Gloucester   [*kneeling*] Oh, you mighty gods! I renounce the
world, and in your sight uncomplainingly rid myself of my
great suffering. Even if I could bear it longer, and not fall
into quarrelling with your great and absolute decrees, the
butt end of my life would fizzle out. If Edgar is alive, oh,
bless him! [*To* **Edgar**] Now, fellow: fare you well.

Edgar   Gone, sir: farewell.

[**Gloucester** *throws himself forward and falls*]

And yet I know not how conceit may rob
The treasury of life when life itself
45   Yields to the theft; had he been where he thought
By this had thought been past. Alive or dead?
Ho, you sir! Friend! Hear you, sir! Speak!
Thus might he pass indeed; yet he revives.
What are you, sir?

Gloucester   Away, and let me die.

50 **Edgar**   Hadst thou been aught but gossamer, feathers, air,
So many fathom down precipitating,
Thou'dst shivered like an egg; but thou dost breathe,
Hast heavy substance, bleed'st not, speak'st, art sound.
Ten masts at each make not the altitude
55   Which thou hast perpendicularly fell:
Thy life's a miracle. Speak yet again.

Gloucester   But have I fallen or no?

Edgar   From the dread summit of this chalky bourn.
Look up a-height: the shrill-gorged lark so far
60   Cannot be seen or heard: do but look up.

Gloucester   Alack! I have no eyes.
Is wretchedness deprived that benefit
To end itself by death? 'Twas yet some comfort,
When misery could beguile the tyrant's rage,
And frustrate his proud will.

65 **Edgar**   Give me your arm:
Up: so; how is't? Feel you your legs? You stand.

Gloucester   Too well, too well.

Edgar   [*pretending to be at a distance*] Gone, sir. Farewell!

[**Gloucester** *throws himself forward, as if over a cliff*]

[*To himself*] Possibly one can be deluded into death when there's no will to live. If he had been where he thought he was, thought would by now be a thing of the past. Is he alive, or dead? [*To* **Gloucester**] Hello, sir! Friend! Do you hear me, sir? Speak! [*To himself*] He might indeed have died. [**Gloucester** *stirs*] But he's recovering! [*Now pretending he is a fisherman at the foot of the cliff*] Who are you, sir?

Gloucester   Go away, and leave me to die.

Edgar   If you'd been anything other than gossamer, feathers, or air, you'd be shattered like an egg after falling from such a height! But you are breathing; you are solid; you aren't bleeding; you can speak; you are in one piece. You have fallen more than the height of ten ships' masts. It's a miracle you are alive. Say something more.

Gloucester   Have I fallen, or not?

Edgar   From the very top of this chalky cliff. Look right up there: you can't see or hear the shrill-voiced lark at that distance. Just look up!

Gloucester   Alas, I have no eyes. Is wretchedness deprived of the benefit of ending itself by death? It was some small comfort when misery could thwart the anger of a tyrant, and frustrate his lofty plans.

Edgar   Give me your arm. [*He helps* **Gloucester** *to stand*] Up, so; how goes it? Can you feel your legs? You are standing up!

Gloucester   Only too well, too well.

Edgar   This is above all
   strangeness.
   Upon the crown o'th'cliff what thing was that
   Which parted from you?

Gloucester   A poor unfortunate beggar.

70 **Edgar**   As I stood here below methought his eyes
   Were two full moons; he had a thousand noses,
   Horns whelked and waved like the enridged sea:
   It was some fiend; therefore, thou happy father,
   Think that the clearest gods, who make them honours
75   Of men's impossibilities, have preserved thee.

Gloucester   I do remember now; henceforth I'll bear
   Affliction till it do cry out itself
   'Enough, enough,' and die. That thing you speak of
   I took it for a man; often 'twould say
80   'The fiend, the fiend': he led me to that place.

Edgar   Bear free and patient thoughts. But who comes here?

[*Enter* **Lear**, *fantastically dressed with wild flowers*]

   The safer sense will ne'er accommodate
   His master thus.

Lear   No, they cannot touch me for coining; I am the King
85   himself.

Edgar   Oh, thou side-piercing sight!

Lear   Nature's above art in that respect. There's your press-
   money. That fellow handles his bow like a crow-keeper: draw
   me a clothier's yard. Look, look! a mouse. Peace, peace! This
90   piece of toasted cheese will do't. There's my gauntlet; I'll
   prove it on a giant. Bring up the brown bills. Oh, well flown

Edgar   This is quite remarkable. On the edge of the cliff, what
was that object who left you?

Gloucester   A poor unfortunate beggar.

Edgar   As I stood here below, I thought his eyes were two full
moons. He had a thousand noses. He had horns that were
bent and twisted like the wavy sea. It was some devil.
Therefore, you lucky old man, assume that the righteous
gods, who are revered for doing the impossible, have
preserved you.

Gloucester   I remember now. In future, I'll bear suffering till it
decides I've endured enough, and lets me die. That thing
you spoke of I thought was a man. It often said, 'The fiend,
the fiend.' He led me to that place.

Edgar   Put your mind at rest. But who comes here?

[**Lear** *enters, ornately dressed with wild flowers. He has lost
his reason*]

No man in his right mind would ever get himself up like this.

Lear   No, they can't accuse me of counterfeiting. I am the
King himself!

Edgar   What a heartbreaking sight!

Lear   In matters of that sort, art takes second place to the real
thing! [*As if to a recruit*] There's your King's shilling!
[*Jumping from one delusion to another*] That man there
handles his bow like a scarecrow. Draw that bowstring out
a full arm's length! [*He spots something at his feet*] Look,
look, a mouse! Sh! Sh! This piece of toasted cheese will
catch it. [*He tears off an imaginary chunk, then suddenly
throws it to the ground*] There's my gauntlet; I'd challenge a
giant even. [*He's a General now*] Bring up the pikemen! [*He
follows an imaginary arrow in its flight*] Oh, well-flown, bird!

bird; i'th'clout, i'th'clout: hewgh! Give the word.

Edgar   Sweet marjoram.

Lear   Pass.

95 **Gloucester**   I know that voice.

Lear   Ha! Goneril, with a white beard! They flattered me
like a dog, and told me I had the white hairs in my beard ere
the black ones were there. To say 'ay' and 'no' to every thing
that I said! 'Ay' and 'no' too was no good divinity. When the
100 rain came to wet me once and the wind to make me chatter,
when the thunder would not peace at my bidding, there I
found 'em, there I smelt 'em out. Go to, they are not men
o'their words: they told me I was every thing; 'tis a lie, I am
not ague-proof.

105 **Gloucester**   The trick of that voice I do well remember:
Is't not the King?

Lear   Ay, every inch a king:
When I do stare, see how the subject quakes.
I pardon that man's life. What was thy cause?
Adultery?
110 Thou shalt not die: die for adultery! No:
The wren goes to't, and the small gilded fly
Does lecher in my sight.
Let copulation thrive; for Gloucester's bastard son
Was kinder to his father than my daughters
115 Got 'tween the lawful sheets. To't, Luxury, pell-mell!
For I lack soldiers. Behold yond simp'ring dame,
Whose face between her forks presages snow;
That minces virtue, and does shake the head
To hear of pleasure's name;
120 The fitchew nor the soiled horse goes to't
With a more riotous appetite.
Down from the waist they are Centaurs,

A bull's eye, a bull's eye! Swish! [*Noticing* **Edgar**] Give the password.

Edgar   Sweet marjoram.

Lear   Pass.

Gloucester   I know that voice.

Lear   [*peering at him*] Aha, Goneril with a white beard! They flattered me like fawning dogs, and told me I was a shrewd one even before I grew my first beard. To think they said 'Yes' and 'No' to everything I said! 'Yes' and 'No' isn't sound theology. When the rain came to drench me once, and the wind made me shiver; when the thunder wouldn't stop when I told it to, then I rumbled them; that's when I smelt them out! Pah, they're not men of their words. They told me I was all-powerful. It was a lie. I'm not immune from sickness.

Gloucester   The tone of that voice I well remember. Are you not the King?

Lear   Yes, every inch a king! When I look hard at a man, see how he trembles! I pardon that man's life. What was your crime? Adultery? You shall not die. Die for adultery? No, even the wren does it, and the little gold-coloured fly has it off in front of my eyes. Let copulation prosper; Gloucester's bastard son was kinder to his father than my legitimate daughters. Get at it, lust, flat out. I need soldiers! Look at that innocent-looking female, whose face suggests she's frigid, who looks so goody-goody, who deplores all sexy talk; polecats and stallions aren't so hungry for it! From the waist down they're animals, albeit they're women higher up.

Though women all above:
But to the girdle do the gods inherit,
125 Beneath is all the fiend's: there's hell, there's darkness,
There is the sulphurous pit – burning, scalding,
Stench, consumption; fie, fie, fie! pah, pah!
Give me an ounce of civet, good apothecary,
To sweeten my imagination.
There's money for thee.

130 **Gloucester**   Oh let me kiss that hand.

Lear   Let me wipe it first; it smells of mortality.

Gloucester   Oh ruined piece of nature! This great world
Shall so wear out to naught. Dost thou know me?

Lear   I remember thine eyes well enough. Dost thou squiny
at me?
135 No, do thy worst, blind Cupid; I'll not love.
Read thou this challenge; mark but the penning of it.

Gloucester   Were all thy letters suns, I could not see.

Edgar   [*Aside*] I would not take this from report; it is,
And my heart breaks at it.

140 **Lear**   Read.

Gloucester   What, with the case of eyes?

Lear   Oh, ho! are you there with me? No eyes in your head,
nor no money in your purse? Your eyes are in a heavy case,
your purse in a light: yet you see how this world goes.

145 **Gloucester**   I see it feelingly.

Lear   What, art mad? A man may see how this world goes
with no eyes. Look with thine ears: see how yond justice rails
upon yond simple thief. Hark, in thine ear: change places,
and, handy-dandy, which is the justice, which is the thief?
150 Thou hast seen a farmer's dog bark at a beggar?

226

The gods hold sway down to the belt; below is all the devil's. *There* is hell; *there* is darkness; *there* is the sulphurous pit – burning, scalding; stench, corruption! [*His mind is tormented with horror and repugnance*] Ugh, ugh, ugh! Pah! Pah! [*To* **Gloucester**] Give me an ounce of perfume, dear chemist, to sweeten my imagination! There's some money for you.

Gloucester   Oh, let me kiss your hand.

Lear   Let me wipe it first. It smells of death.

Gloucester   Oh, what a ruin of a man! So too will the universe come to its end. Do you know me?

Lear   I remember your eyes well enough. Are you squinting at me? No, do your worst, blind sinfulness; I won't indulge. [*Obsessed with* **Gloucester**'s *affliction*] Read this challenge. Note how it's written.

Gloucester   If all the letters were suns, I could not see them.

Edgar   [*aside*] I wouldn't believe this if I heard about it. But it's a fact, and my heart breaks at it.

Lear   Read.

Gloucester   What, with holes for eyes?

Lear   Oh, ho! Is that your game? No eyes in your head, and no money in your purse? Sad for your eyes; bad for your purse. But that's the way of the world, you see.

Gloucester   I see by the feel of things.

Lear   What, are you mad? A man doesn't need eyes to see how this world goes. Look with your ears. See how that magistrate rebukes that humble thief. A word in your ear. Switch places, and – take your choice – which is the magistrate, which the thief? You've seen a farmer's dog bark at a beggar?

Gloucester   Ay, sir.

Lear   And the creature run from the cur? There thou
      might'st behold
      The great image of Authority:
      A dog's obeyed in office.
155   Thou rascal beadle, hold thy bloody hand!
      Why dost thou lash that whore? Strip thine own back;
      Thou hotly lusts to use her in that kind
      For which thou whipp'st her. The usurer hangs the
         cozener.
      Through tattered clothes small vices do appear;
160   Robes and furred gowns hide all. Plate sin with gold,
      And the strong lance of justice hurtless breaks:
      Arm it in rags, a pigmy's straw does pierce it.
      None does offend, none, I say, none; I'll able 'em:
      Táke that of me, my friend, who have the power
165   To seal the accuser's lips. Get thee glass eyes;
      And, like a scurvy politician, seem
      To see the things thou dost not. Now, now, now, now;
      Pull off my boots; harder, harder; so.

Edgar   [*Aside*] Oh, matter and impertinency mixed;
170   Reason in madness.

Lear   If thou wilt weep my fortunes, take my eyes;
      I know thee well enough; thy name is Gloucester;
      Thou must be patient; we came crying hither:
      Thou know'st the first time that we smell the air
175   We wawl and cry. I will preach to thee: mark.

Gloucester   Alack, alack the day!

Lear   When we are born, we cry that we are come
      To this great stage of fools. This's a good block!
      It were a delicate stratagem to shoe
180   A troop of horse with felt; I'll put't in proof,

Gloucester   Yes, sir.

Lear   And the man run away from the cur? That symbolizes
Authority: a dog is obeyed when it's got an official position.
[*Addressing an imaginary officer of the law*] You rascally
constable, stay your blood-stained hand! Why are you
lashing that whore? Strip the skin off your own back; you're
lusting for the very thing you're whipping her for. The big
crooks hang the petty ones. The petty crimes of the poor are
always obvious; robes and fur-lined gowns hide everything.
Cover sin with gold armour and the strong lance of justice
shatters on contact. Cover it with rags, and the puny
weapon of a pigmy will pierce through it. Nobody sins:
nobody, I say, nobody; I'll vouch for them. Take my word for
it, my friend: I who have the power to silence all
prosecutors. Get youself glass eyes. Like a vile opportunist,
pretend to see what you actually cannot. [*As if talking to
his valet*] Now, now, now, now – pull off my boots! Harder,
harder; that's right.

Edgar   [*aside*] Sense and nonsense combined. Sanity in
madness!

Lear   If you want to weep for my misfortunes, have my eyes. I
know you well enough. Your name is Gloucester. You must
be patient. We came crying into this world; you know, the
first time that we smell the air we wail and cry. I'll preach to
you – listen.

Gloucester   Alas, alas the day!

Lear   When we are born, we cry because we've come to this
great stage of fools. [*He stands on a tree stump to continue
his 'sermon'*] This is a good mounting-block! It would be an
ingenious idea to shoe a troop of horses with felt. I must

And when I have stolen upon these sons-in-law,
Then, kill, kill, kill, kill, kill, kill!

[*Enter a* **Gentleman,** *with Attendants*]

Gentleman   Oh here he is; lay hand upon him. Sir,
Your most dear daughter –

185 **Lear**   No rescue? What, a prisoner! I am even
The natural fool of fortune. Use me well;
You shall have ransom. Let me have surgeons;
I am cut to the brains.

Gentleman   You shall have any thing.

Lear   No seconds? All myself?
190 Why this would make a man a man of salt,
To use his eyes for garden water-pots,
Ay, and laying autumn's dust. I will die bravely,
Like a smug bridegroom. What! I will be jovial:
Come, come; I am a king, masters, know you that?

195 **Gentleman**   You are a royal one, and we obey you.

Lear   Then there's life in't. Nay, if you get it, you shall get
it by running. Sa, sa, sa, sa.

[*Exit running. Attendants follow*]

Gentleman   A sight most pitiful in the meanest wretch,
Past speaking of in a king! Thou hast one daughter,
200 Who redeems nature from the general curse
Which twain have brought her to.

Edgar   Hail, gentle sir!

Gentleman   Sir, speed you: what's your will?

Edgar   Do you hear aught, sir, of a battle toward?

give it a try. And when I've crept up behind these
sons-in-law, then [*he jumps down, shouting*] kill, kill, kill,
kill, kill, kill!

[*A* **Gentleman** *enters, with Attendants*]

Gentleman   Oh, here he is. Take hold of him. Sir, your most
dear daughter –

Lear   [*thinking he has been captured in war*] No rescue? What,
a prisoner? I was born unlucky. Treat me well. You shall
have ransom. Get me doctors. My head's split.

Gentleman   You shall have whatever you want.

Lear   No supporters? Just me alone? Why, this would make a
man cry salt tears, to have his eyes used for garden
watering-cans, yes, and to lay the dust of autumn. I shall die
splendidly, like a bridegroom all dressed up. What, I'll be
jovial! Come, come, I am a King, gentleman. Do you realize
that?

Gentleman   You are a royal person, and we obey you.

Lear   Then there's still hope. Come, if you want it, you'll have
to run for it! [*He runs off, making noises like a hunter*] Sa,
sa, sa, sa! [*The Attendants pursue him*]

Gentleman   A most pitiful sight even if it featured the lowliest
of wretches: it's beyond words when it involves a king! You
have one daughter who redeems nature from the universal
curse her two sisters have brought upon it.

Edgar   Greetings, sir!

Gentleman   Sir, my compliments: what can I do for you?

Edgar   Have you heard anything, sir, of an impending battle?

Gentleman   Most sure and vulgar; every one hears that,
Which can distinguish sound.

205 **Edgar**   But, by your favour,
How near's the other army?

Gentleman   Near, and on speedy foot; the main descry
Stands on the hourly thought.

Edgar   I thank you, sir: that's all.

Gentleman   Though that the Queen on special cause is there,
210   Her army is moved on.

Edgar   I thank you, sir.

[*Exit* **Gentleman**]

Gloucester   You ever-gentle gods, take my breath from me:
Let not my worser spirit tempt me again
To die before you please!

Edgar   Well pray you, father.

215 **Gloucester**   Now, good sir, what are you?

Edgar   A most poor man, made tame to fortune's blows;
Who, by the art of known and feeling sorrows,
Am pregnant to good pity. Give me your hand,
I'll lead you to some biding.

Gloucester   Hearty thanks:
220   The bounty and the benison of heaven
To boot, and boot!

[*Enter* **Oswald**]

Oswald   A proclaimed prize! Most happy!
That eyeless head of thine was first framed flesh
To raise my fortunes. Thou old unhappy traitor,

Gentleman   Certainly; it's common knowledge. Everyone's heard about it who isn't deaf.

Edgar   But, if I may ask; how near is the other army?

Gentleman   Very near, and advancing swiftly. We expect to see the main body any hour now.

Edgar   Thank you, sir: that's all.

Gentleman   Though the Queen is here for special reasons, her army has moved on.

Edgar   I thank you, sir.

[*The* **Gentleman** *leaves*]

Gloucester   You ever-merciful gods, take my life. Don't let my evil side tempt me again to die before it's your will!

Edgar   Well, prayed, father.

Gloucester   Now, good sir, who are you?

Edgar   A very poor man, broken by misfortune. Experience of sorrow has predisposed me towards pity. Give me your hand. I'll lead you to some shelter.

Gloucester   Hearty thanks. May the bounty and blessing of heaven reward you, in addition to my gratitude.

[**Oswald** *enters*]

Oswald   A man with a price on his head! Most fortunate! That eyeless head of yours was preordained to make my fortune! You miserable old traitor, think of your sins. [*He draws his*

233

Briefly thyself remember: the sword is out
That must destroy thee.

225 **Gloucester**   Now let thy friendly hand
Put strength enough to't.   [**Edgar** *interposes*]

Oswald   Wherefore, bold peasant
Dar'st thou support a published traitor? Hence;
Lest that the infection of his fortune take
Like hold on thee. Let go his arm.

230 **Edgar**   Chill not let go, zir, without vurther 'casion.

Oswald   Let go, slave, or thou diest.

Edgar   Good gentleman, go your gait, and let poor volk pass.
An 'chud ha' bin zwaggered out of my life, 'twould not ha'
ben zo long as 'tis by a vortnight. Nay, come not near th'old
235 man; keep out, che vor' ye, or ise try whither your costard or
my ballow be the harder. Chill be plain with you.

Oswald   Out, dunghill!

Edgar   Chill pick your teeth, zir. Come; no matter vor your
foins.

[*They fight, and* **Edgar** *knocks him down*]

240 **Oswald**   Slave, thou hast slain me. Villain, take my purse.
If ever thou wilt thrive, bury my body;
And give the letters which thou find'st about me
To Edmund Earl of Gloucester; seek him out
Upon the British party. Oh, untimely death.
245 Death!   [*Dies*]

Edgar   I know thee well: a serviceable villain;
As duteous to the vices of thy mistress
As badness would desire.

Gloucester   What! is he dead?

sword from its scabbard] The sword is out that must
destroy you.

Gloucester   [*ready to die*] Thrust hard with your friendly hand.

[**Edgar** *steps forward in his father's defence*]

Oswald   You impertinent peasant, how dare you defend an
outlawed traitor? Go, before you suffer the same fate as
him. Let go his arm.

Edgar   [*assuming a regional accent*] I'll not let go, sir, without
a better reason.

Oswald   Let go, wretch, or you'll die.

Edgar   Good gentleman, be on your way, and let us poor folk
move on. If I could have been cheated out of my life, I'd
have lost it weeks ago. No, don't come near the old man.
Keep off, I tell you, or I'll test which is harder – your head or
my stick. That's the truth.

Oswald   Get away, you slob!

Edgar   I'll pick your teeth for you, sir. Come on, I'm not scared
of your sword-thrusts. [*They fight;* **Edgar** *knocks* **Oswald**
down]

Oswald   Wretch, you've killed me. Peasant, take my purse. If
you ever hope to prosper, bury my body. Give the letters
you'll find on me to Edmund, Earl of Gloucester. Find him on
the English side. Oh, such untimely death! Death . . . [*He
dies*]

Edgar   I know you well. An unscrupulous villain, as dutiful in
serving the vices of your mistress as wickedness could
desire.

Gloucester   What, is he dead?

Edgar   Sit you down, father; rest you.
250   Let's see these pockets: the letters that he speaks of
May be my friends. He's dead; I am only sorry
He had no other deathsman. Let us see:
Leave, gentle wax; and, manners, blame us not:
To know our enemies' minds, we rip their hearts;
255   Their papers is more lawful.   [*Reads*]

Let our reciprocal vows be remembered. You have many
opportunities to cut him off; if your will want not, time
and place will be fruitfully offered. There is nothing done
if he return the conqueror; then am I the prisoner, and his
260   *bed my gaol; from the loathed warmth whereof deliver*
me, and supply the place for your labour.
        Your wife, so I would say –
        Affectionate servant,
        GONERIL.

265   Oh undistinguished space of woman's will!
A plot upon her virtuous husband's life,
And the exchange my brother! Here, in the sands,
Thee I'll rake up, the post unsanctified
Of murderous lechers; and in the mature time
270   With this ungracious paper strike the sight
Of the death-practised Duke. For him 'tis well
That of thy death and business I can tell.

Gloucester   The King is mad: how stiff is my vile sense
That it stand up, and have ingenious feeling
275   Of my huge sorrows! Better I were distract:
So should my thoughts be severed from my griefs,
And woes by wrong imaginations lose
The knowledge of themselves.

Edgar   Sit down, father, and rest. Let's see what's in these pockets; the letters he referred to might do me some good. [*As he searches, he answers* **Gloucester's** *question*] He's dead. I am only sorry he didn't have some other executioner. [*He finds the letter*] Let's see. [*He breaks the seal*] If I may, dear wax! Don't say this is bad manners; to know what's in our enemies' minds, we rip their hearts. Ripping open their letters is more lawful. [*He reads the contents aloud*]

> *Remember our mutual vows. You'll have many chances to see him off. If you've got the determination, there'll be ample time and opportunity. If he comes back the victor, we shall have achieved nothing. Then I would be his prisoner, and our marital bed would be my gaol. Save me from the intimate horror of that, and assure yourself of physical contentment.*
>> *Your wife, as I would wish, and*
>>> *Devoted lover,*
>>>> *Goneril.*

Oh, how infinite is woman's lust! A plot to kill her virtuous husband, and my brother to replace him! [*Addressing* **Oswald**] Here, on these sands, the unholy burial-place of murderous lechers, I'll cover your body up. When the time is ripe, I'll show this wicked letter to the Duke whose life is threatened. It's fortunate for him that I can report both your death and the business you were about.

Gloucester   The King is mad. How obstinate my mind is, that I should stay sane, and be conscious of my great distress! It would be better if I were mad, then my thoughts and my griefs would be separated, and in my fantasies woes would cease to have any meaning.

[*The sound of drums is heard*]

Edgar   Give me your hand:
    Far off, methinks, I hear the beaten drum.
280 Come, father, I'll bestow you with a friend.

                                 [*Exeunt*]

Scene 7

A tent in the French camp. Enter **Cordelia, Kent, Doctor,** *and*
Gentleman

Cordelia   Oh thou good Kent! How shall I live and work
    To match thy goodness? My life will be too short,
    And every measure fail me.

Kent   To be acknowledged, madam, is o'er-paid.
5   All my reports go with the modest truth,
    No more nor clipped, but so.

Cordelia   Be better suited:
    These weeds are memories of those worser hours:
    I prithee, put them off.

Kent   Pardon, dear madam;
    Yet to be known shortens my made intent:
10 My boon I make it that you know me not
    Till time and I think meet.

Cordelia   Then be't so, my good lord. [*To the Doctor*] How
    does the King?

Doctor   Madam, sleeps still.

15 **Cordelia**   Oh you kind gods,
    Cure this great breach in his abused nature!

Edgar Give me your hand. I think I can hear drum-beats in the distance. Come, father: I'll leave you with a friend.

[*They go*]

Scene 7

A tent in the French camp. **Cordelia, Kent,** *a* **Doctor** *and a* **Gentleman** *enter*

Cordelia Oh, good Kent! How shall I live and work to equal your goodness? My life will be too short, and I'll fail by every standard.

Kent To be appreciated, madam, is to be overpaid. All I've described is the honest truth, no more, no less, just as it is.

Cordelia Change your clothes. These garments are reminders of those bad times. Please, take them off.

Kent With respect, madam. To be recognized now runs counter to my plans. I'd ask the favour of your not knowing me till I think the time is right.

Cordelia So be it, my good lord. [*To the* **Doctor**] How is the King?

Doctor Madam, he's still sleeping.

Cordelia Oh, you kind gods, cure this great fracture in his

Th'untuned and jarring sense, oh, wind up
Of this child-changed father.

Doctor   So please your majesty
That we may wake the King? He hath slept long.

20 **Cordelia**   Be governed by your knowledge, and proceed
I'th'sway of your own will. Is he arrayed?

[*Enter* **Lear** *in a chair carried by Servants*]

Gentleman   Ay, madam, in the heaviness of sleep
We put fresh garments on him.

Doctor   Be by, good madam, when we do awake him;
I doubt not of his temperance.

25 **Cordelia**   Very well.

Doctor   Please you draw near. Louder the music there!

Cordelia   Oh my dear father! Restoration hang
Thy medicine on my lips, and let this kiss
Repair those violent harms that my two sisters
Have in thy reverence made!

30 **Kent**   Kind and dear Princess!

Cordelia   Had you not been their father, these white flakes
Did challenge pity of them. Was this a face
To be opposed against the warring winds?
To stand against the deep dread-bolted thunder?
35   In the most terrible and nimble stroke
Of quick, cross lightning? To watch – poor perdu! –
With this thin helm? Mine enemy's dog,
Though he had bit me, should have stood that night
Against my fire. And wast thou fain, poor father,
40   To hovel thee with swine and rogues forlorn,

240

tormented mind! Tune the discordant senses of this childlike
father!

Doctor   Would your majesty allow us to wake the King? He
has slept long.

Cordelia   Act according to your knowledge of these things. Do
as you think best. Is he dressed?

[**Lear** *enters in a chair carried by Servants*]

Gentleman   Yes, madam. While he was fast asleep we put
clean clothes on him.

Doctor   Be at his side, good madam, when we waken him. I
do not doubt that he'll be normal.

Cordelia   Very well.

[*Soft music is played*]

Doctor   [*to the Servants*] Come nearer. Play louder there!

Cordelia   Oh, my dear father! May my lips convey healing, and
let this kiss cure the damage that my two sisters have done
to you. [*She kisses him on the forehead*]

Kent   Kind and dear princess!

Cordelia   [*stroking his hair*] If they were not of your own
begetting, these snowy locks would merit pity. Was this a
face to battle with antagonistic winds? To withstand the
thunderbolts of bass-rumbling thunder? To be in the midst
of flashes of terrifying lightning? To be up at night – poor
hopeless one! – with this thin head-covering? My enemy's
dog, even if it had bitten me, would have had a place in
front of my fire that night. Were you obliged, poor father, to
slum it with swine and homeless vagabonds, in scanty and

In short and musty straw? Alack, alack!
'Tis wonder that thy life and wits at once
Had not concluded all. He wakes; speak to him.

Doctor   Madam, do you; 'tis fittest.

45 **Cordelia**   How does my royal lord? How fares your majesty?

Lear   You do me wrong to take me out o'th'grave;
Thou art a soul in bliss; but I am bound
Upon a wheel of fire, that mine own tears
Do scald like molten lead.

Cordelia   Sir, do you know me?

50 **Lear**   You are a spirit, I know; where did you die?

Cordelia   Still, still, far wide.

Doctor   He's scarce awake; let him alone awhile.

Lear   Where have I been? Where am I? Fair daylight?
I am mightily abused. I should e'en die with pity
55 To see another thus. I know not what to say.
I will not swear these are my hands: let's see;
I feel this pin prick. Would I were assured
Of my condition!

Cordelia   Oh, look upon me, sir,
And hold your hand in benediction o'er me.
No, sir, you must not kneel.

60 **Lear**   Pray, do not mock me:
I am a very foolish fond old man,
Fourscore and upward, not an hour more or less;
And, to deal plainly,
I fear I am not in my perfect mind.
65 Methinks I should know you and know this man;
Yet I am doubtful: for I am mainly ignorant
What place this is, and all the skill I have
Remembers not these garments; nor I know not

musty-smelling straw? Alas, alas! It's amazing that your life
and your sanity didn't succumb together. He is waking.
Speak to him.

Doctor Madam, do you. It's best.

Cordelia How is my royal lord? How fares your majesty?

Lear It's wrong of you to take me out of the grave. You are a
soul in a state of bliss; but I am in hell, tied to a wheel of
fire. My own tears scald like molten lead.

Cordelia Sir, do you know me?

Lear You are a spirit, I know. Where did you die?

Cordelia [*to the* **Doctor**] He is still confused.

Doctor He's hardly awake. Leave him alone a moment.

Lear Where have I been? Where am I? Is this real daylight? I
was mightily deluded. I'd die with pity to see someone else
like this. I don't know what to say. I'm not sure these are
my hands – let's see. [*He winces as he tests with the point
of a brooch*] I feel this pin-prick. I wish I could sort things
out.

Cordelia Oh, look at me, sir, and hold your hand in blessing
over me!

[**Lear** *looks at her, then falls at her feet*]

No, sir: you must not kneel!

Lear Please, do not mock me. I am a very foolish old man, in
his dotage; over 80 years old, not an hour more or less. To
tell you frankly, I'm afraid I'm not in my right mind. I think I
should know you and this man, but I am uncertain. I'm
entirely ignorant about what this place is, and even if I try
very hard I can't remember these clothes; nor do I know

Where I did lodge last night. Do not laugh at me;
For, as I am a man, I think this lady
70   To be my child Cordelia.

Cordelia   And so I am, I am.

Lear   Be your tears wet? Yes, faith. I pray, weep not:
If you have poison for me, I will drink it.
I know you do not love me; for your sisters
75   Have, as I do remember, done me wrong:
You have some cause, they have not.

Cordelia   No cause, no cause.

Lear   Am I in France?

Kent   In your own kingdom, sir.

Lear   Do not abuse me.

Doctor   Be comforted, good madam; the great rage,
80   You see, is killed in him: and yet it is danger
To make him even o'er the time he has lost.
Desire him to go in; trouble him no more
Till further settling.

Cordelia   Will't please your highness walk?

Lear   You must bear with me.
85   Pray you now, forget and forgive: I am old and foolish.

[*Exeunt* **Lear, Cordelia, Doctor,** *and Attendants*]

Gentleman   Holds it true, sir, that the Duke of Cornwall was
so slain?

Kent   Most certain, sir.

Gentleman   Who is conductor of his people?

90 **Kent**   As 'tis said, the bastard son of Gloucester.

where I stayed last night. Do not laugh at me; as I'm a man, I think this lady is my child, Cordelia . . .

Cordelia   And so I am, I am!

Lear   Are your tears wet? [*He tries them*] Yes, indeed. Please don't weep. If you have poison for me. I will drink it. I know you do not love me. Your sisters have, now I remember, done me wrong. You have some cause. They have not.

Cordelia   [*shaking her head, weeping*] No cause, no cause.

Lear   [*to* Kent] Am I in France?

Kent   In your own kingdom, sir.

Lear   Do not mock me.

Doctor   Take comfort, madam. The delirium you see has subsided in him. It's dangerous to fill in the gaps in his memory. Request him to go in. Don't trouble him any more till he's calmer.

Cordelia   Would your highness like to walk? [*She offers her arm*]

Lear   You must be patient with me. Please now: forget and forgive. I am old and foolish.

[**Lear, Cordelia, Doctor** *and Attendants leave*]

Gentleman   Is it a fact that the Duke of Cornwall was killed like that?

Kent   Absolutely, sir.

Gentleman   Who has taken command of his people?

Kent   The bastard son of Gloucester, so it's said.

Gentleman   They say Edgar, his banished son, is with the Earl of Kent in Germany.

Kent   Report is changeable. 'Tis time to look about; the powers of the kingdom approach apace.

95 **Gentleman**   The arbitrement is like to be bloody. Fare you well, sir.

[*Exit*]

Kent   My point and period will be throughly wrought, Or well or ill, as this day's battle's fought.

[*Exit*]

Gentleman   They say Edgar, his banished son, is with the Earl of Kent in Germany.

Kent   Rumours come and go. We must prepare. The armies of the kingdom will soon be here.

Gentleman   The battle is likely to be a bloody one. Farewell, sir.

[He goes]

Kent   The full stop at the end of my life will be placed for good or ill according to the outcome of today's battle.

[He goes]

Act five

Scene 1

The British camp near Dover. Enter, with drum and colours,
Edmund, Regan, *Officers, Soldiers, and others*

Edmund   Know of the Duke if his last purpose hold,
Or whether since he is advised by aught
To change the course; he's full of alteration
And self-reproving; bring his constant pleasure.

> [*To an Officer, who goes out*]

5 **Regan**   Our sister's man is certainly miscarried.

Edmund   'Tis to be doubted, Madam.

Regan   Now, sweet lord,
You know the goodness I intend upon you:
Tell me, but truly, but then speak the truth,
Do you not love my sister?

Edmund   In honoured love.

10 **Regan**   But have you never found my brother's way
To the forfended place?

Edmund   That thought abuses you.

Regan   I am doubtful that you have been conjunct
And bosomed with her, as far as we call hers.

Edmund   No, by mine honour, madam.

15 **Regan**   I never shall endure her: dear my lord,
Be not familiar with her.

Act five

Scene 1

The British Camp at Dover. Enter **Edmund**, **Regan**, *Officers, Soldiers and others*

Edmund *[to an Officer]* Find out from the Duke if he's sticking to his last plan, or whether he's had any reason to alter course. He changes his mind all the time and is full of insecurity. Bring his final decision.

[The Officer salutes and goes]

Regan Our sister's steward has come to some harm.

Edmund I'm afraid so, madam.

Regan Now, sweet lord, you know that I intend to do you some good. Tell me, honestly, even if it's unpalatable: don't you love my sister?

Edmund In an honourable way.

Regan *[trying to be delicate about personal matters]* But have you never trespassed on my brother-in-law's territory?

Edmund That thought is worrying you.

Regan I fear you may have got very close to her . . . gone all the way . . .

Edmund No, on my honour, madam!

Regan I couldn't tolerate her. Dear my lord, don't be intimate with her.

249

Edmund   Fear me not.
She and the Duke her husband!

[*Enter, with drum and colours,* **Albany, Goneril,** *and Soldiers*]

Goneril   [*Aside*] I had rather lose the battle than that sister
Should loosen him and me.

20 **Albany**   Our very loving sister, well be-met.
Sir, this I hear; the King is come to his daughter,
With others whom the rigour of our state
Forced to cry out. Where I could not be honest,
I never yet was valiant: for this business,
25   It touches us, as France invades our land,
Not bolds the King, with others, whom, I fear,
Most just and heavy causes make oppose.

Edmund   Sir, you speak nobly.

Regan   Why is this reasoned?

Goneril   Combine together 'gainst the enemy;
30   For these domestic and particular broils
Are not the question here.

Albany   Let's then determine
With the ancient of war on our proceeding.

Edmund   I shall attend you presently at your tent.

Regan   Sister, you'll go with us?

35 **Goneril**   No.

Regan   'Tis most convenient; pray go with us.

Goneril   [*Aside*] Oh, ho! I know the riddle. I will go.

[*As they are going out enter* **Edgar,** *disguised.*]

Edmund   Don't worry about me. [*A drum sounds*] Here she is, with the Duke her husband!

[**Albany** *and* **Goneril** *enter, followed by Soldiers*]

Goneril   [*aside*] I'd rather lose the battle than have my sister come between him and me.

Albany   [*bowing politely to* **Regan**] Our very loving sister: greetings. [*To* **Edmund**] Sir, I hear this: the King has gone to his daughter, along with others forced to defect as a result of our harsh rule. I've never had any stomach for shady matters. As for this business, it concerns us only because France invades our land: not that we wish to confront the King and those others whose genuine grievances, I fear, make them opposed to us.

Edmund   Sir, you speak nobly.

Regan   Why bother to say all this?

Goneril   Unite against the enemy; these private quarrels are irrelevant.

Albany   Then let's consult the experts on our tactics.

Edmund   I'll join you at your tent immediately. [*He makes to leave*]

Regan   Sister, you'll go with us?

Goneril   No.

Regan   It's only right that you should. Go with us.

Goneril   [*aside*] Oh yes. I know your game . . . [*She suspects her sister cannot trust her alone with Edmund*] I'll go.

[*Before anyone can leave,* **Edgar** *enters, disguised*]

Edgar   If e'er your grace had speech with man so poor,
Hear me one word.

Albany   I'll overtake you.

                         [*Exeunt all but* **Albany** *and* **Edgar**]

                              Speak.

40 **Edgar**   Before you fight the battle, ope this letter.
If you have victory, let the trumpet sound
For him that brought it: wretched though I seem,
I can produce a champion that will prove
What is avouched there. If you miscarry,
45   Your business of the world hath so an end,
And machination ceases. Fortune love you!

Albany   Stay till I have read the letter.

Edgar   I was forbid it.
When time shall serve, let but the herald cry,
And I'll appear again.

Albany   .Why, fare thee well:
50   I will o'erlook thy paper.

                                   [*Exit* **Edgar**]

   [*Re-enter* **Edmund**]

Edmund   The enemy's in view; draw up your powers.
Here is the guess of their true strength and forces
By diligent discovery; but your haste
Is now urged on you.

Albany   We will greet the time.

                                   [*Exit*]

Edgar   [*to* **Albany**] If your grace would deign to speak to so
poor a man, may I have a word with you?

Albany   [*indicating to the others to carry on*] I'll catch up with
you.

> [**Edmund, Regan, Goneril,** *Officers, Soldiers and Attendants*
> *leave*]

Edgar   [*to* **Albany**] Before you fight the battle, open this letter.
If you win, sound the trumpet to summon me. Humble
though I seem, I can produce a champion who will prove
what is said here. If you lose, you won't be concerned about
worldly things, and there all matters will end. Good luck!

Albany   Stay till I've read the letter.

Edgar   I was forbidden to. At the appropriate time, just let the
herald's trumpet sound, and I'll appear again.

Albany   Well, fare you well. I'll read your letter.

> [**Edgar** *goes*]

[**Edmund** *returns*]

Edmund   The evening is in sight. Bring up your troops.
[*Handing* **Albany** *a note*] Here's the estimate of their
equipment and numbers, determined by our scouts. You
must be quick now.

Albany   We'll rise to the challenge.

> [*He goes*]

55 **Edmund**   To both these sisters have I sworn my love;
　　　　　Each jealous of the other, as the stung
　　　　　Are of the adder. Which of them shall I take?
　　　　　Both? one? or neither? Neither can be enjoyed
　　　　　If both remain alive: to take the widow
60　　　Exasperates, makes mad her sister Goneril;
　　　　　And hardly shall I carry out my side,
　　　　　Her husband being alive. Now then, we'll use
　　　　　His countenance for the battle; which being done,
　　　　　Let her who would be rid of him devise
65　　　His speedy taking off. As for the mercy
　　　　　Which he intends to Lear and to Cordelia,
　　　　　The battle done, and they within our power,
　　　　　Shall never see his pardon; for my state
　　　　　Stands on me to defend, not to debate.

　　　　　　　　　　　　　　　　　　　　　　　　[*Exit*]

Scene 2

A field between the two camps. Alarum within. Enter, with drum
and colours, **Lear, Cordelia,** *and their forces; and exeunt.*

　　　[*Enter* **Edgar** *and* **Gloucester**]

Edgar   Here, father, take the shadow of this tree
　　　　　For your good host; pray that the right may thrive.
　　　　　If ever I return to you again,
　　　　　I'll bring you comfort.

Gloucester　　　　　　Grace go with you, sir!

　　　　　　　　　　　　　　　　　　　　　　　[*Exit Edgar*]

Edmund I have sworn my love to both these sisters. Each is
suspicious of the other, as those who are bitten are wary
of the snake. Which of them shall I have? Both? One? Or
neither? Neither can be enjoyed if both remain alive. To take
the widow would exasperate, infuriate, her sister Goneril.
But with *her* husband still alive, I wouldn't find it easy to
play a winning game. So for now we'll use him as a front
man in the battle. When that's over, it's up to her who
wants to be rid of him to work out how to see him off. As
for the mercy he intends to show Lear and Cordelia, once
the battle's over and they are at our mercy, they'll never see
his pardon. My interests are best served by action rather
than thought.

[*He goes*]

Scene 2

A field between the two camps. Noises of war. **Lear** *and*
Cordelia *cross the stage with some of their army, and leave.*
Edgar *enters with* **Gloucester**

Edgar Here, father, shelter in the shade of this hospitable
tree. Pray that right triumphs. If ever I return to you again,
I'll bring you comforting news.

Gloucester Grace go with you, sir!

[*Edgar leaves*]

[*Alarum; afterwards a retreat. Re-enter* **Edgar**]

5 **Edgar**   Away, old man! Give me thy hand: away!
King Lear hath lost, he and his daughter ta'en.
Give me thy hand; come on.

Gloucester   No further, sir; a man may rot even here.

Edgar   What, in ill thoughts again? Men must endure
10   Their going hence, even as their coming hither;
Ripeness is all. Come on.

Gloucester   And that's true too.

[*Exeunt*]

Scene 3

*The British camp near Dover. Enter, in conquest, with drum and
colours,* **Edmund, Lear** *and* **Cordelia,** *prisoners; Officers, Soldiers, etc.*

Edmund   Some officers take them away: good guard,
Until their greater pleasures first be known
That are to censure them.

Cordelia   We are not the first
Who, with best meaning, have incurred the worst.
5   For thee, oppressed King, I am cast down;
Myself could else out-frown false fortune's frown.
Shall we not see these daughters and these sisters?

[*The sounds of war grow louder. A retreat is sounded.*
Edgar *returns, dismayed*]

Edgar   We must go, old man! Give me your hand. [*He tries to pull* **Gloucester** *to his feet*] Let's go! King Lear has lost. He and his daughter have been captured. Give me your hand. Come on!

Gloucester   [*resisting*] No further, sir. A man can die well enough here.

Edgar   What, depressed again? Men must endure dying just as they do being born. Being prepared for it is what matters. Come on.

Gloucester   That's true, too.

[*He rises to his feet and they leave*]

Scene 3

The British Camp near Dover. Drums and flags herald the entrance of **Edmund** *in victory, and* **Lear** *and* **Cordelia** *in defeat, as prisoners. Soldiers guard them*

Edmund   Some officers take them away. Guard them well, till the wishes of our leaders, who will decide their fate, are known.

Cordelia   We are not the first to suffer the worst from the best of intentions. For you — a suffering King — I am defeated: for myself I could have faced ill-fortune and won. Shall we see these 'daughters', these 'sisters'?

257

Lear   No, no, no, no! Come, let's away to prison;
We two alone will sing like birds i'th'cage:
10   When thou dost ask me blessing, I'll kneel down,
And ask of thee forgiveness: so we'll live,
And pray, and sing, and tell old tales, and laugh
At gilded butterflies, and hear poor rogues
Talk of court news; and we'll talk with them too,
15   Who loses and who wins; who's in, who's out;
And take upon's the mystery of things,
As if we were God's spies: and we'll wear out,
In a walled prison, packs and sects of great ones
That ebb and flow by th'moon.

Edmund   Take them away.

20 **Lear**   Upon such sacrifices, my Cordelia,
The gods themselves throw incense. Have I caught thee?
He that parts us shall bring a brand from heaven,
And fire us hence like foxes. Wipe thine eyes:
The good years shall devour them, flesh and fell,
25   Ere they shall make us weep: we'll see 'em starved first.
Come.

                         [*Exeunt* **Lear** *and* **Cordelia,** *guarded*]

Edmund   Come hither, captain; hark.
Take thou this note;   [*Giving a paper*]
                         Go follow them to prison.
One step I have advanced thee; if thou dost
30   As this instructs thee, thou dost make thy way
To noble fortunes; know thou this, that men
Are as the time is; to be tender-minded
Does not become a sword; thy great employment
Will not bear question; either say thou'lt do't,
Or thrive by other means.

Lear   No, no, no, no! Come, let's be off to prison. We two, alone, will sing like birds in a cage. When you ask a blessing of me, I'll kneel down and ask your forgiveness. That way we'll live, and pray, and sing; and tell each other tales of days gone by; and laugh at courtiers in their fancy clothes; and hear poor wretches discusss the news from court. And we'll talk with them, too: who has failed, and who succeeded; who's in favour, and who's out; and – as if we were God's spies – solve the mysteries of the universe. In the confines of our prison, we'll go through many a gang of high and mighty ones, who come and go by the month.

Edmund   [*to the Officers*] Take them away.

Lear   The gods themselves endorse such sacrifices as yours, Cordelia. [*She starts to weep*] Have I made you cry? [*He puts his arm around her*] To separate us, a man would need a burning torch from heaven – to drive us apart with fire, like a fox smoked from its lair. Wipe your eyes. They'll rot before they'll make us weep! We'll see them starved first! Come!

[**Lear** *and* **Cordelia** *leave under guard*]

Edmund   [*to an* **Officer**] Come here, Captain. Listen. [*Giving him a paper*] Take this note. Follow them to prison. I've promoted you once already. If you follow these instructions, you'll do well for yourself. Know this: men must take advantage of their opportunities. To be tender-hearted is not becoming in a soldier. This great assignment brooks no argument: either say you'll do it, or prosper by some other means.

35 **Officer**   I'll do't, my lord.

   Edmund   About it; and write happy when thou hast done.
      Mark, I say, instantly, and carry it so
      As I have set it down.

   Officer   I cannot draw a cart nor eat dried oats;
40   If it be man's work I'll do't.

                                                      [*Exit*]

   [*Flourish. Enter* **Albany, Goneril, Regan,** *Officers, and
   Soldiers*]

   Albany   Sir, you have showed to-day your valiant strain,
      And fortune led you well; you have the captives
      Who were the opposites of this day's strife;
      I do require them of you, so to use them
45   As we shall find their merits and our safety
      May equally determine.

   Edmund   Sir, I thought it fit
      To send the old and miserable King
      To some retention and appointed guard;
      Whose age had charms in it, whose title more,
50   To pluck the common bosom on his side,
      And turn our impressed lances in our eyes
      Which do command them. With him I sent the Queen;
      My reason all the same; and they are ready
      To-morrow, or at further space, t'appear
55   Where you shall hold your session. At this time
      We sweat and bleed; the friend hath lost his friend,
      And the best quarrels, in the heat, are cursed
      By those that feel their sharpness;
      The question of Cordelia and her father
      Requires a fitter place.

Officer   I'll do it, my lord.

Edmund   Get on with it then. Be well contented when you've
done it. Note — I said *immediately*. Carry it out according to
my instructions.

Officer   I can't pull a cart, nor live on dried oats like a horse:
so if it's man's work, I'll do it.

[*He goes*]

[*Trumpets sound. Enter* **Albany, Goneril, Regan,** *Officers
and Soldiers*]

Albany   [*to* **Edmund**] Sir, you've shown your valiant side
today, and fortune has taken care of you. You have the
captives who were our enemies in today's battle: I require
them from you, to do with them what their deserts, and our
safety, shall equally determine.

Edmund   Sir, I thought it appropriate to send the old and
miserable King to some confinement, under guard. The
emotional appeal of his age, and even more so his title,
could win the hearts of the common people, and turn
against us the lances of the conscripted soldiers under our
command. With him I sent the Queen, for the same reason.
They are ready tomorrow, or later, to appear wherever you
intend to hold your trial. Right now, we sweat and bleed.
Friend has lost friend. Even the best of causes can be
misjudged by injured parties acting in the heat of passion.
The issue of Cordelia and her father requires a more suitable
place.

60 **Albany**   Sir, by your patience,
   I hold you but a subject of this war,
   Not as a brother.

   Regan   That's as we list to grace him;
   Methinks our pleasure might have been demanded,
   Ere you had spoke so far. He led our powers,
65 Bore the commission of my place and person;
   The which immediacy may well stand up,
   And call itself your brother.

   Goneril   Not so hot;
   In his own grace he doth exalt himself
   More than in your addition.

   Regan   In my rights,
70 By me invested, he compeers the best.

   Albany   That were the most, if he should husband you.

   Regan   Jesters do oft prove prophets.

   Goneril   Holla, holla!
   That eye that told you so looked but a-squint.

   Regan   Lady, I am not well; else I should answer
75 From a full-flowing stomach. General,
   Take thou my soldiers, prisoners, patrimony;
   Dispose of them, of me; the walls are thine;
   Witness the world, that I create thee here
   My lord and master.

   Goneril   Mean you to enjoy him?

80 **Albany**   The let-alone lies not in your good will.

   Edmund   Nor in thine, lord.

   Albany   Half-blooded fellow, yes.

   Regan   [*To* **Edmund**] Let the drum strike, and prove my title
      thine.

Albany Sir, just a moment. I regard you as a subject in this war – not as an equal.

Regan It's up to us to decide how to rank him. I think our wishes might have been consulted before you had said so much. He led our armies, and acted with the authority of my rank and person. Such representation might well stand up and call itself your equal.

Goneril Not so fast. He ranks higher in his own right rather than because of any titles *you* have given him!

Regan In exercising my rights, with my approval, he equates with the best.

Albany That would only be so if he married you.

Regan Many a true word is spoken in jest!

Goneril [*sarcastically*] Well, well, well . . . Chance would be a fine thing!

Regan Madam, I am not well: otherwise I'd give you a piece of my mind. [*To* **Edmund**] General, take my soldiers, my prisoners, my inheritance. Do as you wish with them, and me. I surrender myself: may the world be witness that I hereby create you my lord and master.

Goneril Do you intend to marry him?

Albany [*rebuking his wife sharply*] It's not for you to say yes or no!

Edmund Or you, lord –

Albany Bastard, it is!

Regan [*to* **Edmund**] Let the drum sound and proclaim that what is mine, is yours.

Albany   Stay yet; hear reason. Edmund, I arrest thee
On capital treason; and, in thy attaint,
This gilded serpent.   [*Pointing to* **Goneril**]

85   For your claim, fair sister,
I bar it in the interest of my wife;
'Tis she is sub-contracted to this lord,
And I, her husband, contradict your banns.
If you will marry, make your loves to me;
My lady is bespoke.

90 **Goneril**   An interlude!

Albany   Thou art armed, Gloucester; let the trumpet sound:
If none appear to prove upon thy person
Thy heinous, manifest, and many treasons,
There is my pledge;   [*Throws down a glove*]
                         I'll make it on thy heart,
95 Ere I taste bread, thou art in nothing less
Than I have here proclaimed thee.

Regan   Sick! Oh, sick!

Goneril   [*Aside*] If not, I'll ne'er trust poison.

Edmund   There's my exchange: [*Throws down a glove*]
                         what in the world he is
That names me traitor, villain-like he lies.
100 Call by the trumpet: he that dares approach,
On him, on you, who not? I will maintain
My truth and honour firmly.

Albany   A herald, ho!

Edmund   A herald, ho, a herald!

Albany   Trust to thy single virtue; for thy soldiers,
105 All levied in my name, have in my name
Took their discharge.

Regan   My sickness grows upon me.

Albany   Hold it: listen to reason! Edmund, I arrest you for
capital treason; and as your accessory [*he points to*
Goneril], this deceptively-beautiful serpent. [*To* **Regan**] As
for your claim, fair sister, I rule it out of order in the interests
of my wife. She's the one who is under contract to this lord,
and I – her husband – contradict your banns. If you want to
marry, address your proposals to me. My lady is already
spoken for.

Goneril   Such drama!

Albany   You are armed, Gloucester. Let the trumpet sound. If
no-one appears to prove in combat with you your vile,
undeniable and many treasons, there is my challenge! [*He
throws down a gauntlet*] I'll prove it on peril of your life,
before ever I break bread again, that you are in every way
what I have here described you.

Regan   [*holding her forehead*] Sick, oh, I'm sick!

Goneril   [*aside*] If not, I'll never trust poison . . .

Edmund   There's my response. [*He throws down his own
gauntlet in exchange*] No matter who he is that calls me
traitor, he lies like a villain! Let the trumpet sound a call.
Whoever dares to come forward: I will defend my truth and
honour against him, against you, and against anybody.

Albany   [*calling*] A herald, there!

Edmund   A herald, there, a herald!

Albany   Trust to your personal valour, because your soldiers –
all levied in my name – have accepted their discharge from
me.

Regan   [*about to fall*] I'm feeling worse.

Albany   She is not well; convey her to my tent.

[*Exit* **Regan**, *led*]

[*Enter a* **Herald**]

Come hither, herald. Let the trumpet sound,
And read out this.

110   **Officer**   Sound, trumpet!   [*A trumpet sounds*]

Herald   [*Reads*] *If any man of quality or degree within the lists*
of the army will maintain upon Edmund, supposed Earl of
Gloucester, that he is a manifold traitor, let him appear by the
third sound of the trumpet. He is bold in his defence.

Sound!   [*First trumpet*]
Again!   [*Second trumpet*]
Again!   [*Third trumpet*]

[*Trumpet answers within*]

[*Enter* **Edgar,** *armed, with a trumpet before him*]

115   **Albany**   Ask him his purposes, why he appears
Upon this call o'th'trumpet.

Herald   What are you?
Your name, your quality, and why you answer
This present summons?

Edgar   Know, my name is lost;
120   By treason's tooth bare-gnawn, and canker-bit:
Yet am I noble as the adversary
I come to cope.

Albany   Which is that adversary?

Edgar   What's he that speaks for Edmund, Earl of
Gloucester?

Albany   She isn't well. Convey her to my tent. [*Officers support her and lead her out*]

[*A* **Herald** *enters*]

Come here, herald. Let the trumpet sound, and read this out. [*He hands over* **Edgar**'s *challenge*]

Officer   Sound, trumpet! [*A trumpet sounds*]

Herald   [*reading*] *If any man of rank or distinction, presently enlisted in the army, will maintain that Edmund, supposed Earl of Gloucester, is an all-round traitor, let him appear by the third sound of the trumpet. He will defend himself boldly. Sound!*

[*The trumpet sounds for the first time*]

Again!

[*The second trumpet sounds*]

Again!

[*The third trumpet sounds. There is a pause, and then an answering trumpet is heard from nearby.* **Edgar** *enters, armed, preceded by a trumpeter*]

Albany   [*to the* **Herald**] Ask him what is his purpose in appearing after the trumpet-call.

Herald   Who are you? Your name? Your rank? Why do you respond to this summons?

Edgar   Know that my name is not on record. Treason has destroyed it. Yet I am as noble as the adversary I come to fight.

Albany   Who is that adversary?

Edgar   Who represents Edmund, Earl of Gloucester?

Edmund   Himself: what say'st thou to him?

Edgar   Draw thy sword,
125   That, if my speech offend a noble heart,
      Thy arm may do thee justice; here is mine:
      Behold, it is the privilege of mine honours,
      My oath, and my profession: I protest,
      Maugre thy strength, place, youth, and eminence,
130   Despite thy victor sword and fire-new fortune,
      Thy valour and thy heart, thou art a traitor,
      False to thy gods, thy brother, and thy father,
      Conspirant 'gainst this high illustrious prince,
      And, from the extremest upward of thy head
135   To the descent and dust below thy foot,
      A most toad-spotted traitor. Say thou 'No,'
      This sword, this arm, and my best spirits are bent
      To prove upon thy heart, whereto I speak,
      Thou liest.

140 **Edmund**   In wisdom I should ask thy name;
      But since thy outside looks so fair and war-like,
      And that thy tongue some say of breeding breathes,
      What safe and nicely I might well delay
      By rule of knighthood, I disdain and spurn;
      Back do I toss these treasons to thy head,
145   With the hell-hated lie o'erwhelm thy heart,
      Which, for they yet glance by and scarcely bruise,
      This sword of mine shall give them instant way,
      Where they shall rest for ever. Trumpets, speak.

      [*Alarums. They fight.* **Edmund** *falls*]

Albany   Save him! Save him!

Goneril   This is practice, Gloucester:
150   By the law of war thou wast not bound to answer

268

Edmund [*stepping forward*] He himself. What have you to say to him?

Edgar Draw your sword, so that if what I have to say offends a noble heart, your valour may bring you justice. Here is mine. [*He draws his sword from its scabbard*] Behold! To draw it is the privilege of my rank, my vows, and my knighthood. I declare – notwithstanding your strength, position, youth, and eminence – despite your victorious sword, your brand-new good fortune, your valour and your courage – that you are a traitor! You have betrayed your gods, your brother and your father. You have conspired against this illustrious high-born prince, and from the top of your head to the dust below your feet, you are a most infamous traitor! Deny it, and this sword, this arm, and my best endeavours are determined to prove to that heart of yours, to which I speak, that you lie!

Edmund Common sense tells me I should ask your name. But as your exterior looks so good and valiant, and because your speech has a touch of good breeding about it, though I could with all propriety postpone this combat – according to the rules of knighthood – this I disdainfully refuse to do. I throw these accusations of treason back at you, together with the hateful-as-hell charge of lying. Though right now they pass you by unscathed, my sword will thrust them home where they belong, and put them to rest forever. Trumpets: speak!

[**Edmund** *and* **Edgar** *fight.* **Edmund** *falls, wounded*]

Albany Save him! Save him!

Goneril This is trickery, Gloucester. By the code of arms, you were not obliged to fight with an unknown enemy. You are

An unknown opposite; thou art not vanquished,
But cozened and beguiled.

Albany   Shut your mouth, dame,
Or with this paper shall I stop it. Hold, sir;
Thou worse than any name, read thine own evil:
155   No tearing, lady; I perceive you know it.

Goneril   Say, if I do, the laws are mine, not thine:
Who can arraign me for't?

Albany   Most monstrous! Oh!
Know'st thou this paper?

Goneril   Ask me not what I know.

[*Exit*]

Albany   Go after her: she's desperate; govern her.

[*Exit an Officer*]

160   **Edmund**   What you have charged me with, that have I done,
And more, much more; the time will bring it out:
'Tis past, and so am I. But what art thou
That hast this fortune on me? If thou'rt noble,
I do forgive thee.

Edgar   Let's exchange charity.
165   I am no less in blood than thou art, Edmund;
If more, the more thou hast wronged me.
My name is Edgar, and thy father's son.
The gods are just, and of our pleasant vices
Make instruments to plague us;
170   The dark and vicious place where thee he got
Cost him his eyes.

not defeated, but cheated and deceived!

Albany   Shut your mouth, woman, or I'll stop it with this
letter. [*It is* Goneril*'s to* Edmund*; the one which* Edgar *found
on* Oswald *in Act 4 Scene 6. To* Edgar] Hold your sword, sir.
[*To* Goneril] Wicked beyond all words: read your own evil!
[Goneril *tries to grab the paper*] No snatching, lady! I
suspect you know what it is.

Goneril   What if I do? The law belongs to me, not you. Who
could prosecute me for it?

Albany   How utterly monstrous! Oh! *Do* you know this letter?

Goneril   [*hysterical now*] Don't ask me what I know!

[*She leaves distraught*]

Albany   Follow her. She's desperate. Take charge of her.

[*An Officer leaves*]

Edmund   [*To* Albany] What you have charged me with, I have
done: and more, much more. Time will reveal all. It's over
now, and so am I. [*To* Edgar] But who are you, who has the
advantage over me? If you are noble, I forgive you.

Edgar   Let's exchange courtesies. I am no less noble than you
are, Edmund. If I'm more, you have wronged me all the
more. My name is Edgar, and I'm your father's son. The
gods are just. They use the vices we take pleasure in as the
means to punish us: conceiving you cost him his eyes.

Edmund   Thou hast spoken right, 'tis true.
The wheel is come full circle; I am here.

Albany   Methought thy very gait did prophesy
A royal nobleness: I must embrace thee:
175   Let sorrow split my heart, if ever I
Did hate thee or thy father.

Edgar   Worthy prince, I know't.

Albany   Where have you hid yourself?
How have you known the miseries of your father?

Edgar   By nursing them, my lord. List a brief tale;
180   And when 'tis told, oh, that my heart would burst!
The bloody proclamation to escape
That followed me so near – oh, our lives' sweetness,
That we the pain of death would hourly die
Rather than die at once! – taught me to shift
185   Into a madman's rags, assume a semblance
That very dogs disdained: and in this habit
Met I my father with his bleeding rings,
Their precious stones new lost; became his guide,
Led him, begged for him, saved him from despair;
190   Never – oh fault! – revealed myself unto him,
Until some half-hour past, when I was armed;
Not sure, though hoping, of this good success,
I asked his blessing, and from first to last
Told him my pilgrimage: but his flawed heart,
195   Alack, too weak the conflict to support,
'Twixt two extremes of passion, joy and grief,
Burst smilingly.

Edmund   This speech of yours hath moved me,
And shall perchance do good; but speak you on;
You look as you had something more to say.

Edmund   You've said right. It's true. The wheel of fortune has
turned a full circle. I am back at the bottom.

Albany   [to **Edgar**] I thought your very walk suggested a royal
nobleness. My welcome to you. [*They embrace in soldierly
fashion*] May sorrow be my lot if ever I hated you or your
father.

Edgar   Wise prince, I know that.

Albany   Where did you hide yourself? How did you know
about your father's sufferings?

Edgar   By nursing them, my lord. Listen to a brief story, and
when I've told it, would that my heart would burst! To
escape the threat of death that was so close upon me – oh,
how sweet life is, in that we suffer the pain of death by the
hour rather than die suddenly! – I learned to dress in the
rags of a madman, and to assume a character that even
dogs despised. And in this clothing I met my father with his
bleeding sockets, his eyes newly blinded. I became his
guide, led him, begged for him, and saved him from despair.
I never, foolishly, revealed myself to him till some
half-an-hour ago, when I was in armour. Not certain of this
fortunate outcome, though hoping for it, I asked his
blessing, and told him of my journeying from first to last. But
his injured heart, alas, too weak to carry the strain, torn
between the two extremes of passion – joy and
grief – burst with happiness.

Edmund   This speech of yours has touched me, and it could
perhaps do some good. Proceed. You look as though you
have more to say.

200 **Albany**   If there be more, more woeful, hold it in;
　　　　For I am almost ready to dissolve,
　　　　Hearing of this.

Edgar　　　　　　This would have seemed a period
　　　　To such as love not sorrow; but another,
　　　　To amplify too much, would make much more,
205　　And top extremity.
　　　　Whilst I was big in clamour came there in a man,
　　　　Who, having seen me in my worst estate,
　　　　Shunned my abhorred society; but then, finding
　　　　Who 'twas that so endured, with his strong arms
210　　He fastened on my neck, and bellowed out
　　　　As he'd burst heaven; threw him on my father;
　　　　Told the most piteous tale of Lear and him
　　　　That ever ear received; which in recounting
　　　　His grief grew puissant, and the strings of life
215　　Began to crack: twice then the trumpets sounded,
　　　　And there I left him tranced.

Albany　　　　　　　　But who was this?

Edgar　　Kent, sir, the banished Kent; who in disguise
　　　　Followed his enemy king, and did him service
　　　　Improper for a slave.

[*Enter a* **Gentleman,** *with a bloody knife*]

Gentleman　　Help, help! Oh, help!

Edgar　　　　　　　　What kind of help?

220 **Albany**　　　　　　　　Speak, man.

Edgar　　What means this bloody knife?

Gentleman　　　　　　'Tis hot, it smokes;
　　　　It came even from the heart of – Oh, she's dead.

Albany [*to* **Edgar**] If there's more to report that's more harrowing, keep it to yourself. I'm almost at the point of tears, hearing of this.

Edgar Those who cannot cope with sorrow would think of this as a breaking-point. To add more woe by giving details would generate further suffering, and go beyond all bearing. While I was bawling out my grief a man arrived who, having seen me in my wretchedness, would have avoided my loathsome company. But seeing who it was that suffered so, he wrapped his strong arms around my neck, and bellowed out as if he'd burst the heavens. He embraced my father, and told the most pitiful tale about Lear and himself that ever anyone heard. In the telling of it, his grief overwhelmed him, and his hold on life began to slip. Then the trumpet sounded twice; and there I left him, unconscious.

Albany But who was this?

Edgar Kent, sir, the banished Kent, who in disguise followed the King from whom he was alienated, serving him beyond the duties even of a slave.

[*A* **Gentleman** *enters, carrying a bloodstained knife*]

Gentleman Help, help, oh, help!

Edgar What kind of help?

[*The* **Gentleman** *is too choked to answer*]

Albany Speak up, man!

Edgar Why this bloodstained knife?

Gentleman It's warm . . . it's steaming . . . it came from the heart of . . . [*He cannot find the words*] Oh, she's dead!

ACT FIVE   Scene 3

Albany   Who dead? Speak, man.

Gentleman   Your lady, sir, your lady: and her sister
225   By her is poisoned; she confesses it.

Edmund   I was contracted to them both: all three
Now marry in an instant.

Edgar   Here comes Kent.

[*Enter* **Kent**]

Albany   Produce the bodies, be they alive or dead;

[*Exit* **Gentleman**]

This judgment of the heavens, that makes us tremble,
230   Touches us not with pity. [*To* **Kent**] Oh, is this he?
The time will not allow the compliment
Which very manners urges.

Kent   I am come
To bid my King and master aye good night;
Is he not here?

Albany   Great thing of us forgot!
235   Speak, Edmund, where's the King? And where's Cordelia?
Seest thou this object, Kent?

[*The bodies of* **Goneril** *and* **Regan** *are brought in*]

Kent   Alack, why thus?

Edmund   Yet Edmund was beloved:
The one the other poisoned for my sake,
And after slew herself.

240   **Albany**   Even so. Cover their faces.

Edmund   I pant for life; some good I mean to do
Despite of mine own nature. Quickly send,

276

Albany   Who is dead? Speak, man!

Gentleman   Your wife, sir, your wife. And she has poisoned your sister-in-law. She confessed it.

Edmund   I was engaged to them both. All three of us will now be married at the same time . . .

Edgar   Here comes Kent.

[**Kent** *enters*]

Albany   Bring in the bodies, alive or dead.

[*The* **Gentleman** *leaves*]

This judgment of heaven, fearful though it is, arouses more of our pity. [*To* **Kent**] Oh, is this the man? This is not the right time for the normal courtesies.

Kent   I have come to bid my King and master an everlasting good night. Is he not here?

Albany   A serious oversight! Speak, Edmund! Where is the King? And where is Cordelia? [*The bodies of* **Goneril** *and* **Regan** *are brought in*] Do you see this, Kent?

Kent   Alas: what's caused this?

Edmund   So Edmund was indeed loved! One poisoned the other for my sake, and afterwards killed herself.

Albany   Indeed so. Cover their faces.

Edmund   I pant for life. I mean to do some good, in spite of my nature. Send quickly – hurry now! – to the castle. I've given

> Be brief in it, to th'castle; for my writ
> Is on the life of Lear and on Cordelia.
> Nay, send in time.

245 **Albany**   Run, run! Oh, run!

Edgar   To who, my lord? Who has the office? Send
Thy token of reprieve.

Edmund   Well thought on: take my sword,
Give it the captain.

Edgar   Haste thee, for thy life.

[*Exit Officer*]

250 **Edmund**   He hath commission from thy wife and me
To hang Cordelia in the prison, and
To lay the blame upon her own despair,
That she fordid herself.

Albany   The gods defend her!
Bear him hence awhile.

[*Edmund is borne off*]

[*Enter* **Lear,** *with* **Cordelia** *dead in his arms*]

255 **Lear**   Howl, howl, howl! Oh, you are men of stones!
Had I your tongues and eyes, I'd use them so
That heaven's vault should crack. She's gone for ever.
I know when one is dead, and when one lives;
She's dead as earth. Lend me a looking-glass;
260 If that her breath will mist or stain the stone,
Why, then she lives.

Kent   Is this the promised end?

Edgar   Or image of that horror?

orders for the deaths of Lear and Cordelia. Get there in time.

Albany   Run – run! Oh, run!

Edgar   To whom, my lord? Who is in charge? Send your token, indicating a reprieve.

Edmund   Well said. Take my sword. Give it to the captain.

Edgar   [*passing the sword to an Officer*] Hurry, on your life! [*The Officer runs off*]

Edmund   [*to* **Albany**] He has orders from your wife and me to hang Cordelia in the prison, and to say her despair led to her suicide.

Albany   The gods protect her! [*To Servants*] Take him away for a moment. [**Edmund** *is carried off*]

[**Lear** *enters, with* **Cordelia** *dead in his arms*]

Lear   Howl, howl, howl, howl! Oh, you are made of stone! If I had your tongues and eyes, I'd use them so the roof of heaven would crack! She's gone forever. I know when one is dead, and when one lives. She's as dead as earth. Lend me a mirror. If her breath will mist or stain the glass, why, then she lives!

Kent   Is this the end of the world?

Edgar   Or a copy of that horror?

Albany   Fall and cease.

Lear   This feather stirs; she lives! If it be so,
It is a chance which does redeem all sorrows
That ever I have felt.

265 **Kent**   [*Kneeling*]   Oh my good master!

Lear   Prithee, away.

Edgar   'Tis noble Kent, your friend.

Lear   A plague upon you, murderers, traitors all!
I might have saved her; now she's gone for ever!
270 Cordelia, Cordelia! Stay a little. Ha!
What is't thou say'st? Her voice was ever soft,
Gentle and low, an excellent thing in woman.
I killed the slave that was a-hanging thee.

Officer   'Tis true, my lords, he did.

Lear   Did I not, fellow?
275 I have seen the day, with my good biting falchion
I would have made them skip: I am old now,
And these same crosses spoil me. Who are you?
Mine eyes are not o'th'best: I'll tell you straight.

Kent   If fortune brag of two she loved and hated,
280 One of them we behold.

Lear   This is a dull sight. Are you not Kent?

Kent   The same;
Your servant Kent. Where is your servant Caius?

Lear   He's a good fellow, I can tell you that;
He'll strike, and quickly too. He's dead and rotten.

285 **Kent**   No, my good lord; I am the very man, –

Lear   I'll see that straight.

Albany   May the heaven's fall, and all things cease!

Lear   [*testing to see whether* **Cordelia** *is breathing*] This
feather moves! She's alive! If so, it is a piece of luck that
cancels out all the sorrows that I have ever felt.

Kent   [*kneeling*] Oh, my good master!

Lear   [*pushing him aside anxiously*] Go away!

Edgar   [*explaining*] It's the noble Kent, your friend.

Lear   Damn you! Murderers, traitors, all of you! I might have
saved her. Now she's gone forever. Cordelia, Cordelia, stay
a while! [*He puts his ear to her lips*] What's that you say?
Her voice was always soft, gentle and low: an excellent
thing in a woman. [*Proudly*] I killed the wretch who was
hanging you!

Officer   It's true, my lords: he did.

Lear   Didn't I, man? I've seen the day when, with my good
sharp sword I would have made them jump! I am old now,
and these ailments of mine get in the way. [*He peers at*
Kent] Who are you? My eyes are not as good as they might
be; I'll tell you straight –

Kent   If Fortune should boast of two men she both loved and
hated, we are looking at one of them now.

Lear   – my sight is poor. [*After a pause*] Aren't you – Kent?

Kent   I am. Your servant, Kent. Where is your servant called
Caius?

Lear   [*recognizing the name* **Kent** *used when disguised*] He's a
good fellow, I can tell you that! He'll fight, and quickly, too!
[*Sadly*] He's dead and rotten.

Kent   No, my good lord. I am the man –

Lear   [*not able to grasp what* **Kent** *says*] I'll see to that in a
moment –

Kent   That from your first of difference and decay,
Have followed your sad steps –

Lear   You are welcome hither.

Kent   Nor no man else. All's cheerless, dark, and deadly:
290   Your eldest daughters have fordone themselves,
And desperately are dead.

Lear   Ay, so I think.

Albany   He knows not what he says, and vain is it
That we present us to him.

Edgar   Very bootless.

[*Enter an* **Officer**]

Officer   Edmund is dead, my lord.

Albany   That's but a trifle here.
295   You lords and noble friends, know our intent;
What comfort to this great decay may come
Shall be applied: for us, we will resign,
During the life of this old majesty,
To him our absolute power: [*To* **Edgar** *and* **Kent**]
                              You, to your rights,
300   With boot and such addition as your honours
Have more than merited. All friends shall taste
The wages of their virtue, and all foes
The cup of their deservings. Oh, see, see!

Lear   And my poor fool is hanged! No, no, no life!
305   Why should a dog, a horse, a rat, have life,
And thou no breath at all? Thou'lt come no more,
Never, never, never, never, never!
Pray you, undo this button: thank you, sir.
Do you see this? Look on her, look, her lips,
Look there, look there! [*Dies*]

Kent   – who has followed in your sad steps from the very
beginning of your declining fortunes.

Lear   You are welcome here.

Kent   The very man. All is dreary, dark, and funereal. Your
eldest daughters have put an end to themselves, and in
hopeless desperation are dead.

Lear   [*uncomprehending*] Yes, so I believe.

Albany   He doesn't know what he is saying. It's no use our
talking to him.

Edgar   No use at all.

[*An* **Officer** *enters*]

Officer   Edmund is dead, my lord.

Albany   That's of small importance here. Lords and noble
friends, know our intentions. We shall provide what comfort
we can for this noble ruin of mankind. As for us, we shall
abdicate our absolute power to this old majesty during the
remainder of his life. [*To* **Edgar** *and* **Kent**] As for you: resume
your rightful places, with such additional titles as your noble
deeds have more than earned. All friends shall be rewarded
for their loyalty, and all foes punished as they deserve to be.
Oh, look, look!

Lear   And my poor child is hanged! No, no, no life! Why should
a dog, or a horse, or a rat have life, and you no breath at all?
You'll come no more: never, never, never, never! [*He
struggles with his collar*] Please, undo this button. [**Albany**
helps him] Thank you, sir. [*He imagines* **Cordelia** *is showing
signs of life*] Do you see this? Look at her – look – her lips!
Look there, look there! [*The excitement overwhelms him,
and he dies*]

310 **Edgar**   He faints! My lord, my lord!

Kent   Break, heart; I prithee, break!
Edgar   Look up, my lord.

Kent   Vex not his ghost: oh, let him pass; he hates him
         That would upon the rack of this tough world
         Stretch him out longer.

315 **Edgar**   He is gone, indeed.

Kent   The wonder is he hath endured so long:
         He but usurped his life.

Albany   Bear them from hence. Our present business
         Is general woe. [*To* **Kent** *and* **Edgar**] Friends of my soul,
            you twain
320   Rule in this realm, and the gored state sustain.

Kent   I have a journey, sir, shortly to go;
         My master calls me, I must not say no.

Edgar   The weight of this sad time we must obey;
         Speak what we feel, not what we ought to say.
325   The oldest hath borne most: we that are young
         Shall never see so much, nor live so long.

[*Exeunt, with a dead march*]

Edgar   He's fainted! [*Shaking* **Lear**] My lord, my lord!

Kent   May he suffer no more!

Edgar   Come on, my lord!

Kent   [*drawing him away*] Don't trouble his parting soul. Let him go. Only an enemy would prolong the torture.

Edgar   He's dead, indeed.

Kent   The surprising thing is that he has endured his suffering so long. He lived on borrowed time.

Albany   Bear them away. General mourning is now our immediate concern. [*To* **Kent** *and* **Edgar**] Kindred souls: you two shall rule this kingdom, to shoulder the burden of our ruined state.

Kent   [*hinting at his death*] I have a journey to make, sir, soon. My master calls me. I must not deny him . . .

Edgar   We must respond to the burdens of these sad times, and speak frankly, not expediently. The oldest have suffered most. We who are young will never see as much as they have seen, or live so long.

[*The bodies are all taken up, and everyone leaves at a dead march*]

Activities

Characters

Search the text (either the original or the modern version) to find answers to the following questions. They will help you to form personal opinions about the major characters in the play. *Record any relevant quotations in Shakespeare's own words.*

King Lear

1   At the beginning of the play Lear (aged 'fourscore and upward, not an hour more or less') is 'every inch a King'. In his opening speech in *Act I Scene 1*

    a   How does he display the 'authority' which Kent (in *Act I Scene 4*) recognizes as one of Lear's major characteristics?

    b   At what point does 'majesty fall to folly'?

2   Kent accuses Lear of 'hideous rashness'. Why was it unwise to

    a   subdivide the kingdom?

    b   subdivide it unequally?

    c   subdivide it according to 'how nature doth with merit challenge'?

3   **a**   At the end of *Act I Scene 1*, what do we learn from Goneril and Regan of Lear's

       i   temper

      ii   judgement

     iii   parental partiality

    in formal days?

    b   Give specific examples of Lear's 'imperfections of long-engraffed condition' as demonstrated in this scene.

c Show from two of Gloucester's comments in *Act I Scene 2* that Kent was not alone in thinking Lear acted rashly.

4 'By day and night he wrongs me', says Goneril in *Act I Scene 3*. List the 'gross crimes' of which Lear is accused in this scene and decide whether Goneril is

  a speaking the truth;

  b justified in her actions.

5 **a** At the beginning of *Act I Scene 4*, Lear is seen enjoying retirement.

    i In what ways is he still acting like a king?

    ii What evidence is there that his happiness is clouded?

    iii Why does the dialogue with the Fool create conflict in his mind?

  b By the end of the scene, Lear is emotionally distraught. Find examples of his use of

  (i) sarcasm (ii) anger (iii) threats (iv) curses (v) tears (vi) self-reproach (vii) self pity

  in responding to Goneril's provocations.

6 **a** Lear's progress towards madness is accelerated in *Act II Scene 4*. Show how stress is evident in

  (i) his expressions of incredulity (ii) his physical discomfort (iii) his sense of impotence (iv) his attempts at self-control.

  b By the end of the scene, Lear's 'let me not be mad' of *Act I Scene 5* has changed to 'Oh Fool, I shall go mad'. Find evidence of mental torment in

  (i) the stocking of Kent (ii) Regan and Cornwall's delayed appearance (iii) Regan's defence of Goneril (iv) Goneril and Regan's progressive reduction of Lear's hundred knights.

Activities

7 In *Act III Scene 2* Lear's rage and sorrow is directed at the storm.

    a Show how he is obsessed with

        i the theme of ingratitude. What does he call upon nature to do?

        ii his weakness and old age. What is his plea before the justice of the gods?

    b Of what is his resolution to 'say nothing' an ironic echo?

    c i Why might his speech denouncing hypocrites and sinners be said to mark the beginning of his redemption?

        ii How does his treatment of the Fool confirm that Lear is beginning to look upon his fellow-men in a new way?

8 **a** At the beginning of *Act III Scene 3*, in the midst of the storm and suffering from 'this tempest in my mind', Lear's understanding increases. How is this shown by

        i the order in which Lear invites his companions to enter the hovel?

        ii his thoughts on 'poor unaccommodated man'?

        iii his actions?

    b Identify the points at which

        i Lear's 'wits begin t'unsettle' in *Act III Scene 3*

        ii Revenge is replaced by justice as a means of dealing with the 'she foxes', in *Act III Scene 6*.

    c What do the three 'justices' have in common who 'try' Goneril and Regan?

9 Lear's next appearance is in *Act IV Scene 6*. He is mad. As a result of his experiences and losing his mind, what has he learned about

    a flattery?

b the limitations of power?

c tolerance?

d the nature of authority?

e the nature of vice?

f the nature of justice?

g hypocrisy?

h patience?

10 In *Act IV Scene 7* Lear recovers from his madness in the company of Cordelia.

    a What, according to Kent in *Act IV Scene 3*, has kept Lear from Cordelia until now?

    b At their reunion, the Doctor observes: 'the great rage, you see, is killed in him'. Illustrate the truth of this, from Lear's awakening to his exit on Cordelia's arm.

11 The battle over and lost, Lear is a prisoner in *Act V Scene 3*. Which of his lines show that he

    i has learned humility?

    ii has rejected the false values of court life?

    iii has regained his dignity?

12 At the end of the play, Lear enters carrying the dead body of Cordelia.

    a There is evidence that he has once again retreated from reality as a result of suffering. Give examples.

    b What has he done which is reminiscent of Lear in his prime?

    c Why is the moment of his death an apt one?

Goneril and Regan

1 Their public speeches near the beginning of *Act I Scene 1* contrast sharply with their private ones at the end.

a Goneril appears to take flattery as far as it will go in expressing her love for her father.

  i How does Regan succeed in capping her?
  ii At this point, is there any recognizable difference in the characters of the two sisters?

b What evidence is there

  i that they have been keeping a critical eye on their father?
  ii that they do not respect him?
  iii that they do not appreciate what he has given them?

c From the evidence in this dialogue, and especially the last two lines of the scene, decide which sister is the dominant one.

2 It is to his elder daughter Goneril that Lear first goes after resigning the throne.

a Read *Act I Scene 3*, and list

  i Lear's alleged offences;
  ii Goneril's plans for dealing with him.

b What do you deduce about her character?

3 a Goneril challenges Lear in *Act I Scene 4*.

  i Compare her accusations with those in *Act I Scene 3*. Have they changed?
  ii What is consistent about her manner towards her father?

b She also stands up to her husband Albany. How is it made clear that she is the dominant partner?

4 In *Act IV Scene 1* Regan and her husband visit Gloucester.

a How does Regan's relationship with Cornwall differ from her sister's with Albany?

b How can we tell that Regan has a prejudiced and distorted attitude to her father and his knights?

c At this point in the play, how would you describe Regan's attitude to Gloucester?

5 **a** Find evidence in *Act II Scene 2* and *Act II Scene 4* to confirm Regan's assertion in *Act I Scene 1*: 'I am made of that self metal as my sister'.

 b i How do the two sisters act in concert in *Act II Scene 4*?

 ii Which sister seems, on balance, to be the more obsessed with the danger of Lear's followers?

6 **a** Both sisters take a life during the course of the play.

 i Compare the circumstances and contrast the methods employed by each.

 ii Is Goneril's suicide consistent with her character?

 b Both sisters fall in love with Edmund.

 i Deduce from this the qualities in a man they both admire.

 ii Examine Goneril's attitude to her husband in *Act I Scene 4*, *Act IV Scene 1*, and *Act V Scene 3*. What qualities in a man does she despise?

 c Both sisters are 'jealous of the other, as the stung are of the adder' (Edmund, *Act V Scene 1*).

 i Check the meaning of these words in the modern translation, then trace the course of the 'jealousy' in *Act IV Scene 2*, *Act IV Scene 5*, *Act V Scene 1* and *Act V Scene 3*.

 ii Both Goneril and Regan are demonstrably bad daughters and bad sisters. One plans to have her husband murdered (check *Act IV Scene 2* and *Act IV Scene 6*); the other has a sadistic trait (check *Act II Scene 2* and *Act III Scene 7*). Is either less pernicious than the other?

Cordelia

1 That Cordelia was Lear's favourite daughter is confirmed

three times in *Act I Scene 1*: find the relevant evidence in speeches by

(a) Goneril; (b) the King of France; (c) Lear himself.

2   That Cordelia is Lear's most virtuous and loving daughter is confirmed

   a in *Act IV Scene 3*. How does Cordelia's reported response to the news of Lear's maltreatment show both her feelings, and her natural disinclination to reveal them in public?

   b in *Act IV Scene 4*. How does Cordelia show her love both emotionally and practically?

   c in *Act IV Scene 7*. What examples are there of her (i) goodness (ii) kindness (iii) compassion (iv) tenderness (v) forgiving nature?

3   That Cordelia is loved and respected by others is demonstrated in *Act I Scenes 1 & 4*

   a by Kent. How does he compliment her?

   b by the King of France. What value does he put upon her?

   c by the Fool. What effect does Cordelia's departure have on him?

4   **a** Twice in *Act I Scene 1* Cordelia refers to her natural reticence. Find the lines, and

   b check them against Lear's description of her speaking voice in *Act V Scene 3*. Then

   c comment on the aptness of the King of France's analysis of her character in *Act I Scene 1*.

5   In spite of saying so little, and appearing only four times in the play, Cordelia shows she has several very positive characteristics.

   a She is honest. What is the best example of this?

   b She deplores insincerity. How does she make this plain (i) to the Duke of Burgundy? (ii) to her sisters?

   c She respects integrity. How do we know she recognizes the goodness of Kent?

d She is loyal. Where does Lear say she has good reason not to be?

e She is philosophical. How is this demonstrated by her last speech in the play?

Kent

1 Kent has the first words in the play, and almost the last. In *Act I Scene 1*, he is fearlessly outspoken; from his speeches choose

 a three words or phrases which confirm his loyalty to the King;

 b three words or phrases which show his clear understanding of Lear's wrongheadedness;

 c three words or phrases which indicate his understanding of Goneril and Regan.

2 a Outspokenness is also a major characteristic of Kent in disguise. How does this work

   i to his advantage in *Act I Scene 4*, and

   ii to his disadvantage in *Act II Scene 2*?

 b In the latter scene, Cornwall speaks of Kent's 'saucy roughness'. Find examples of this in

   i his argument with Oswald;

   ii his retorts to Cornwall and Regan.

3 Between *Act III Scene 1* and *Act V Scene 3*, Kent's role is one of protector and correspondent, working on behalf of Lear's cause.

 a In the storm scene (*Act III Scene 6*) he stands out as being the only rational man at the trial. His suggested cure for Lear's insanity is the same as the Doctor's in *Act IV Scene 4*: what is it?

 b In *Act III Scene 1* and *Act IV Scene 3*, Kent establishes links with Cordelia and the French invading army at Dover.

What is said at the beginning of *Act IV Scene 3* and the end of *Act IV Scene 4* to clear Kent of the charge of treason?

4 What is the evidence in *Act V Scene 3* that Kent sees his service to the King as extending beyond the grave?

The Fool

1 a The Fool first appears in *Act I Scene 4*.

　　i How many times does Lear have to call for him before he appears?

　　ii What is the Knight's explanation for the Fool's absence, and what does it tell us about the latter's feelings?

b Immediately, the Fool begins to jest about foolishness

　　i to Kent (and again in *Act II Scene 4*). Explain why.

　　ii to Lear. What does he say that merits Kent's remark: 'This is not altogether fool, my lord'?

c Collect further examples of the Fool's oft-reiterated theme, in this scene and the others in which he appears.

2 a Another of his targets is Truth (and its counterpart Falsehood). How many references to it can you find in *Act I Scene 4*?

b Find examples of Truth conveyed by means of

　　i jokes and conundrums;

　　ii songs;

　　iii wise sayings.

c In the circumstances, why does Goneril say he is 'more knave than fool'?

3 The Fool's second appearance, in *Act I Scene 5*, follows Lear's humiliation at the hands of Goneril.

a Why do you think the Fool's first joke is about brains?

   b What message is he trying to convey in his jokes about crab-apples, noses, and snails?

   c Which of the Fool's remarks is close to the unvarnished truth?

   d Mark the text at points where the Fool diverts Lear from brooding about his troubles.

4 **a** As Lear becomes more isolated and tormented, the Fool works harder to sustain him, maintaining his pointed jokes, puns and witticisms as the King progresses towards madness. In *Act II Scene 4*

     i How many jokes does he make at Lear's expense?

     ii How many at Kent's?

     iii Is there a significance in the switch of emphasis?

   b As Lear departs into the storm, the Fool is his only companion. According to the Gentleman in *Act III Scene 1*, what is his function now?

5 The storm scenes (*Act III Scenes 2; 4; 6*) are those in which Lear's 'wits begin to turn' and he goes mad.

   a The Fool suffers from the same physical discomfort as his master. Which lines in *Act III Scene 2* show that they have come close together through hardship?

   b What incident in *Act III Scene 4* is close enough to farce to relieve the dramatic tension?

   c Which line spoken by the Fool in Edgar's presence emphasizes the levelling effect of their situation?

   d How does the Fool's presence at the mock trial of Goneril and Regan help to bring out the full pathos and tragedy of Lear's condition?

6 The Fool's last words in the play ('And I'll go to bed at noon') can be interpreted many ways. Here are two of them:

   a 'If you are having your evening meal in the morning, then my bedtime will be noon' (i.e., a straightforward quip).

b 'I shall not live much longer' (i.e., using the word 'bed' as a euphemism for 'grave').

Those who favour (a) point out that the Fool's dramatic usefulness is at an end, so Shakespeare gives him no more lines to say. Those who favour (b) say Lear's 'And my poor fool is hanged' (*Act V Scene 3*) proves that he committed suicide; though the word 'fool' could mean 'my child', and therefore refer to Cordelia.

c What is your opinion?

Gloucester

1 Gloucester opens the play by making light of a 'pleasant vice' which resulted in the birth of the illegitimate Edmund. Look up Edgar's words to the dying Edmund in *Act V Scene 3*: show how they confirm the former's belief that 'the Gods are just' in dealing with immorality.

2 Edmund describes Gloucester as 'a credulous father'. Trace the tricks Edmund uses to deceive Gloucester in *Act I Scene 1* and *Act II Scene 2*

a Is his success due

    i entirely to his manipulative skills, or,

    ii have recent events made the old Earl vulnerable?

b Show that Gloucester's mind is in a state of turmoil after Lear's abdication.

3 Gloucester seems weak, letting others make decisions for him.

a To Edmund, he says 'frame the business after your own wisdom' in *Act I Scene 2*; and he refers to Cornwall as 'The noble Duke my master' in *Act II Scene 1*. What is ironic about his dependence on these two men?

b Consider his protest at the stocking of Kent. Do you think he did all he could in the circumstances?

  c Read the dialogue between Lear and Gloucester in *Act II Scene 4* concerning Cornwall's slighting of the King. Does Gloucester's exit line imply that he lacks the courage to take sides?

4 By *Act III Scene 2* Gloucester has had further experience of Goneril and Regan, and time to think.

  a Explain what is praiseworthy about his resolution.

  b Explain what is unfortunate about his choice of confidant.

  c Explain how he puts his decision to aid Lear into practice.

5 In *Act III Scene 7* Gloucester suffers cruelly for his loyalty.

  a Illustrate

    i his dignity whilst under threat;

    ii his strong moral values.

  b Later, in *Act IV Scene 1*, he says 'I stumbled when I saw'. What is the first truth he learns after losing his sight?

6 Blindness brings despair to Gloucester.

  a In *Act IV Scene 1*, which lines sum up his pessimistic philosophy?

  b What is his purpose in seeking to be guided towards Dover?

7 *Act IV Scene 6* sees Gloucester, led by Edgar, 'at the top of that same hill', which he is told overlooks the sea.

  a Explain why it is necessary for Edgar to mislead his father.

  b Choose two statements by Gloucester, one after Edgar's successful ruse, and one after his meeting with Lear, to show that he has rejected the pessimism of *Act IV Scene 1*.

  c i On what occasion in *Act V Scene 2* does Gloucester relapse into melancholy?

    ii What observation revives him?

8 Gloucester's death is reported by Edgar in *Act V Scene 3*. What was the cause of it?

Edmund

1 We meet Edmund at the very beginning of the play, when Gloucester speaks for him, and we learn of his illegitimacy. Find two reasons why

   a he might be forgiven for having a jaundiced view of society;

   b he might be forgiven for his subsequent lack of filial loyalty.

2 In his soliloquy in *Act I Scene 2, lines 1–22* Edmund speaks for himself.

   a To whose 'law' does he say his 'services are bound'?

   b List his arguments for appealing to the gods to 'stand up for bastards'.

3 a Edmund's villainy has a strong element of wit about it. Find examples in *Act I Scene 2*, with reference to

   i his deception of Gloucester and manipulation of Edgar;

   ii his sceptical references to astrology;

   iii his use of irony.

   b Which lines summarize his case for intrigue against 'a credulous father and a brother noble'?

   c In *Act II Scene 1*,

   i how many examples of his cunning trickery can you find?

   ii which of Gloucester's lines indicate that Edmund has succeeded?

   iii which lines of Cornwall's advance his prospects even further?

4 In *Act III Scene 5*, Edmund tells Cornwall: 'I will persevere in my course of loyalty, though the conflict be sore between that and my blood'.

   a Consider

   i what he has previously said in *Act III Scene 3*;

   ii his behaviour in *Act III Scene 7*;

    iii   Regan's report of his murderous intentions in *Act IV Scene 5*.

b   Is there any evidence of conflicting loyalty?

5   Both Goneril and Regan fall in love with Edmund.

    a   Find the evidence in *Act IV Scene 2*, *Act IV Scene 5*, and *Act V Scene 1*, and

    b   decide from Edmund's soliloquy at the end of *Act V Scene 1* how far their love is reciprocated.

6   By the end of the play, Edmund has been both victor and vanquished.

    a   In victory, what is his most wicked deed?

    b   In defeat, what good does he do 'despite of mine own nature'?

    c   Do the words he utters in his dying moments – 'Yet Edmund was beloved' – provide any clue about either his past behaviour or his deathbed reformation?

Edgar

1   Edgar plays a number of roles throughout the play.

    a   In *Act I Scene 1* he is simply the Earl of Gloucester's legitimate son. How much older is he than Edmund?

    b   In *Act I Scene 2* he is in disgrace. How does Edmund account for the ease with which this is accomplished?

    c   By *Act II Scene 3* he is Poor Tom: 'Edgar I nothing am.'

        i   Describe his appearance.

        ii   Using the information in *Act III Scene 4*, list his sufferings and show why 'unaccommodated man is no more but such a poor, bare, forked animal' as he is.

        iii   Explain why Lear finds him a congenial companion, and how Lear's suffering helps Edgar endure his own.

    iv Show from Edgar's words in *Act IV Scene 1* that he has the courage and the philosophy to overcome despair.

2 **a** Edgar is changed for the better when he appears in *Act IV Scene 6*, although he denies this to his blind father.

    i From whom did he obtain his superior clothes?
    ii In what ways is his speech different?

  b i What is Edgar's purpose in 'trifling thus with his (i.e. Gloucester's) despair'?
    ii Explain his method of procedure.

  c Which lines of Gloucester's prove that the ruse has worked?

3 **a** In his final role in the play, Edgar is a man of action.

    i What is his first valorous deed on behalf of his father in *Act IV Scene 6*?
    ii What is the second, before the battle, in *Act V Scene 1*?
    iii What is the third, after the battle?

  b i Show from the speeches of Edmund and Albany at the end of the play that Edgar has royal dignity.
    ii In the Quarto edition of the play (1608), the last lines of *King Lear* are given to Albany. Do you agree with the Folio editors that the words are more appropriately given to Edgar?

Structure, themes and imagery

1   The play has both a main plot and a sub-plot. Identify the main characters in each.

2   Show how in each there is

a	a foolish father	**i**	disguise
b	loyalty	**j**	homelessness
c	disloyalty	**k**	madness, real or feigned
d	rejection of the good	**l**	redemption through suffering
e	trust in the bad		
f	banishment	**m**	experience of abject poverty
g	greed		
h	deceit	**n**	loving care shown by a rejected child
		o	violent death
		p	death caused by emotional stress

3   Complete the following:

    a   Whereas one father has all daughters, the other has . . .

    b   Whereas one suffers madness, the other suffers . . .

    c   Whereas there is rivalry between sisters in one, there is rivalry between . . . in the other.

    d   Whereas in one a son leaves home, in the other . . . leaves home.

    e   Whereas daughters betray their father in one, a . . . betrays his father in the other.

    f   Whereas one family is wiped out, in the other . . . survives.

    g   Whereas in one, a fool helps a King, in the other a madman helps . . .

4 The theme that initiates events in the play is that of the generation gap; the relationship of parent and child, and the duties and obligations that flow from the blood-bond. Find examples of parent/child relationships involving

(a) gratitude/ingratitude (b) kindness/cruelty (c) trust/deceit (d) legitimacy/illegitimacy (e) duties/freedoms (f) respect/contempt (g) hatred/love

5 Self-knowledge, and the pursuit of truth, go hand in hand with the development of the plot.

a Lear goes mad before he comes to his senses. Find examples of his progress from folly to wisdom in the following scenes:

(i) *Act 1 Scene 1*; (ii) *Act 1 Scene 4*; (iii) *Act 2 Scene 4*; (iv) *Act 3 Scenes 2 and 6*; (iv) *Act 4 Scenes 6 and 7*

b Gloucester loses his sight before he can 'see'. Trace the stages through which he passes (noting in particular how he learns to accept Edgar's dictum 'Ripeness is all') in the following scenes:

(i) *Act 1 Scenes 1 and 2*; (ii) *Act 2 Scene 1*; (iii) *Act 3 Scenes 3 and 4*; (iv) *Act 3 Scene 7*; (v) *Act 4 Scene 1*; (vi) *Act 4 Scene 6*; (vii) *Act 5 Scene 2*.

6 a The largest theme of all is that of the nature of man, both in terms of the individual and the way he behaves (often hypocritically) in organized society. The following speeches are central; they are all spoken by Lear:

   i 'Reason not the need . . .' (*Act 2 Scene 4*). What *is* 'the need'?

   ii 'Let the great Gods . . . find out their enemies now' (*Act 3 Scene 2*). What *are* their enemies?

   iii 'Poor naked wretches . . .' (*Act 3 Scene 4*). What is to be learned from them?

   iv 'What, art mad? . . . harder, harder; so.' (*Act 4*

Scene 6) What has Lear learned about power, corruption, and the dispensation of justice?

b How many relevant pieces of wisdom can you find amongst the songs and sayings of the Fool?

7 Animal imagery abounds in *King Lear*. To convey the inhumanity of human behaviour and its similarity to wild life, over sixty different creatures are mentioned. Trace the following to their sources, and explain their significance in the context of the play:

(a) 'monster ingratitude'; (b) 'serpent's tooth'; (c) 'wolvish visage'; (d) 'like a vulture'; (e) 'most serpent-like'; (f) 'like rats . . . like dogs'; (g) 'those pelican daughters'; (h) 'rash boarish fangs'; (i) 'Tigers, not daughters'; (j) 'be-monster not thy feature'; (k) 'dog-hearted daughters'.

How many more can you find?

8 **a** Look up Gloucester's speech in *Act 1 Scene 2*: 'These late eclipses in the sun and moon . . .'

    i How many words can you find that imply discord, social breakdown, and fractured relationships?

    ii Which speech of Edmund's in the same scene catalogues 'these divisions'?

b 'Division' is echoed in figurative expressions throughout the play. Place the following examples in context and explain the force of the imagery:

    i 'These hot tears which break from me perforce . . .' (*Act 1*)

    ii 'Like rats, oft bite the holy cords a-twain . . .' (*Act 2*)

    iii 'Crack Nature's moulds . . .' (*Act 3*)

    iv 'She that herself will sliver and disbranch from her material sap . . .' (*Act 4*)

    v 'The strings of life begin to crack . . .' (*Act 5*)

9 Imagery based on physical suffering is recurrent in *King Lear*. The torment endured by Lear and Gloucester, and the savagery of the play as a whole, is reflected in terms of

303

'a human body in anguished movement: tugged, wrenched, beaten, pierced, stung, scourged, dislocated, flayed, gashed, scalded, tortured and finally broken on the rack' (Caroline Spurgeon: *Shakespeare's Imagery*).

a Trace the following examples to their contexts, and explain their appositeness. They are all from Act One.

   i   . . . 'wrenched my frame of nature from the fixed place'

   ii   . . . 'Th'untented woundings of a father's curse Pierce every sense about thee!'

   iii   . . . 'with her nails she'll flay thy wolvish visage'

b Find further examples, guided by Miss Spurgeon's list.

10 In his opening address to the Court in *Act 1 Scene 1*, Lear says he will 'divest' himself of 'rule, Interest of territory, cares of state'. Imagery based on clothing (or references to it) can be found throughout the play.

a Find examples from speeches by the following:

   i   France, in *Act 1 Scene 1*;

   ii   Cornwall, in *Act 2 Scene 2*;

   iii   Lear, in *Act 3 Scene 4*;

   iv   Lear in *Act 4 Scene 6*.

b Explain why clothes have a symbolic significance in relation to the play's major themes.

Textual questions

Read the original Shakespeare and (if necessary) the modern transcription, to gain an understanding of the speeches and extracts below. Then concentrate entirely on the original in answering the questions.

1 *Thou, Nature, art my goddess (Act 1 Scene 2)*

    a Edmund has said very little up to this point, and what he has said would accord with customs in polite society. What is the element of shock built into these first words of his soliloquy?

    b A soliloquy can either be regarded as 'thinking aloud, alone' or 'confiding inner thoughts to a wider audience'. If you were playing the part of Edmund, would you treat these lines as private musings, or as an opportunity to address the audience?

    c Why is custom said to be 'a plague'?

    d Why is 'moonshines Lag of a brother' more wittily suggestive than 'younger than a brother'?

    e Edmund repeats 'base' five times, 'bastard' three times, and 'bastardy' and 'baseness' once each, all in the space of twenty-two lines. What effect does this have on what in former times would have been a series of words with derogatory connotations?

    f What effect on the meaning of 'legitimate' does Edmund's reference (i) to conception in and out of wedlock and (ii) his repetition of the word as adjective and noun five times have on its normally-favourable meaning?

    g Why might an audience at this stage in the play's development side with a character who has announced his villainous intentions?

2 *These late eclipses in the sun and moon (Act 1 Scene 2)*

a Gloucester believes there is an astrological explanation for the troubles of his time. What is Edmund's viewpoint on the subject?

b 'Nature' is a word frequently used throughout the play; here it means 'man's reason'. Collect as many references to nature as you can find, and interpret each one according to the context in which it appears.

c Several items in Gloucester's catalogue of woe are directly related to the circumstances of the play. Explain each.

d Gloucester uses the word 'nothing'. So do Lear and Cordelia in *Act 1 Scene 1*. (i) How many times can you find the word employed in *King Lear* and (ii) can you explain why it should be so significant a word?

3 *I heard myself proclaimed (Act 2 Scene 3)*

a Why 'happy' hollow?

b Edgar mostly uses words of one or two syllables in this soliloquy. (i) How does this help to emphasize important information and (ii) how does this help to emphasize the words which are exceptions to the rule?

c Edgar is planning to be 'Poor Tom' here. Compare what is said of him, and by him, in *Act 3 Scene 4*. Does he carry out his plans to the letter?

d The play is set in Ancient Britain: what evidence is there here that Elizabethan audiences did not object to anachronisms?

e Re-read *Act 1 Scene 2*: what is ironic about Edgar's choice of name for his new identity?

4 *I prithee, daughter, do not make me mad (Act 2 Scene 4)*

a In this speech, Lear says 'I can be patient'. 'Patient' and 'patience' are words with many echoes throughout the play. Find as many as you can.

b Here patience is shown in the way Lear's outbursts are followed by checks. Mark the text (i) where you believe Lear raises his voice in anger, and (ii) where he disciplines himself with self-control.

c (i) Some lines are effective here because they are antithetical: that is, one half of the line is balanced against the other. Find examples, and say how they add to the pathos of Lear's words.

(ii) Sometimes Lear's mounting anger results in repetition in sets of three words or phrases. Find two examples.

d How does Lear make his critical points perfectly clear whilst affecting not to?

5 *Oh, reason not the need (Act 2 Scene 4)*

a The first lines relate significantly to the process whereby Lear's folly is redeemed. Explain why.

b Lear only once refers to 'God' in his speeches. Here, as elsewhere, he addresses 'heavens' and 'you gods'. Sometimes in the play the gods are regarded as malevolent (find Gloucester's anguished cry in *Act 4 Scene 1*), and sometimes benign (note his retraction in *Act 4 Scene 6*). What position does Lear take here?

c How is Lear's pathetic impotence conveyed (i) in disjointed sentences and (ii) by a short line?

d If you were producing the play, would you have Lear leave the stage in tears, or not? Discuss the alternatives and give reasons for your decision.

6 *Blow, winds, and crack your cheeks! (Act 3 Scene 2)*

a The Elizabethan theatre had primitive sound effects, and performances took place on fine days in the open air. How does Shakespeare

  i create the illusion of a storm by means of words, and

  ii succeed in conveying a sense of Lear's impending mental breakdown?

b The passionate force of Lear's ranting is conveyed by the verbs he uses to command the elements.

  i List them, and

  ii show how water, fire, explosion and destruction are called upon to carry out his orders.

c In this speech, some lines are composed of multi-syllabic and/or hyphenated words; others are mainly mono-syllabic.

  i Which are best suited for abusive purposes?

  ii Which are evocative and descriptive?

7 Examine the following key speeches in similar detail:

a *Poor naked wretches, whereso'er you are (Act 3 Scene 4)*

b *Wisdom and goodness to the vile seem vile (Act 4 Scene 2)*

c *Come on, sir, here's the place: stand still (Act 4 Scene 6)*

d *Ay, every inch a king (Act 4 Scene 6)*

e *And the creature run from the cur (Act 4 Scene 6)*

f *Pray do not mock me (Act 4 Scene 7)*

g *No, no, no, no! Come, let's away to prison (Act 5 Scene 3)*

h Lear's last speeches, from *Howl, howl, howl* to *Look there, look there! (Act 5 Scene 3)*

Examination questions

The following are typical of the kind of examination questions set by the major examining boards.

1 *King Lear* is a play based on family relationships. How do the parallel stories of Lear and Gloucester support this viewpoint?

2 'The essence of tragedy is the vindication of human nobility and greatness.' How far is this true of *King Lear*?

3 To what extent was Lear 'a man more sinned against than sinning'?

4 What resemblances and differences does Shakespeare display in the characters of Lear's three daughters?

5 In what ways do the Fool and Gloucester add to the dramatic effect of *King Lear*?

6 Show by means of precise reference and illustration how the sub-plot emphasizes the central theme of *King Lear*.

7 Discuss any *two* of the following: (i) the animal imagery in *King Lear* (ii) the importance of the Fool's patter before and during the storm (iii) Edgar's feigned madness (iv) Kent's loyalty.

8 The following remarks are applied to King Lear; say what you think they mean and how far they are true: (i) 'He hath ever but slenderly known himself' (ii) 'The best and soundest of his time hath been but rash' (iii) 'He but usurped his life'.

9 How does Shakespeare achieve both intense horror and acute pathos in the storm scenes of *King Lear*?

10 Show how suffering is an integral part of the tragedy of *King Lear*.

11 What part does Nature play in *King Lear*?

12 Consider *two* of the following as examples of different kinds of villainy: (i) Edmund (ii) Goneril (iii) Regan (iv) Cornwall.

13 'This is not altogether fool, my lord.' In what ways is the Fool wiser than Lear?

14 'You do me wrong to take me out o'th'grave.' In what ways is the reborn Lear a better man than the one who died in the storm?

15 For over 100 years, *King Lear* was performed with a happy ending and the storm scene cut. Assess the importance of what was lost.

One-word-answer quiz

1 Into how many parts did Lear originally divide his kingdom?

2 How many knights did Lear wish to have in his train?

3 How many were denied him in his first fortnight of retirement?

4 How many did Regan offer him at first?

5 What was her final offer?

6 Until what time was Kent to sit in the stocks, according to Cornwall?

7 In the storm scene, who is first to find Edgar in the hovel?

8 What was Edgar wearing when disguised as Poor Tom?

9 Who 'oft prove prophets'?

10 To how many of his daughters does Lear kneel?

11 What was the Prince of Darkness called, besides Modo?

12 What did Lear have in his countenance that Kent would fain call master?

13 What is obeyed in office?

14 How many 'red burning spits' would Lear have liked to hiss in upon his daughters?

15 What was the surname of the Marshal of France?

16 What did Edmund give the Captain who went to save the lives of Lear and Cordelia?

17 What did Kent give to the Gentleman who went to see Cordelia at Dover?

18 How many days was Kent allowed to prepare for banishment?

19 For how many days did the Fool pine after Cordelia?

20 For how many years had Poor Tom been mad, according to Edgar?

21 For how many years had Edmund been abroad?

22 What article did Lear ask for in his dying moments?

23 What did the Fool take Goneril for in the trial scene?

24 Who showed his father 'a child-like office'?

25 Who said she had been 'worth the whistle'?

26 What was Kent's assumed name?

27 How many times did the trumpet sound before Edgar appeared to fight Edmund?

28 Who does Lear call the 'hot Duke'?

29 What was Edmund's goddess?

30 How many knights were 'hot questrists' after Gloucester?

31 Who signed herself 'Your wife, so I would say, Affectionate servant'?

32 How old was Kent?

33 What did Lear say can be made out of nothing?

34 Who told Edgar that Nero was an angler in the Lake of Darkness?

35 Who wrote the letter which Kent holds when in the stocks?

What's missing?

Complete the following quotations:

1 Oh! How this mother swells up toward my heart; . . .
2 I have no way, and therefore want no eyes; . . .
3 Come, let's away to prison; We two . . .
4 The gods are just, and of our pleasant vices . . .
5 This shows you are above, You justicers . . .
6 As flies to wanton boys are we to the gods . . .
7 This is the excellent foppery of the world . . .
8 Her voice was ever soft, Gentle and low . . .
9 Let it be so; . . .
10 Not only, sir, this your all-licensed Fool . . .
11 They durst not do't; They could not, would not do't . . .
12 No, they cannot touch me for coining . . .
13 Cry to it, nuncle, as the cockney did to the eels . . .
14 This is most strange, That she . . .
15 Poor naked wretches, whereso'er you are . . .
16 Pray, do not mock me: I am a very foolish fond old man . . .
17 Howl, howl, howl! Oh, you are men of stones: . . .
18 Return to her? And fifty men dismissed? No, . . .
19 There thou might'st behold The great image of Authority . . .
20 How, how Cordelia! Mend your speech a little . . .
21 Men must endure Their going hence, even as . . .
22 I am made of that self-metal as my sister . . .
23 Truth's a dog must to kennel; . . .
24 Yet better thus, and known to be contemned, Than . . .
25 Better thou Hadst not been born than . . .

26 Ay, every inch a king: . . .

27 Wisdom and goodness to the vile seem vile; . . .

28 Thy dowerless daughter, King, thrown to my chance . . .

29 Idle old man, that . . .

30 I am a man More . . .

31 It is the stars, The stars above us, govern our conditions . . .

32 Thou, nature, art my goddess . . .

33 Oh, reason not the need: . . .

34 When we our betters see bearing our woes . . .

35 Pat he comes, like the catastrophe of the old comedy: . . .

Other plays in the
SHAKESPEARE MADE EASY
series